SASINDA FUTHI SISELAPHA (STILL HERE)

SASINDA FUTHI SISELAPHA (STILL HERE)

Black Feminist Approaches
to Cultural Studies in South Africa's
Twenty Six Years Since 1994

**Derilene (Dee) Marco, Tiffany Willoughby-Herard,
and Abebe Zegeye, eds.**

AFRICA WORLD PRESS

TRENTON | LONDON | CAPE TOWN | NAIROBI | ADDIS ABABA | ASMARA | IBADAN | NEW DELHI

AFRICA WORLD PRESS
541 West Ingham Avenue | Suite B
Trenton, New Jersey 08638

Book design: Dawid Kahts
Cover design: Asharful Haq

Catalogue-in-Publication Data may be obtained from the Library of Congress.

ISBNs: 978-1-56902-649-6 (HB)
       978-1-56902-650-2 (PB)

Table of Contents

Section Two: Redress is Medicine

Section Three: Unsettling Laughter

Section Four: The White Writing Offensive

Post-Script

Notes on Terminology

Sasinda and Siselapha

Zethu Cakata

Ukusinda is a Nguni term that means "to survive" something bad/a tragedy.

Sasinda—means we survived. It is closer to "we are still here," rather than ukusinda. Sasinda means we survived to tell the tale and learn from the lessons of the experience. Ukusinda or surviving a tragedy could be perceived as a second lease at life, a moment when one stops taking life for granted because you have seen how brittle it is. As writers we work from our experience as survivors of a brutal past. We draw strength from the memory.

Siselapha—literally means we are still here. In the context of colonization this construct speaks to the ability to refuse death or erasure in spite of the brutal measures. It follows that death is not an end of life but a continuation in a different realm. Hence the assertion "soyisa ukufa" which means we defeated death. Therefore even those whose souls were separated from the body are still here working to ensure that African people continue to live. Siselapha speaks to the resilience of African people against the brutal onslaught; the resilience of the mortal and those in the world of the spirit. It is also an assurance that we shall never die. It gives meaning to the idea that the current uprisings, both in the environment (through natural disasters) and in the spaces of learning, are the rise of the ancestors demanding justice.

Which Black Feminism?

Tiffany Willoughby-Herard

In the past, women of color feminisms and Black feminisms have fought for scholarly recognition and an almost invisible space in basement narrows and the hideaway fastness of academe.[1] Yet following the lead of the younger activists and culture workers who organize Afro-Futurist assemblies, marches, demonstrations, and anti-violence political education of every stripe, a liberatory queer Black transfeminism seems to be what most people globally are more invested in. This explains a resounding, ongoing, and robust discussion about the limits of Black feminism and one of its main theoretical contributions (and how it has been institutionalized and defanged at North American universities)—the concept, intersectionality. For some intersectionality is largely a hopelessly identitarian, multiculturalist, "normatively malleable" foil for homonationalism and pinkwashing.[2] In the face of this necessary and robust debate and its sites of prominent characterization we insist that Black feminisms and women of color feminisms are linked research terms that have been the generative origin for many other accounts of dynamic structural approaches and yet in the instance of titling this collection, we return to Black feminist approaches to re-center the political, the ethical, and all the manifestations of the immaterial, the non-human, and the spirit. Indeed our cover image sutures and the included contributions are grounded in a wide-ranging invocation of Black feminist praxis and concept-building. If the tension is about the scale of the personal, subjective, interpersonal, on the one hand, and the scale of the structure and institution, on the other, we say, instead, we must have both of these *and* the scale of the immaterial and non-human, the psyche, and the spirit, as well, too.[3] Gendered racial violence has historically been deployed at multiple dynamic interacting scales (global, local, national, regional, and at the level of the psychic, libidinal, and cosmological)[4] of structural intersectionality[5] that produce interstitiality,[6] in-betweeness, and a static stationary position where bodies that are gendered as Black[7] are often trapped and carry the tainted markings of immobility (at the same time that Black place is always available for theft).[8] In the contemporary period power continues to operate through new forms while benefiting from the ongoing legacies of imperialism, capitalism, militarism, enslavement, segregation, immigration restriction, medical and pharmaceutical and biopolitical aparhtheid, detention and carcerality. In this book, scholars are drawing both on genealogies of Black feminisms and women of color feminisms and their concerns with disabusing us of the most damaging features of the institutionalization of gender. Such genealogies have provided us with critiques of gender as property, gender as excuse for suppressing cultural tools of survival and world-making/world-breaking, gender as providing cover for typecasting the sexual, household, communal, representational, and public lives of all kinds of people. Because of the complexity of the South Africa and the complexity of the world that we have apportioned to us in very unequal portions, drawing on both of these feminist genealogies and their rich internal tensions and irresolutions has been productive. These interventions are Black, politicized, and ungendered in the most deliberately rebellious senses of the refusal of gender. We agree at minimum, that gender is a site of ongoing racial sexual colonial imposition. It does us no good. We mean to hail those who are concerned both with the world of rememory and healing and "getting on with it [that is building and breaking]"[9] and those concerned with the systematic undoing of the world that organizes itself around subjection and legitimizing those expressions of violence. Following, Robert Farris Thompson there is a "flash of the spirit" here. There is also the refreshing breath of stories by time-traveling, continent-whirling grandmothers dancing across these pages much like the inspired political education documented by Randall Robinson and David Covin in their newest creative offerings.[10] And we insist on having communion and being regenerated by all that is good and worthy of return.

Endnotes

1   Jasmine Syedullah's conceptualization of a "loophole of retreat" is a generative departure for this. See Syedullah's *"IS THIS FREEDOM?" A political theory of Harriet Jacobs's loopholes of emancipation.* 2014, UC Santa Cruz, PhD dissertation.

2   Lindsay, Keisha. "God, gays, and progressive politics: Reconceptualizing intersectionality as a normatively malleable analytical framework." *Perspectives on Politics*, 11.2, 2013, pp. 447-460; Nash, Jennifer C. "Re-thinking intersectionality." *Feminist review*, 89.1, 2008, pp. 1-15; Puar, Jasbir K. "'I would rather be a cyborg than a goddess': Becoming-intersectional in assemblage theory." *PhiloSOPHIA*, 2.1, 2012, pp. 49-66.

3   Horton-Stallings, LaMonda. *Funk the erotic: Transaesthetics and black sexual cultures.* University of Illinois Press, 2015.

4   Blackwell, Maylei. "Weaving in the spaces: Indigenous women's organizing and the politics of scale in Mexico." *Dissident Women: Gender and Cultural Politics in Chiapas*, 2006, pp. 115-156.

5   Isoke, Zenzele. *Urban black women and the politics of resistance.* New York, Springer, 2013.

6   Spillers, Hortense J. *Black, white, and in color: Essays on American litera-ture and culture.* University of Chicago Press, 2003.

7   Snorton, C. Riley. *Black on both sides: A racial history of trans identity.* University of Minnesota Press, 2017.

8   Perry, Keisha-Khan Y. *Black women against the land grab: The fight for racial justice in Brazil.* University of Minnesota Press, 2013.

9   Oyĕwùmí, Oyèrónkẹ́. Personal Conversation. 2018. January. Pretoria, South Africa.

10   Thompson, Robert Farris. *Flash of the Spirit: African and Afro-American Art and Philosophy.* New York, Vintage, 1984; Covin, David. *Raisins in Milk.* Sacramento, Blue Nile Press, 2018; Robinson, Randall. *Makeda.* Sacramento, CA, Open Lens, 2011.

Introduction

This Country is Not My Body:
Caricatures, Shreds, Still Here, Black Feminist and Women of Color Feminist Approaches to the Study of Culture Twenty Six Years After 1994

Tiffany Willoughby-Herard,
Derilene (Dee) Marco,
Abebe Zegeye[1]

If we want humanity to advance a step further, if we want to bring it up to a different level than that which Europe has shown it, then we must make discoveries.

Frantz Fanon[2]

Six years after the twenty-year anniversary of the "end of apartheid," this volume offers a purview of the nearly three decades between the end of official institutionalized racial segregation and the imaginary, and meanings associated with South Africa *since 1994.* We focus primarily on works of literary, cultural and visual arts and humanistically-oriented social sciences, with a decidedly African feminist/Black women's consciousness sensibility. Our positionality is part of a gendered African studies genealogy devoted to careful attention to how our contemporaries make art, make the sacred, laugh at and unstitch power in the context of enduring colonial, libidinal, and material economies. The authors unapologetically remain within their own constellations, authorize kinship and anti-imperialist community, and yet are experimental and innovative while also avoiding the escapism of colonial nostalgia and/or useless guilt.

We urge readers to consider this volume and read it alongside an earlier contribution in the journal, *African Identities*, titled, Twenty Years of South African Democracy. The special issue, which appeared on the mark, in 2014,[3] deals with similar concerns. In this volume we invite and invoke thinking through and with, the shards of debris and presences within what has acceptably become a term and an evolving sensibility, "post-apartheid." It became apparent that there was a distinct need for continual engagement around what constitutes "post-apartheid," as a geographical space and nation, and how this been formulated as a sensibility (ongoing) across genres of culture work. These issues remain contentious and often simply off kilter, to say the least.

The twenty year anniversary in 2014 was marked and celebrated differently from the ten year anniversary. At twenty cultural critics imagined that most cultural studies work would reflect national symbolism of an even further-evolved society that was no longer struggling through the earliest milestones of political transformation but which had now found a real foothold and sense of direction. Yet twenty-six years on, South Africa also finds itself in a situation far less ideal than the national phantasm of the Rainbow Nation. Indeed the era after 1994 is marked most decisively by ambivalent sensibilities. It is perhaps contending with such an atemporal position has made available new discoveries necessary to a time such as this (*a la* Fanon), discoveries that can only emerge as the visions of the present. This volume does some of its work surreptitiously by querying the very concept of "post-apartheid" in order to raise questions about what that concept obscures. We have begun to unearth the rootedness of this concept by alluding to it with more skepticism and suspicion, and by not specifying it numerically instead of as if it has been achieved. Though legal theorists and other kinds of scholars and history-makers have insisted on the reality of the post-apartheid period, analyses of culture point to the ways in which it remains conjectural and still unsettled.

With the creation of Madiba's New South Africa, the pervasive mood was hopefulness, levity, and artistic innovation. Now, the opposite seems to be the case. Or to put it more precisely—more than twenty years on—the hope, levity, and innovation is tempered with more forthright discussion about what institutional and administrative democracy in this global context can and cannot yield. Such complexities require turning toward reflection on art, creativity, language, memory, healing, and culture. The chapters in this volume are invested in complex narratives of *being* and *being in* "post-apartheid" South Africa.

The ever-burning narrative that South Africa simply cannot escape, nor seemingly work past, is a combination of racial inequality and racism. But there are also over-determined narratives about postcolonial African leadership and patriarchy—narratives which all to often *fail* to register the intense ongoing anti-colonial social and political work on race and gender justice. This ongoing work and cultural struggle must not be overlooked, but neither must it be romanticized because it's handmaidens and laborers and advocates pay high costs in isolation for bearing the burden of political visions of democracy that have as yet still been unfulfilled. While several of the authors included in this volume provide empirical data on the public disdain for Black cultural production within high status arenas of control and evaluation, others focus on the creativity and knowledge that Black people in South Africa have produced in the face of this ongoing set of conditions.

In the essays included, scholars take up pressing questions like: 1) Why are Black women artists—visual and literary—still being viewed by major critics as contributing very little? 2) Why are films and novels about the apartheid era still prioritizing white loss and trying to hail whites-only audiences? 3) Why have Black women culture workers been suppressed as thinkers and scholars? 4) How have contemporary African artists sustained their autonomy, navigated the consumerism of the art world, rejected being included as kitsch, and also commented on ethical imaginaries? 5) In what ways can laughter and comedy be more effective for developing fellow feeling and courage than collective expressions of spectacular anguish and hurt? 6) How do we do the work of creating new spaces for reflecting on the meaning of our work for the rights of the most despised people in order to "make new discoveries" as Fanon called us to do? Certainly, these are potent examples—of the work of race and gender justice as endlessly generative areas of thinking.

The contributors in this volume deal with some of these concerns and are in dialogue with each other, as well as with other such scholarly heavy lifting, which takes place around South Africa and on the continent. They constitute contributions to a flourishing African Humanities. Although the volume is framed as one that thinks through some of what constitutes the cultural terrain of twenty six years on, it is as invested in thinking through the postcolonial as a position for and about the continent. A number of the essays speak to iterations of discontent that are found in different geographical spaces on the continent. To take up the charge in the opening quotation from Fanon, we need to *make new discoveries*. This edited volume is part of the ongoing work of thinking through new and ongoing discoveries while also being wise to old wine in new bottles.

The Cultural Period After 1994

The essays here cover a range of cultural works: visual art, film, poetry, literature and cultural praxis and positions more broadly. The papers are all concerned with critical considerations of the challenges of the postcolonial and/or post-1994. Abebe Zegeye's paper,[4] for example, is an intricate commentary and analysis of Sarah Nuttall's classic *Entanglement* in which, he argues, Nuttall weaves a thread of equalizing Black and white pain and struggle in post-apartheid. He extends his analysis to what he calls, "the intellectual project [...] of the Truth and Reconciliation Commission of South Africa." Through close analysis of Nuttall's arguments, Zegeye concludes that *Entanglement* entrenches the notion that "race and class analysis of post-apartheid South Africa are obsolete frameworks," a position that Zegeye argues is an (unacceptable) form of white minority apology. No matter how knotted histories of peoples may be, the fact of entanglement or observations about multiple forms and experiences of pain do not necessarily correct the consistent desire to deem all things Black antediluvian and pre-modern. In fact the attempt to portray "white misery"—the long history of white on white violence under racial settler colonialism, most often comes with crafty reminders to repress expression of Black injury and fragmentation.[5] Institutionalized antiblack harm is not supposed to be spoken of, challenged, or explored as a site of meaning production. In short, reference to any forms of white misery typically demands sympathy with white supremacy.[6] Explained formally, white misery is:

> (1) the rediscovery of white people as flesh who arrived there through alleged competition with black people reduced to flesh [...] (2) concerned with when and how white misery returns [...] (3) [a study about] whom and how does white vulnerability suggest a relationship of shared status with blackness? (4) [a reflection on the multiple] ways [that] white vulnerability meant to guarantee black suffering as natural and reasonable while simultaneously rendering black racial resistance as unthinkable.[7]

Such entanglements and cognitive associations remind of histories of injured white people during histories of racial colonialism in Europe but then evacuate the history of those injuries in order to fill histories with ideological referents to Blackness as justified inferiorization. This history must be handled with more grace and sophistication in every instance. Entanglements that do such ideological work must be understood differently from visions of emancipation for they are not emancipatory. Instead they provide cover for an endless range of forms of anti-Black violence.

Critic and poet Natalia Molebatsi's "Healing Perspectives of a Black womxn poet: Writing the unborn and the dead" is a welcome contribution by a living contemporary creative writer laboring against the false binaries created between writing creatively and curating and writing as a critical scholarly respondent. Analyzing the poems, "Listen up child" (2008)[8] and "Summers at your feet" (2010),[9] the poet explains how the global black urban proverb attributed to actor and businessman, Will Smith, "If you stay ready, you don't have to get ready" has such resonance. The proverb is calling people to understand the context of living and that living well requires preparation and courage and assurance in the face of abuse. This is an insight, particularly relevant to black motherhood, viewing an unborn infant—the inspiration of "Listen up child"—as such a powerful force in the universe, as such an augur and cypher for memory. In "Summers at your feet," Molebatsi reflects on her grandmother's life and the painful embodied transition from black successful working class, middle class urban dwelling and land holding African people in the period before and immediately after the catastrophe of the 1913 Land Act. The poet resolves the dislocations of her grandmother having ended up in the subordinate position as a domestic worker with the uncanny testimony of "wanting to be you" to live that life, to understand that life, to feel the sorrows that emerged as songs—as a way into closeness and understanding, and perhaps being able to grieve the dreams deferred in her grandmother's life that were planted so lovingly and dedicatedly in Molebatsi's own blessed life.

Molebatsi's scholarly attention to memory punctures and provides a nuanced account of how the last twenty six years has been experienced in an embodied fashion by cultural producers and the biological families that they came from and that which protected their gifts. Though the scholarship on memory has been explored at all sorts of levels and scales Molebatsi's two poems on generations provoke readers by reflecting on the influence that generations have on each other. Molebatsi argues, such a hold on and mandate for each other—that the generation of the dead and the unborn have on each other—often is better interpreted by the body of the poet. In the two poems, Molebatsi describes being a medium and translator for trans-generational memories. While the open-ended language of poetry and speech itself may be an imperfect language and semiotics for communication, for Molebatsi whose expressed goal is healing the trauma of apartheid that exists and persists still, poetry and the audiences and practitioners that are hailed by the nurturing of poets handle the predicaments of memory in ways far more sophisticated than when memory is captured by the goals of the state. While the state uses ceremony and ritual to prove that the past has been overcome, is gone away, and so draws on memory in pompous and symbolic fashion, Molebatsi and the generation of poets that she seeks to document are not concerned with dispensing with the past. Instead they bend time, break temporality, and wrinkle space, with a deliberate attention to holding the disassociative experience of lacking the handles of time and pursuing futuring.

These poems invite us to sit in the predicaments of allegedly unreliable black female memory;[10] *embodied, captivating, exercising authority, and marshaling the sublime and the uncanny. Poor, old, dusty, vilified black women's memories of the world. Unloved, unwanted, unchosen*[11]—*and the very things which are desired the most by us and by the world that seeks to eat us.*

We suggest reading the essays by Zegeye and Molebatsi in conversation with June Jordan's devastating critique of rights-bearing liberal national discourse in "Poem About My Rights" (2005). What Jordan teaches us through her poem is certainly that forms of oppression are linked and mutually constituted. But, Jordan also demonstrates effectively that erstwhile entanglements might be better understood through the ethically clarifying language of relationality. "Relationality is constantly shifting…not an excuse for presuming a commonality among all racialized peoples, but a clear-eyed appraisal of the dividing line between valued and devalued, which can cut within, as well as across, racial groupings."[12] Through their interventions into the ways that the legal-religious sphere of the Truth and Reconciliation Commission operated, Zegeye and Molebatsi , point us to cross generational memory and artistic practice as a politics not to be underestimated—a politics that indicts rights bearing discourses for their inability to shore up or even approximate dignity and self-worth. June Jordan explained:

> I am the history of rape
> I am the history of the rejection of who I am
> I am the history of the terrorized incarceration of
> myself …
> I have been the meaning of rape
> I have been the problem everyone seeks to
> eliminate by forced
> penetration with or without the evidence of slime and/
> but let this be unmistakable this poem
> is not consent I do not consent
> to my mother to my father to the teachers to
> the F.B.I. to South Africa to Bedford-Stuy
> to Park Avenue to American Airlines to the hard on
> idlers on the corners to the sneaky creeps in
> cars
> *I am not wrong: Wrong is not my name*
> My name is my own my own my own
> and I can't tell you who the hell set things up like this
> but I can tell you that from now on my resistance

my simple and daily and nightly self-determination
may very well cost you your life[13]

To consider situated meanings of the body and healing beyond white minority apology or what Mamta Accapadi has called "white tears"[14] is taken up in another work of black feminist positionality in this collection. Derilene Marco's chapter on the film adaptation of *Disgrace* (2008) invites readers to keep in mind the links between slave narratives and young Black women's bodies in the film. Marco, also, through a seemingly morbid construction, suggests that young white women, as subjects and victims can also take on new identities. As Lucy Lurie says to her father David in *Disgrace*, "perhaps this is the price of staying in this place." 'This place' is South Africa. Marco employs scholar Meg Samuelson's articulation of Lucy Lurie's "Rainbow Womb" as a key framework for evaluating the film.

Marco also reminds us of the history of the "grassroots women's organizing within broader housing struggles" that found a powerful enunciation in the founding of *SPEAK* magazine (1982-1994) and the book reflecting on that history, Shamim Meer's *Women SPEAK – reflections of our struggles 1982-1997*.[15] Marco picks up on the founding of *Agenda* in 1978 and a long legacy of Black women's political visions of governance without sexual violence. The Black women-led struggle against sexual violence is not a phenomenon of the post-apartheid period alone. When Yvette Christianse wrote in *Unconfessed* (2006) that it must be known "what this place had made of her all these years," she was insisting that what was considered *good order and national security under apartheid* pressed sexual violence into the flesh and psyche of Black women.[16] Everyday practices of moving in the world and across racialized space attempted to suppress the struggle against state sexual violence. That this venomous social practice endures in the lives of "Born Frees"—who also exist in no small way because their lives are said to pivot around and signify the meaning of the past—is no surprise to any of us. If the novel upon which the film adaptation is based—Coetzee's *Disgrace*— was a white supremacist cautionary tale about post-apartheid nation building and articulated white fears about black governance as sexually excessive and destructive, then Christianse's *Unconfessed* provides a countervailing account that sends sexual violence and rape—as projects of conquest back to their source. Those who insist on silence about rape as a form of white nationalist state-making and those who insist that battles against sexual assault in South Africa have only emerged since 1994 have not made the transition called for by Fanon "to make new discoveries."

Rape is political warfare [...] Colonialism is about making war on people and seeing every [person] as a "combatant" [...] surviv[ing] rape [is] primarily [a] political act…there is nothing to prevent [rape] from being [mis]construed as a private act of vengeance or humiliation: or simply a gendered act that targets unique biological characteristics and social categories rather than something with long-range harm to entire communities. Rape […] represse[s] sexual autonomy and violate[s] the bodily integrity of the persons that experience it [while] caus[ing] irreparable personal and communal and social harm. It function[s] to keep women and men away from the battlefield, away from the consciousness and resistance that [a]re central to the work of […] struggle. Rape [i]s an attempt to stifle women's participation in any type of revolutionary movement to improve their life conditions […] as caretakers of major networks [rape] function[s] […] like other types of torture and produce[s] what Fanon called, "depersonalized people" whose misery [may be] internalized and delinked from other systems of colonial oppression.[17]

By addressing how rape is figured in literature and on screen, Marco is entering a canon of scholars like Meer, Zoe Wicomb, Zmitri Erasmus, Yvette Abrahams, and Pumla Gqola who have been explicit about the nature of apartheid—and everything in *its wake* as Christina Sharpe reminds— as a power relation of sexualized perpetual war. For those with the moral authority to insist that sexual violence be understood as ontologically significant for post-1994 world-making, taking up this enduring question is a blood-stained retort to more placid definitions of post-apartheid democracy. Marco reminds us that the film like the novel place a premium on protagonist David Lurie's point of view: Lurie's experience of being helpless to protect his daughter, his experience of predation on young Black women, and his inability to recognize or undo how racialized sexual violence is sutured with power and masculinity in South Africa. Viewers are supposed to identify with David Lurie who is a libertine—but a white one—and his critique of black governance as inherently "primitive […] beast-like, vengeful and crass," shaped by "violent taking (the rapists) or conspicuous consumption (Petrus)" by some nightmare myth of black masculinity. Marco provides a close reading of the stalled imaginary of *Disgrace*, a dystopia where men negotiate over the protection of white women's "Rainbow wombs," and where Black people play supporting characters to forms of white self-emergence. As cultural readers of the present, we all "get it" that generational guilt and soiled wombs are being carried into the post-apartheid period but as Marco explains, only the white wombs are legible as injury, for the black wombs are deemed, in this racist phantasm, to produce toxic and dangerous black masculinity.

Peter Hudson passed away on June 22, 2019, before this book had been released. We honour him and his work by including the piece in this collection. We suggest reading Peter Hudson's "Colonialism and Capitalism in South Africa Today" alongside Zethu Cakata's "South Africa Belongs to All who speak Colonial Languages," a critical interrogation of the position of language in the new South Africa. Hudson's critical reflection on the relationship between what he calls "the residual," remainders of colonialism invites a complex engagement with capitalism, democracy and race relations in South Africa. Both these works also remind us of the work of colonialism that set in place the scaffolding for the further atrocities seen during apartheid. Though each of these papers sees the colonial project in different guises, each one also makes work of not making that historical act the point of fixation. These papers thus still form a crucial part of our investment in not only thinking through the fissures left by apartheid but also thinking through some of the sensibilities of the present. Hudson answers the question of whether Colonialism of a Special Type still obtains in the period after the introduction of a democratic South Africa by concluding that the white unconscious is a singular site for the production and rebirthing of colonial power coupled with white ownership of land, status, and prestige. Thus, he offers us a careful and systematic methodology for considering the quality and meanings of a democratic transition that still faces new productions of racial colonial power.

Cakata's linguistic research on proverbs, idioms, and figurative language more generally, demonstrates that "Language exclusion in education is therefore a deliberate strategy to exclude indigenous people from formalizing their production of knowledge…from inserting their worlds and their experiences as knowers." Cakata explores specific concepts like the word "tribe" and conducts empirical analysis of the most popular psychology textbooks to explain how African higher education students are taught and evaluated on the basis of reinforcing myths about white supremacy and African inferiority.

Cakata's study of what has become a new variation of a historic exclusionary language policy is concerned with the "erosion, inferiorisation and marginalization…endured during the colonial era", demonstrates how post-apartheid policy and constitutionalism have occurred while African people have remained "appendages of the western world". This finding has particular significance for higher education transformation projects as it compels us to consider not only state capture and that form of political corruption but also consciousness and *linguistic capture*, if you will, and the detriment and injury that these forms of power leave behind. Colonial education as it lives on after 1994 is "aimed at making African children not… learn to understand their world but [making African children understand] the world of others so they may contribute into maintaining the colonial order". Post-1994 laws such as The *Language in Education Policy* (1997) and the *Language Policy for Higher Education* (2002) reflect enduring commitments to institutionalized linguistic discrimination. Criteria like "affordability" and "practicality" undermine even the most basic application of these laws. Such linguistic discrimination, argues Cakata, has resulted in African people "being [merely] accommodated," a cruel form of tolerance reserved for guests that have over-stayed their welcome. Analyzing the figurative language of idiom and proverbs in isiXhosa, Cakata explores what is currently being lost in the current approach and what critical linguistic pedagogies can recover in the classroom. Shoring up the teaching of African languages, says Cakata, will result in a wide range of gains including grounding classroom education in "African experience and knowledge forms […] wisdom […] an understanding of nature […] reference points [about how] to be human in the world" and affirming worldviews that reflect people's ways of knowing. Ultimately, Cakata describes the current situation with language policy in South Africa as a distortion of culture that justifies and imposes Eurocentric bias.

In a different tone, Ashraf Jamal's "Gradations in a Blur" explores the developments of what is called (and which has fixed associations), 'African Art', and the boxing in of such works, particularly from and in a Western imagination. Using the London-based annual African Art exhibition, 1:54, Jamal asks "How 'African' is African art? How transcultural? How diasporic? Are our South African artists as disposed to the blithe ease and banality of the familiar?" Jamal explores Ghanaian sculptor El Anatsui—known alternately as the "art worlds recycling conscience" and a critic of the libidinal claims made by consumerism—using William Boshoff's *Blind Alphabet* as a theoretical vantage point for understanding the commodification and success of contemporary African art work and its critical reception. In a context in which Africa continues to be consumed as a "site for a brute unconscious," Jamal probes, how we understand the art collectives, and anti-gallery spaces that emerge all over the continent and which garner critical attention among elite art buyers and critics while also smashing (and sometimes merely re-jiggering) "the masters tools." Jamal notes that contemporary African art (like its predecessors in the earlier days of slavery, colonialism and genocide) continues to comment on the nature of many human conditions, to inspire ethical imaginaries, and to sustain principled material relations. This current turn seeks to correct earlier museum practices of including African art as curio, outlandish, and inevitably foreign to draw an ever-tighter boundary around European modernism. Yet even such correctives fail to consider the enormity of the legacies of European modernism and the creative worlds—characterized in this moment by indeterminacy and play and better ideas—stifled by its claims of provenance. New audiences and cross-cultural parallels make it possible to enter the global art market with new types of leverage against the interests of capitalism but which also may hollow out the struggles and histories that compelled artists to make their interventions in the first place. Such a contemporary condition, Jamal argues, is better interpreted as "blindsight"—the capacity to navigate physical obstacles and affective registers beyond conventional sight. For the sighted Boshoff's *Blind Alphabet* (which invited blind people to be its primary and critical audience) "proved obstructive...[and] also spurred a new perception." Asking provocative questions that "cause uneasiness in the clan"[18] about the leadership and first principles that may come from contemporary African art once it decides who its audiences are and what its project is, readers will end this meditative essay coming a bit closer to comfort with "synaesthesia at work."

The dramatic arts, especially the labors of comedy and the invocations of humour, also provide an essential toolkit for wrestling with the apparitions of the present—the remnants of flesh awaiting ceremonies of enrobing.[19] While none of us ought to be about the business of making light of the present and the past, Jamal's insistently hopeful contemplations about the South African art scene keenly set the stage for Bhavisha Panchia's essay, "To Make Light of a Dark World: Contemporary South African Art in Review." Panchia makes a provocative argument for the use of laughter, humour, and play as strategies that have sometimes been used successfully since 1994, and other times not. Thus, the analysis engages questions of how and where we might be able to see the incorporation of lightness in artworks as ways of exploring current sensibilities. Panchia's attention to the ways in which humour is called to mediate the social helps us make sense of the relationship between Albie Sach's bitter caricatures of "more fists and spears and guns, the better" and Søren Kierkegaard's explanation of the connectedness between deep suffering and the authoritative use of comedy. Panchia attends to the distinctive aspects of comedy and humor in the visual arts, signaling a deep tendency in the present that cautions against the naming of notorious forms of everyday apartheid violence by artists. While humor remains as a signature part of the cache of forms of aesthetic resistance, Panchia argues for humor in order to redirect and suppress a focus on the normalization of pain. Panchia disabuses readers of a belief in the affective capacity of spectacular anguish and collective expressions of hurt as a means for developing fellow feeling and courage. Satire and laughter, instead, become the more powerful touchstones for depicting "everyday life of Cape communities in ways that were resilient, dignified, and nuanced" in the work of Peter Clarke and for interpreting "imaginative renditions that stretch beyond the veracity of the world at hand" in Tommy Motswai's work.

If Bhavisha Panchia and Ashraf Jamal's essays probe questions around the use of strategies in the South African and African art world and in specific artists' works, then Sharlene Khan's work takes this further yet. Khan's work here is the most succinct and faithful use of Patricia Hill Collins in South African visual culture scholarship to date. Following Pumla Gqola, Khan links Collins to Desiree Lewis, and Yvette Abrahams, but in this case in a narrow field of visual arts and the study of museum and art critcism. Khan observes "the re-centering of bodies-of-colour to a position from which to theorise are aspects that can be strongly evidenced in the visual arts globally, and increasingly, in post-apartheid South Africa." Khan's wonderful exegesis and deft theoretical analysis provides medicine, healing, direction, and champions the dialogic practices that animate these artists call for unapologetic Black love. Framed in Black feminist theory, Khan makes a series of arguments for re-telling Black women's stories in the artworks of Mary Sibande and Senzeni Marasela. Khan draws on Audre Lorde's concept of "bio-mythography" to weave together a complex series of arguments around and within (postcolonial) masquerade, subjectivity, narrative, and memory.

Lorde's biomythography calls art critics to historicize their own identity as both individuals, and as members of society. Such a process of historicization of identity unsettles the normalization of sensationalized dying, implacably dead, and incomprehensibly angry Black bodies. Such a process of historicization she excavates the macabre sensibility and fatalism that divorces art criticism from its own capacity to recognize feeling in Black bodies represented visually. This is a sophisticated and complex rendering of how South African apartheid gendered and raced artists in that society. Biomythography allows readers to engage their own process of black feminist decolonization and rejecting what T. Denean Sharpley-Whiting has called "anti-black femininity."[20] The process of de-naturalizing racist indignities that reside in the mind, hold the promise to decolonize visual. Khan's decolonizing visual culture criticism allows her to unearth and critique the necropolitics of the visual cultural practices of apartheid law, governmentality, and sociality. Thus, Khan's art criticism sees value and excellence in the works of black women artists that other art historians may not wish to see. Quite unlike the boredom and tedium line of critique and the scolding reminders to get over the past already, Khan attests that Black women visual artists' pay an exquisite price to make art while facing the accusations of being overly identified with grievance—as if that injury has no social meaning.[21] Khan's approach, then, is replying to Hegel's notorious caricatures about Africa being separate from history and the capacity for world consciousness. Khan means to root out lines of critique organized through name-calling and deliberate attempts at spirit injury. Khan's use of biomythography illuminates how the notion that Black women artists are boring is often a *prelude to lethal violence*. Given that being viable for the artworld's commodity market is also a prelude to other forms of self-implicating lethal violence,[22] certainly the artists and their provocative questions are deserving of far more serious engagement. Khan provides a powerful model of such scholarly rigor.

Khan's retort to these kinds of lines of criticism provokes earth-shattering epistemological questions. What might become of visual culture criticism and scholars if they refused to claim and displace the pain of others? What might become of visual culture criticism and scholars if they bore witness to the pain of others? What might become of visual culture criticism and the scholars who deploy it if they examined their boredom with black people's accounts and theories about their own suffering?

Not only do the artists that Khan explores "deploy autobiographical witnessing and personal testimonies as narrative giving more individual and textured accounts of life under apartheid [but they used] masquerading as a particularly sound rejoinder to the Black-African body as a motif of ethnographic research and pseudo-scientific colonial-racist imaginative projection." Khan argues that embodied interrogation and the use of dialogue in assessing knowledge claims demonstrates the altruistic and empathic ethos of examining lived experience. That is, such self-regard as agents of knowledge and such rigorous self-examination is organized around gaining the tools to work collectively to challenge intersecting structural forms of oppression as they are experienced most devastatingly in the material world, the psyche, land, and in the body. Thus, Khan suggests that black women visual artists: 1) navigate both spaces that affirm them and spaces that disrespect and undermine them and 2) struggle toward black feminist consciousness as a tool for inhabiting the complexity of singular and plural 'I's.

While others may call these intellectual labours tedious or anti-theoretical, in actuality, they constitute a rigorous set of ethical practices that are absolutely critical for addressing the actual damage created by interlocking and shifting systems of oppression across space, time, and visual discourse. How can anyone truly commit to changing social and collective practices that have so deeply shaped South African society and the world—like apartheid—without embodied interrogation, an ethic of personal accountability, using dialogue to assess knowledge claims, and rigorous self-examination—a few of the foundational Black feminist methodological principles? This is a methodology of social change. Perhaps this is why unlike those who seek to remind us that our lives bore them, the conditions under which we survive must be carefully examined so that we come to commit to making liveable lives for ourselves especially when we are being told that democratic transition has been achieved and we know that our democratic visions have yet to be met.

Dawes is tired of Black feeling. Others hope to instruct, guide, tutor, mold, correct, uplift, and make Black feeling resspectable. Neither line of critique is willing to witness, be with, or learn from these types of Black feeling. The interpretive and analytical work of being willing to witness, be with, or learn from these types of Black feeling is castigated. Perhaps, to witness and learn from these works may take a more precise interior examination, set of visual cultural practices, and ethical principles—a willingness, as Ernesto Martinez has theorized, to "make sense."[23]

Khan, like other women of color visual artists turned critics, has forged these practices and principles in plain sight and allowed her critical vision to thrive in hard fought battles in the theory-building by women of color visual artists for decades now. Their attention to power relations and epistemology has a storied provenance in cultural studies. These are not expressions of narcissism but *again by following Collins*, these new discourses by the still marginalized are examinations of the power relations which validate who is believed and which accounts are deemed knowledge production.[24] Certainly none of us would agree that the South African or European art market place (and their practices, regulatory mechanisms, and systems of standardization and reward) are dominated by women of color visual artists. Instead, the art world continues to regard as boring, tedious, and simply ungrateful the artistic production of those who continue to be crowded out and included on terms of disrespect, public disregard and tokenism. Such artistic weapons as the boldness and inventiveness of women of color artists are not being dismissed because they are dull, banal, or repetitive. Rather these women of color artists, suggests Khan, are being rejected because phenomenon like the making of roti by some black women's hands is a potent fact and reminder about the material and immaterial origins of artistic innovation and meaning. Indeed, the rarefied world where what black women visual artists make with their hands does not belong is on the verge of collapse, made sluggish by the indefensibility of its own dualistic claims. Khan invites us to struggle over whether the accounts of aesthetic reflection made by a body named Senzeni or a body named Sibande shall matter or whether only the accounts of white writing and male writing will be the tools for examining the period after 1994.

Robert Muponde's essay on white writing in postcolonial Zimbabwe and post-apartheid South Africa offers another feature of the debates over which accounts will matter in the analysis of the two decades that have passed. White emergence, white need, and whiteness overall are explored through what Muponde calls, 'double dipping' or 'going native.' Muponde questions accounts that "mak[e] the perspective of one who has gone native central, and the stories and actions of the native population … encountered incidental." Muponde reprises earlier critiques of vacuous celebrations of crossing the color line that unwittingly (and sometimes quite intentionally) prop up the rigidification of binarized social sexual categories without transforming the power differentials that undergird them.[25] Drawing on two literary texts, John Eppel's *Absent: The English Teacher* (2009) and Antjie Krog's *Begging To Be Black* (2009), Muponde employs a postcolonial position to ask a rather controversial question of whether 'going black', by white writers, is a possible "social prophylactic" in the context of the ongoing crises of belonging and race in Zimbabwe and South Africa. Marked by Aime Cesaire's 1955 notion of a historical process of "thingification" of dynamic living cultures, such accounts point to enduring calls for the "regeneration of the white race" and the securit[ization of] imperial cultures."[26] White characters in these novels are subject to countless forms of objectification through the "rhetoric of rarity and antiquity," "fetish," and "curio." Eppel draws white characters who root themselves in Zimbabwe through their settler pioneer ancestors and who cannot connect to "conscious inspiration from and nostalgia for black African political figures and ancestral history." Eppel's character, George Jorge George, is as unable to make amends as "gone native" characters like *The Fiddler* (1929) by famous early twentieth century novelist Sarah Gertrude Millin.[27] Muponde writes that Eppel's protagonist felt "deeply grounded and that, if properly propagated and tended, he could be nourishing to community. He seeks a route out of a whiteness beyond the borders of the colonial legacy, although curiously enough, he does not talk about being nourished by the same black community…a glaring absence of mutality."

Instead in Eppel's writing, as Muponde explains, the most significant thing to know is that African people inherited literacy and creative expression, governance of the multiple and the individual, as well as basic foodstuffs— like maize—*from Europe*. There can be no basis for mutuality or learning in such an account, there can only be the humiliation and debasement that Eppel's character experiences as a destitute houseboy, destitute both because of the work he does and because that work is beneath the gendered racial inheritance mobilized by white nationalist fanatics. While Eppel's protagonist wants the fact of his degradation in status and class to stand in for analysis of racial conflict, Krog wrestles with "pain and loss, brutality and genocide" through guilt and nostalgia. Guilt and nostalgia, however, cannot redeem the fact that the "victims of holocaust" in South Africa do not control the land, money, and their own bodies in a society that created itself through massive group harm against them. Revealing that whiteness as innocence is a globe-trotting and dangerous trope, Krog wants to engage in "black[ness] as the new locus of an inimitable humanism and viable politics" but stumbles in traveling to Germany, a place where racism continues to be a foundation stone of state and juridical necropolitics, anti-Islamic white nationalist citizen-making, and forced removals hiding under the cover of pink washing. [28] Not only this but, Muponde explains that Germany is not a way out of the "quagmire of whiteness" since the perpetrators and their descendants continue to be "firmly in control of the state, its economy, language and culture." In Krog's writings, white nostalgia and white guilt, are coupled with a sanitized overly pacific black charismatic male political class not with "the underclasses associated with township 'necklace murders' and violent service delivery protests"—the classic mode of colonial settler society *in toto*. With Eppel and Krog we find that white destitution, for the former, and white desires for interrelatedness, for the latter, lead us back again to entanglement of the Nuttall sort. Such political and cultural projects proceed as if they have no histories and no ethical or material stakes.

We close the book with a group of commissioned and curated creative pieces and cross-genre testimonies written by undergraduate students in California reflecting on feminist pedagogy experiments with Winnie Madikizela-Mandela's *491 Days: Prisoner Number 1323/69*, reprinted by Ohio University Press with a Foreword by Ahmed Kathrada (2014). To be read as part of the various women of color feminist provocations and Black feminist invocations by our more established contributors, their insights and artwork reflect the continued relevance of memoirs by political prisoners as feminist political, cultural, and social theory in the classroom. As we continue to celebrate the life of this tremendous and complicated force for social change, we must remember to share Madikizela-Mandela's writings and those of other political activists and freedom fighters in our classrooms. Ariana Bolton's blog entry, Callan Grace Garber's redacted pages and writing in the voice of Winnie remembering her children, Adita Mayer's visual diary, Maya Green's painting, and Lara Nguyen's "Frequently Asked Questions" all use the experimental dynamics of the epistolary that are central to Madikizela-Mandela's *491 days*. These young creatives upend how we interact with the world with pre-determined answers by presenting this text through their quadruply-mediated world. They offer courageous calls to action steeped in simple reminders about pedagogy, curriculum building practices, and the publishing habits of those in power who would reduce brutality to footnotes, and confine our words to simple bodily tics and affectations. Haunting poems, choreopoems, and literary criticism by Alexa Dorsett-Levingston, Sydney Diane Lara, Alyana Reid, Maya Green, RM Corbin and Kamerahan Francisco-Latiti form a crucial part of our intention with this book: to take seriously the emerging but present sensibilities in this post-apartheid era wherever it emerges.

Abebe Zegeye, Tiffany Willoughby-Herard, Derilene Marco, Ashraf Jamal, Peter Hudson, Bhavisha Panchia, Sharlene Khan, Natalia Molebatsi, Zethu Cakata, Robert Muponde, Alyana Reid, Aditi Mayer, Lara Nguyen,

Ariana Bolton, Callan Grace Garber, Alexa Dorsett-Levingston, Kamerahn Francisco-Latiti, Sydney Diane Lara, R M Corbin, and Maya Green, experiment with and interpret the ethical and material stakes of the art we make. We may yet have the last laugh, black wombs and all.

Endnotes

1   The authors wish to extend thanks to the anonymous reviewers of this essay, the Academic Writers Studio team of Laura Holliday and Berkeley Goodloe, to Editorial Research Assistant and Los Angeles-based teacher, Amber Gordon, to LaShonda Carter, Jeanne Scheper, and Jos Charles. This research has been funded by the University of California, Irvine, Humanities Center, the Humanities Commons, the Deans of the Schools of Social Science and Humanities, the Department of African American Studies, the PhD Program in Culture and Theory; and by the University of the Witwatersrand School of Literature, Language, and Media Studies.

2   Fanon, Frantz, *The Wretched of the Earth*. Fraçois Maspéro, ed. 1961. Transcribed by Dominic Tweedie, *marxists.org*, https://www.marxists.org/subject/africa/fanon/conclusion.html. Accessed October 4, 2018.

3   In the ensuing years, we have lost friends, celebrated the birth and growing of children and grandchildren and been witness to tremendous global upheaval and revolutionary movements.

4   Willoughby-Herard, Tiffany, "Black Rainbows: Militant White Women Writers, Post-Racial Discourse, and the Stakes of Race, Class, and Gender in South Africa." *Journal of Contemporary Thought*. Rajagopalan Radhakrishnan, ed. vol. 39, Special Issue: Speaking Truth to Power, 2014, pp. 197-218.

5   Willoughby-Herard, Tiffany. *Waste of a White Skin: The Carnegie Corporation and the Racial Logic of White Vulnerability*. University of California Press, 2015, xiv.

6   Ibid, 8-9.

7   Ibid.

8   Molebatsi, Natalia. (2008 [2013]). Listen up child. *Mahala*. September 27, 2013. http://www.mahala.co.za/art/listen-up-child/ Accessed October 4, 2018; See also Poetry for Life http://www.poetryforlife.co.za/index.php/poem-selection/south-african-selection/118-listen-up-child Accessed Oct 4, 2018.

9   Molebatsi, Natalia (2010).

10   Willoughby-Herard has an extensive critique of the notion of black memory as especially and uniquely unreliable in "Black Rainbows," 209.

11   Winkle-Wagner, Rachelle. *The unchosen me: Race, gender, and identity among Black women in college*. Johns Hopkins University Press, 2010.

12   Hong, Grace Kyungwon, and Roderick A. Ferguson. "Introduction." *Strange affinities: The gender and sexual politics of comparative racialization*. Duke University Press, 2011, pp. 10-11.

13   Jordan, June. "Poem About My Rights." *Directed By Desire: The Collected Poems of June Jordan*. Port Townsend, WA, Copper Canyon Press, 2005.

Copyright © 2005 by The June M. Jordan Literary Trust. Used by permission of The June M. Jordan Literary Trust, www.junejordan.com. https://www. poetryfoundation.org/poems-and-poets/poems/detail/48762, Accessed April 7, 2017.

14   Accapadi, Mamta Motwani. "When White Women Cry: How White Women's Tears Oppress Women of Color." *College Student Affairs Journal,* vol. 26, No. 2, Spring 2017, pp. 208-215. Accessed February 23, 2014.

15   Meer, Shamim. "African Feminist Thinkers: Our Voices." *African Gender Institute.* University of Cape Town, http://agi.ac.za/teaching-material/shamim-meer. Accessed April 5, 2017.

16   Christianse, Yvette. *Unconfessed.* New York, Other Press, 2006, p. 2.

17   Willoughby-Herard, Tiffany. "'The Rape of an Obstinate Woman': Frantz Fanon's Wretched of the Earth." *Shout Out: Women of Color Respond to Violence.* Barbara K. Ige and Maria Ochoa, eds. Berkeley, CA, Seal Press, 2008, pp. 274-5.

18   Knight, Etheridge. "The Idea of Ancestry." *The Essential Etheridge Knight.* The University of Pittsburgh Press,1986. All rights are controlled by the University of Pittsburgh Press; used by permission of the University of Pittsburgh Press. https://www.poets.org/poetsorg/poem/idea-ancestry. Accessed May 1, 2017.

19   Swarns, Rachel L. "Mocked in Europe of old, African is embraced at home at last." *New York Times,* May 4, 2002, p. 3; Hearst, David. "Colonial Shame: African Woman Going Home after 200 years." *The Guardian,* April 30, 2002, p. 13; Willis, Deborah, *Black Venus 2010: They Called Her "Hottentot."* Philadelphia, Temple University Press, 2010.

20   Sharpley-Whiting, T. Denean. "Anti-Black Femininity, Mixed-Race identity: Engaging Fanon to Read Capecia." *Frantz Fanon: A Critical Reader.* Lewis Gordon, T. Denean Sharpley-Whiting, and Renee White, eds. Hoboken, NJ, Blackwell Wiley, 1996, pp. 155-163.

21   Eze, Emmanuel, *Race and the Enlightenment.* Oxford, Blackwell, 1997, pp. 111-116, pp. 126-127.

22   Thinking with performance studies as resistance scholars who balance between the limits and possibilities of navigating the terrain of survival as Black creatives. Sharpe, Christina. *Monstrous intimacies: Making post-slavery subjects.* Duke University Press, 2010; Scheper, Jeanne. *Moving Performances: Divas, Iconicity, and Remembering the Modern Stage.* Rutgers University Press, 2016; Kilomba, Grada. *Plantation memories: episodes of everyday racism.* Münster, Unrast, 2008.

23   Martínez, Ernesto Javier. *On Making Sense: Queer Race Narratives of Intelligibility.* Stanford University Press, 2012.

24   2000/2009, p. 270.

25   Jared Sexton's *Amalagamation Schemes: Antiblackness and the Critique of Multiracialism* (University of Minnesota Press, 2008) is most powerful when critiquing the global and cross-temporal misunderstandings about mixed race identity as a new-found political possibility that provides a backdoor way out

of naming and addressing the philosophies and practices of eugenics and anti-blackness. Sexton insists, instead, that this very old social phenomenon far from being an index of the meaning of love or the nature of human relations is typically marshaled by the state to silence the political claims of those designated for naturalized discrimination and medicalized subordination. In other words, to have parents of two different racial designations provides one very important and politically salient point that the state and society still regard racial designations as a key biometric tool for surveillance and for transmitting racialized carcerality to manage demographic populations. Sometimes the state will designate mixed race people as heroes and promises of modernity and futurity and at other times the very same state will designate mixed race people and their parents as the shame of the nation. This phenomenon is so deeply embedded in the modern history of the state that suggesting that it offers a newfound political *solution* is both ahistorical and anti-scientific.

26   Huhndorf, Shari M. *Going Native: Indians in the American Cultural Imagination*. Ithaca/London, Cornell University Press, 2001. Cited in Muponde. For Cesaire see *Between Colonizer and Colonized*. http://staff.kings.edu/cristoferscarboro/HNRS%20204/Cesaire.html. Accessed June 27, 2017.

27   Millin, Sarah Gertrude. *The Fiddler*. London, Constable and Co., 1929.

28   El-Tayeb, Fatima. "Time travelers and queer heterotopias: Narratives from the Muslim underground." *The Germanic Review: Literature, Culture, Theory*, vol. 88, no. 3, 2013, pp. 305-319; Bruce-Jones, Eddie. "German policing at the intersection: race, gender, migrant status and mental health." *Race and Class*, vol. 56, no. 3, 2015, pp. 36-49; Snorton, C. Riley and Jin Haritaworn. "Trans Necropolitics." *Transgender Studies Reader*, vol. 2, New York, Taylor and Francis, 2013, pp. 66-76. For more research on a wide range of cases where whiteness as innocence is used to establish plantation slavery again and consolidate racial hierarchies see Gerald Horne's *The White Pacific: US imperialism and Black slavery in the South Seas after the civil war*. University of Hawaii Press, 2007; *Mau Mau in Harlem?: the US and the liberation of Kenya*. New York, Springer, 2009; *The deepest south: the United States, Brazil, and the African slave trade*. NYU Press, 2007. Horne's accounts of "blackbirding" and the ease of travel given to U.S. planters (who received financial reparations after the US Civil War) and then used those infusions of capital to re-establish plantations in Brazil, Kenya, and Fiji remind us that moving to new places—or *racial capitalism on the move*—replicates the worst aspects of racial hierarchy again.

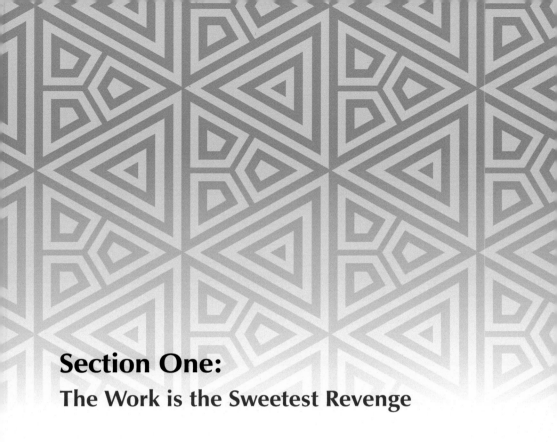

Section One:
The Work is the Sweetest Revenge

1

Thinking Through Black Feminist Creative Theorisation through the Postcolonial Masquerades of South African Visual Artists Mary Sibande and Senzeni Marasela

S. Khan[1]

> *A woman "brings her story into the story."*
>
> Minh-ha[2]

Introduction

In 2001, South African White[3] male "cultural writer" Nick Dawes, on viewing South African Coloured woman visual artist Berni Searle's work *Snow White* at the Venice Biennale, had this to say about the work in which Searle, kneeling naked on the floor in a darkened space, has flour falling on and all around her (which she then proceeds to knead into dough):

> Would that the same could be said of Berni Searle's *Snow White*. Indeed, as one stands poised between the two screens that comprise the video installation, a single question imposes itself: 'And who among you, when the public asks for something to chew on, would give them a video of Berni Searle making roti?' [...] Instead one simply sighs in affirmation: indeed race, gender and domestic labour cut across the body of the black but not-quite-black woman in complicated ways. Indeed woman's work has a transformative and even sacramental character, but how tedious the lecture, how dully the point is inscribed

on tape, and how easily we could have read it in a book, mirror on the wall, wicked queen and all. The perfectly banal surface of identity politics, of a comfortable academic discourse on hybridity, smoothes everything over here. In the end we are standing in front of yet another video of a naked woman performing a repetitive task, and we are bored beyond words.[4]

Dawes' statements reflect a historical juncture at which White practitioners and theorists in South Africa are tiring of works and discourses dealing with identitarian fictions after the advent of post-apartheid seven years earlier and are keen to move to a post-racial phase. He is, as he states, bored with another woman-of-colour struggling to articulate, creatively and visually, how social oppressions intersect around her. But who is the "we" that is invoked here? Clearly the "we" of Dawes' statement does not include the curatorial team who found Searle's work interesting enough to exhibit at the Venice Biennale. In South Africa, the "we" of the art audience, as I have argued elsewhere (Khan 2015), reveals the racial polemic of a South African art world governed by a White monied habitus and, more recently, by a small black bourgeoisie. This was pointed out in 2001 by South African black feminist Desiree Lewis in her article entitled "The Conceptual Art of Berni Searle":

> His [Dawes'] critique ends up revealing far less about Searle's art than it does about his entitlement, his subject position and the South African art world in relation to socially marginal artists. Dawes' reduction of Searle's art to obsolescence is ultimately a claim that it falls beyond standards shaped by an elite, speaking on behalf of 'the public', that continues to define spurious notions of universality and artistic excellence (111).

In the article, Lewis reads the work through various black-African feminist perspectives showing how the "lack" lay not in the work itself, but in the viewer's inability to decode the work outside of hegemonic Western art framings.

Fast forward to 2016, and the re-centring of bodies-of-colour can be strongly evidenced in the visual arts globally through the strategy of performative fictive masquerading. Visual artists Berni Searle, Mary Sibande, Nandipha Mntambo, Tracey Rose, Senzeni Marasela, Lebohang Kganye, Donna Kukuma and many others, have become well-known names in the South African arts field, suggesting that the art market is anything but bored with displays of women-of-colour subjectivities. "Masquerading" here is defined as the donning of costumes and make-up by visual artists, along with the use of props, to enact and stage characters, often engaging their own bodies in front of a photographic/video camera or live performance.

The breakdown of apartheid in the early 90s saw artists using their bodies as sites of critique in unprecedented ways. Performance art entered the South African visual arts gallery as a tour de force. In particular, the Black-African body as a motif of anthropological research, pseudo-scientific colonial-racist imaginative projection, but also autobiographical witnessing, has become contested in South African narrativisation, as personal testimonies give more individual and nuanced accounts of life under apartheid. Masquerading's performative playing reflects the many spaces this body inhabits, both physically in the space(s) of post-apartheid, post-colonial[5] South Africa, as well as Africa and a globalised, technologized world. The 2000s have seen many young women-of-colour visual artists employing masquerading, and it is within these multiple spaces that I seek to theorise the idea of visual arts "postcolonial masquerading" as a subversive strategy able to *reveal* various social scripts.

Cultural scholar Niti Sampet Patel in her book *Postcolonial Masquerading: Culture and Politics in Literature, Film, Video, and Photography* (2001, 120-121) proposes the term "postcolonial masquerading" as a tool for post-colonial people to visualise the social categories that construct their bodies/identities, and to decolonise their own minds and histories. She argues that it can form communities of resistance and self-definition via an aesthetics aimed at them and through cultural productions produced for them (rather than global, capitalised markets). Patel draws on postcolonial literary theorist Homi. K. Bhabha's book *The Location of Culture* (1994) where he proposes that an ambivalent identification can possibly be redeemed into a political act of subversion. Patel (xx) heeds Bhabha's call to "read between the lines", which informs his notion of hybridity, and which he proposes has capacity for intervention, as Other denied/repressed knowledges come to impinge and question authorised knowledge.

Patel attempts to demonstrate the potential of postcolonial masquerading and ambivalence, not just in terms of the centralised perspectives of the characters, content and audience identification, but in the aesthetic considerations of the chosen genres. Through her various reflections on the differing strategies of masquerade employed in the field of film, video, literature and photography, Patel locates its potential for subversiveness and resistance in its "contradictory, representational, and performative nature." She regards masquerade as a powerful metaphor:

> [T]hrough which we can understand both the material and aesthetic strategies of varied postcolonial texts and discourses. The trope permits a critical re-examination of the predicaments of postcolonial identities and dislocations in an increasingly aggressive, neo-colonial global world. At the same time it contains within it notions of *changeability*, *metamorphosis*, and *contradiction* (119-120).

Patel believes that by not reducing postcolonial readings to binaries of either/ or, she can create dynamic/incompatible/complex ways of "articulating and unmasking postcolonialities", and states that "masquerade thrives on specificity and locality" rather than generalization on traversing borders, subjectivities, and even disciplines (xiv).

Thus, far from feeling bored or irritated by the many manifestations of personal narratives on offer through performative fictive postcolonial masquerading, this text looks at the work of two South African visual artists, Mary Sibande and Senzeni Marasela, and how their use of biography, storytelling and masquerading can be read through black-African feminist and postcolonial theories. I argue that these visualisations rile against collective imaginations of "Africans," "blacks," and "women" to create complex, contradictory Subject positions. These engagements with identitarian fictions are discussed in relation to the visual strategies and concept of 'postcolonial masquerading' and what is offers for both artists and audiences in its critical play.

Black feminist creative theorisation and insider/ outsider positions

Who is the black woman? What does she want? Is she one or many things? Has she something we could call 'an identity', which remains 'given' beneath all the shifting appearances? Or is her identity always a performance, a masquerade?

Stuart Hall and Mark Sealy[6]

Black feminist, African feminisms, Third World/postcolonial feminisms, and intersectionality studies complicate narratives of gender by insisting that the categories of race-sex-class-sexuality-ethnicity-religion-location do not function independently in women-of-colours' lives, but are interlocking matrices of domination that result in multiple intersecting oppressions.[7] The site of the "everyday" becomes important for "women-of-colour" in their Self-determination and Self-definition.[8] In her book *Black Feminist Thought: Knowledge, Consciousness, and the Politics of Empowerment* (2000/2009), African-American sociologist Patricia Hill Collins explores the development of US black feminist thought. A large part of Collins' book is dedicated to showing the extensive trajectory of African-American women speaking about their experiences not only in academia, but in many other sites like blues, jazz and rap music, storytelling, literature, poetry, religion, and daily conversations and behaviour. Some of the tenets of Collins' black feminist epistemology include: lived experience as a criterion for knowledge,[9] the use of dialogue in assessing knowledge claims, the ethic of personal accountability, and black women as agents of knowledge. She argues that many black women scholars draw on their own lived experiences and those of other black women when deciding on their research areas, and the kinds of methodologies they use. I am interested in her assessment that black women researchers often harness narrative methodology in their engagement with fellow black subjects, as I notice similar trends in the South African art field where many women-of-colour employ various forms of narration in their practices.[10]

Collins' ideas are exemplified in the work of South African black-African feminists Desiree Lewis, Pumla Gqola and Yvette Abrahams, and their engagement with artistic creations as sites of critical reflection. Gqola (2001; 2006) believes that creative works, as sites for theorisation and knowledge production, propose a way out of Western philosophical dualism between theory and praxis. Creative spaces offer freedom of the imagination, which is sometimes stifled in academic discourses:

> By "creative theorization," I intend the series and forms of conjecture, speculative possibilities opened up in literary and other creative genres. Theoretical or epistemological projects do not only happen in those sites officially designated as such, but emerge from other creatively textured sites outside of these (Gqola 2006, 50).

Gqola, Lewis and Abrahams' creative theorisations on women-of-colour cultural productions, both in South Africa and internationally, have some of the following common features: women-of-colour centred narratives produced by women-of-colour artists who seem to be *addressing* (but not limiting themselves to) audiences-of-colour who understand the nuances of their work and permit a *dialogue* with their work (rather than an objectification of their bodies and work); the use of *autobiography* as the intersection of larger social histories with individual and familial histories; the *"everyday"* as a site of theorisation as to the intersectionality of oppressive and affirmative practices; the use of the *black body* as a site of performative interrogation; *differences and contradictions* as fundamental in theorisation to show the heterogeneity of women-of-colours' lives; the value of the *emotional* as a form of knowledge; and *an ethics of caring and personal accountability* about how their works fit into the larger histories of their communities, and visual legacies of women and black bodies. Such premises can be viewed as what sociologist Himani Bannerji (1995) has called "situated critiques", which are not just informed by the experiences of "an isolated self, but from my sense of being in the world, presuming the same for others, and [having] tried to think through as best as I can the making of these experiences" (13). It is this sense of making situated critiques in changing times that many South African visual artists share – of trying, in hindsight, to comprehend apartheid trauma and the instability and unknown of post-apartheid.

Gqola often echoes African womanist Molara Ogundipe's words that African feminists need to theorise out of our "epicentres of agency, looking for what is meaningful, progressive and useful to us as Africans" (2006, 49). This idea is pivotal to the artists discussed below as we shall see that the Black woman's body is quite literally used as an epicentre from which to theorise. For these artists, these acts of creation are an attempt to understand their lives and histories, which doesn't necessarily lead to final conclusions, but rather to "re-creating", to a continuous destabilisation of hegemonic discourses. Of course, dealing with one's own communities and histories is never easy, in that one is invested and implicated in the research and the outcomes, and has a responsibility in what one says about ourselves (even as one attempts at some kind of "objectivity"). Vietnamese-American filmmaker and theorist Trinh T. Minh-ha proposes that far from the implicated "insider" researcher being a weighted position, this creates a complex position of the Inside-Outsider/ Outside-Insider. Trinh T. Minh-ha says of this task:

> The moment the insider steps out from the inside, she is no longer a mere insider (and vice versa). She necessarily looks in from the outside while also looking out from the inside. Like the outsider, she steps back and records what never occurs to her the insider as being worth or in need of recording. But unlike the outsider, she also resorts to non-explicative, non-totalizing strategies that suspend meaning and resist closure (1991, 74).

The use of Inside-Outsider/Outside-Insider positions is an interesting way of reading the use of the "insider" performed body of South African visual artists who, in visualising apartheid's identitarian fictions, have also found engaging complex ways of interrogating them. Two artists who exemplify such practices are Mary Sibande and Senzeni Marasela in their use of "fictional" Selves and in their placement of stories of their mothers at the epicentres of their inquiries. Engaging some of the creative features of women-of-colour centred narratives discussed above, I want to show how the use of Self and "I" narratives contribute to nuanced validation processes.

Inside-outsider: Mary Sibande and *Sophie*

South Africa has a long history of in-house domestic work since Dutch and British colonialism. Domestic work remains one of the staple areas of formal and informal employment for Black women in middle-class households in South Africa. Despite their presence in many public/private spaces, domestic workers are ambivalent figures which occupy an "outsider-within" status in the South African mindscape. Scholar of English Anne McClintock in her book *Imperial Leather: Race, Gender and Sexuality in the Colonial Context*, says of the domestic worker:

> Laboring by day to uphold the white cult of domesticity, black women are shunted by night to tiny backyard *khayas* (homes) without water, sanitation, heat or light. The furtive intimacies between black women and their white charges; the forbidden liaisons between black women and their white male employers; the fraught relations of acrimony, strained intimacy, mistrust, condescension, occasional friendships and coerced subservience that shape relations between African women and their white mistresses ensure that the colonial home is a contest zone of acute ambivalence (1995, 271).

McClintock's statement points to the way race-gender-class intersects in the figure of the "maid," and the fraught contra-bond power relationships between South African women themselves. The lives of domestic workers under colonialism and apartheid were characterised by contradictions. They attended to the welfare of White families, but often at the expense of time with their own. They had to be available whenever needed, and yet, while bodily present, forced to remain invisible, absent in their individualism. They represented "savages"[11] who, nonetheless, could be entrusted to raise White children. Domestics had to be "sanitised" in various ways. They had to wear specific attire for their employment; be discreetly housed outside in a small room and often not allowed to entertain visitors even if these were a husband or children. They also had to drink and eat from specific dishes and cutlery assigned to them, and almost always take on a name that the *baas* and *madam* could pronounce easily enough.

In the 2000s, Mary Sibande, the daughter of a line of domestics created the ultimate domestic worker, which has gained huge popularity in both the local and international art circuit. Sibande's mother, grandmother and great-grandmother were domestic workers. Sibande's grandmother narrated to her that her great-grandmother was called "Tsheledi Fanedi" in SeSotho, but as her "masters" couldn't remember or pronounce her name, they re-named her "Elsie" (Sibande 2013). "And so she died as Elsie," relates Sibande, reminding us, once again, of the power of naming, of those with the power to re-name grown men and women, whose ethnic names are endowed with cultural significance. Reducing them linguistically to "my boy" and "my girl" is an act of language that claims ownership over certain bodies, that gives particular persons the status of property.

When Sibande created her now iconic domestic worker, she named her "Sophie", an English/ Spanish/French derivative of the Greek word for "wisdom." Sibande, herself, found that Sophie represented a wealth of accumulated stories that she unearthed from her mother and grandmother about the conditions of their lives, and how they had managed to succeed despite the limitations imposed on their lives (Sibande is the first person in her family to study beyond high school and to go to university). Sophie becomes the embodiment of countless narratives that came before. She represents the hopes, dreams and aspirations of Black women beyond their actual lives. Dressed in the colonial fetish of the clean white apron and head doek[12], and an African Zionist/Victorian-inspired frock of royal blue, which grows ever larger and represents the layers of stories that she encompasses (but which also physically limits and weighs her down), Sophie dares to dream beyond the role that has been ordained for her skin colour, gender, class, and by the Bantu Education Act.[13] Cast in life-size sculptures worked in Sibande's hands, and modelled on her, or later performed by Sibande's body (enacted in digital photographs), Sophie is in excess of all the categories that contain her ("Black", "woman", "poor", "maid"). Everything about her is *more than*—whether she is praying, sewing, taking a break, stopping to smell the flowers, conducting an orchestra, or charging on a horse like White men generals (Figs.1-5), Sophie becomes a signifier for dreams and imaginations that are not dependent on her reality. Even while recognising the unrealistic aspirations of this poor Black woman under apartheid, Sibande's masquerade doesn't hold Sophie back or condemn her for her flights of fantasy. Dreaming itself becomes a subversive moment for Sibande.

In *They Don't Make Them Like They Used To* (2009, Fig.4), Sophie is caught unawares in a daydream when she is supposed to be working. Captured in the stillness of the digital photographic moment, she stands (forever) eyes closed, deep inside her. Whether she is the invisible shadow behind Superman mending his costume in her hands or is envisioning herself in the (un)wanted role of Superwoman, Sophie could, simplistically read, represent the affirmative role played by mothers as the backbone of households. Read differently, however, Sophie could also be exposing the "Black Superwoman" [14] myth that various black women theorists have criticised: the one called upon to bear the burdens of providing for so many in her family; of seeing endlessly to the needs of another paying family; of being herself and not, a schizophrenic demand placed on her to negotiate

Fig.1. Mary Sibande, *The Reign* (2010) © [Mary Sibande]

Fig.2. Mary Sibande, *I Put a Spell on Me* (2009) © [Mary Sibande]

Fig.3. Mary Sibande, *Silent Symphony* (2010) © [Mary Sibande].

daily in her life; of being an othermother,[15] looking after the welfare of Black communities more generally; to being silenced under the overwhelming strain of all these roles in her masquerade of standing by[16] the Black man, Black family and Black community.

This "playing" of multiple, sometimes invisible and contradictory, roles is often disavowed by employers who trust and believe in the "knowability" of their domestic workers, and, yet, at the same time feel a subliminal recognition of "the stranger in one's home" that unnerves and disconcerts. McClintock states that domestic workers in private spaces were capable of many small subversive acts:

> In colonial homes, African women perform myriad such small acts of refusal: in work slowdowns, in surreptitiously taking or spoiling food, in hiding objects, in chipping plates, in scolding or punishing children, in revealing domestic secrets, in countless acts of revenge that their white employers identify as laziness, clumsiness, incompetence, gossip, and theft (1995, 272).

Similarly, Sophie's daring to dream can be read as an act of subterfuge. Sophie declares her humanity in opposition to the very title of the work, which suggests that she is a mere product of labour, one that is defective or of inferior quality to the kind of trope the White madam/baas holds in mind.

Moreover, Sophie is "cheeky" in her masquerading fantasies of occupying the position of the madam. In *I'm a Lady* (2009, Fig. 5) Sophie seems to be mimicking the leisurely pose of her madam, replete with a dainty umbrella. What could be dismissed as a kind of cooning or colonial mimicry, could also be read as the ultimate subversion of placing her body within the intimate wear of the madam's, trying to imagine herself as overseer of her own territory. It could also quite simply evidence a woman wanting to wear the latest fashions of the day. South African photographer Santu Mofokeng's *Black Photo Album/Look at Me* (1997) shows a history of cross-cultural fashion in images of Black South African middle-class families wearing modern English garb, posing for cameras from the 1890s onwards. His work evidences the cultural influence of European bourgeoisie society on middle-class Black societies, who identified with modernity and the cultural fashions of the day. Such visualisations were invisiblised during colonialism and apartheid in favour of depictions of Black Africans in their ethnic/tribal attire, and as distinctly "unmodern natives."[17] Sophie makes visible these hidden modern impulses and mixed cultural influences that were part of life, but wilfully suppressed by racist ideologies.

Sophie is not just a woman of her times though—she is an amalgamation of the women who came before, of Sibande herself (whose bodily masquerades act like a medium and conduit for cross-generational dialogue), and those

Fig.4. Mary Sibande, *They Don't Make Them Like They Used To* (2009), © [Mary Sibande]

Fig.5. Mary Sibande, *I'm a Lady* (2009), © [Mary Sibande]

who will come after Sibande. Sibande uses her Inside-Outsider performances to elucidate a fictive emotional life about domestic workers that is usually hidden or overlooked in their hyper-visible/invisibilised presence—we think we know "our girl," but Sophie's flights of fancy show us we never do.

Outside-insider: Senzeni Marasela, *Theodorah* and *Sarah*

It is this very "knowability" of the hyper-visible Black woman that Senzeni Marasela's avatar Theodorah consistently denies the viewer in *Theodorah Comes to Johannesburg* series (2004, Figs.6-8). In a set of digitally staged photographs, Marasela, dressed in her mother's yellow dress and head doek, retraces her mother's steps in Johannesburg and attempts to see the city through her eyes. Marasela's mum moved from the rural Eastern Cape to Johannesburg after marriage, and apartheid Johannesburg was a trauma that she could never deal with. She lived in constant fear of arrests which she saw in the city, and once witnessed someone being beaten to death in the 60s (2013). These external circumstances, combined with her own diagnosed schizophrenia, made Johannesburg an aggression she eventually couldn't confront, and has never been to since the 80s. In the *Theodorah* series, Marasela, on behalf of her mother, visits historical sites such as the Hector Pietersen memorial;[18] the Apartheid Museum[19] in Soweto; and the once derelict skeletal structure of the Turbine Hall,[20] an obsolete power station in central Johannesburg. She also visits everyday non-descript places such as an abandoned run-down shop in Kliptown, the bustling migrant trading quarters at Diagonal Street and Jeppestown, and she is even seen contemplating graffiti on a wall and having a quiet sit down in a park.

In this series, we never see Theodorah/Marasela's face. We only follow her gaze as she becomes disillusioned with Joburg[21] and the modernist capitalist dream. She feels alone against the tide of masses and time, signalling the physical, emotional and mental toll these forces take on Black people who try to survive them. When asked why she takes these trips as her mum/for her mum, Marasela says it's to acknowledge that her mother's experience of apartheid happened: "Because I guess apartheid for most people who might not have experienced harshness, might not have seen it, it's part myth, part horror. It's very difficult to conceive of it as something real, that could possibly happen, you know, on the scale it did" (2013). Marasela feels the need to validate her mother's trauma as something beyond her schizophrenia, as an external condition imposed on Black South Africans. Deconstructionist Jacques Derrida reminds us that apartheid was "… an evil that cannot be

Fig.6. Senzeni Marasela, *Theodorah Comes to Johannesburg* (Hector Pietersen Memorial, Soweto) (2004), © [Senzeni Marasela]

Fig.7. Senzeni Marasela, *Theodorah Comes to Johannesburg* (Diagonal Street) (2004), © [Senzeni Marasela]

Fig.8. Senzeni Marasela, *Theodorah Comes to Johannesburg (Zoo Lake)* (2004), © [Senzeni Marasela]

summed up in the principal and abstract iniquity of a system. It is also daily suffering, oppression, poverty, violence, torture inflicted by an arrogant white minority … on the mass of the black population" (1983, 293). It is these scenes of everydayness, the space of daily threat and quiet menace that Marasela captures in these unspectacular photographs – the landscapes that haven't changed, and, yet, are probably unrecognisable to someone who has not been to Johannesburg's city centre since the 80's, when White business and the financial district relocated to the suburbs "abandoning" the city centre to informal Black trading and small businesses. Once stigmatised as a zone of crime, an area to be avoided by the middle-class, the Johannesburg CBD (Central Business District) today, while undergoing gentrification, still bears the stigmas and visible scars of its past. This is true of Marasela's mum and also the larger South African psyche.

Marasela recognises the impossibility of her task—she cannot really re-create her mother's experiences because she is of another generation marked so differently by South Africa's history. She can only re-create an imagination of her mother's stories, a kind of personal memorial image acknowledging apartheid as not just a physical brutalisation, but as a continued mental violation, indicating the kind of wounding spoken about by Abrahams (1997; 2003) when she deals with discourses and feels herself inseparably implicated in the stories of her people, the KhoiKhoi, and Sarah Baartman. For Abrahams people-of-colour are subjected to a psychic violence when they are told racist stories about themselves, when there is a disjuncture in the official racist narratives about oppressed people, in which they cannot recognise themselves. Marasela's work creates a tension between the narrations of public wounding and her private one, and one can only imagine the pain felt by Marasela, as a child, visualising these horrific incidents and her mother's desolation. In negotiating this tension, between fact and fiction, oral narratives and official memorial projects, imagination and fantasy, she reclaims her own and her mother's subjective experiences as part of South Africa's untold histories.

While Marasela's photographic *Theodorah* series invokes personal psychological and emotional alienation, her series *Sarah, Theodorah and Senzeni in Johannesburg* (2011) extends this performative masquerading into reclamations of historical narratives of "troubled"/"troubling" Black women in fictive public scenes of women bonding. Marasela and Theodorah, in a gesture that brought me to tears on first viewing, publicly clothe Sarah Baartman and then lead her through present-day Johannesburg (Figs.9-10). Baartman's tragic life story highlights sexual and racial exhibitionism, racist science, colonial abuse and denigration of Black subjects. In Marasela's fictions though, they explore the city together, understanding the changing landscape, finding strength and safety in each other's presence. Her red, menstrual-like, fertile embroidery[22] and ink lines trace a history of limitations and over-coming narratives, from Baartman, to her own mother, to herself. Even though contemporary artwork is often associated with the "I" of the individual creator, Marasela refuses this individuation to invoke historical legacy and identify with the social struggles of women who came before. The multiple "I's" in this narrative also offer these Black women's bodies some kind of protection in South African public space where they continue to be incredibly vulnerable.

Fig.9. Senzeni Marasela, *Covering Sarah IV* (one of a triptych) (2011), © [Senzeni Marasela]

Fig.10. Senzeni Marasela, *Visit to Joburg IV* (2011), © [Senzeni Marasela]

Bio-mythographical story-telling and truth-fictions

In both Sibande and Marasela's still fixed photographic images, (re)
staged activities, whether grand or subtle, are shrouded in silence (for
example Sophie dreaming or Marasela sitting on a park bench). These are
not silences that extinguish voices but are rather contemplative silences that
Gqola (2006) speaks of when she echoes the sentiments of black feminist
Nthabiseng Motsemme, who believes that "the mute always speaks": "It
is rather to remind us that under conditions of scarcity and imposed limits,
those who are oppressed often generate new meanings for themselves around
silences. Instead of being absent and voiceless, silences in circumstances of
violence assume presence and speak volumes" (Motsemme quoted in Gqola,
2006, 50). Motsemme's idea reminds us that even though bodies can be
made invisible or silent in discourses, their presence always articulates a

counter-discourse. Sophie, Baartman, Theodorah and Marasela are threats posed by Black women narratives against sanitised European "civilisation" histories, as their stories reflect the brutality of the colonial and apartheid regimes.

Both Marasela and Sibande counter the invisibilisation of ordinary Black women—who were neither activists, nor simply victims—by forcing their oral personal narratives and points of view onto the visual landscape in an attempt to validate their experiences and contributions to their individual family and South African society at large. They visually translate and materialise spoken biographical truth-fictions, giving them tangibility and qualification. McClintock notes: "Oral memory is a refusal of the dismemberment of history, a laborious life-giver. ... It is a device against oblivion, a strategy for survival" (1995, 317). Oral testimonies situate "non-heroes" into South Africa's history-in-the-making, fracturing it into a plethora of unspectacular ordinary narratives. They provide an everyday-ness to the grand narrative of apartheid, giving textures and complexity to women-of-colours' subjectivities. Trinh T. Minh-ha believes that such memory-making process which emanates from women's personal story-telling breaks down boundaries and either/or dualisms into "both-and"[23] narratives by engaging both a plural and singular "I", and a plural and singular "you":

> Diaries, memoirs, and recollections are widely used by marginalized people to gain a voice and to enter the arena of visibility. ... Memories within come out of the material that precedes and defines a person. When she creates, they are the subsoil of her work. Thus, autobiography both as singularity and as collectivity is a way of making history and of rewriting culture. Its diverse strategies can favour the emergence of new forms of subjectivity: the subjectivity of a non-I/plural I, which is different from the subjectivity of the sovereign I (subjectivism) or the non-subjectivity of the all-knowing I (objectivism) (1991, 191-192).

Subjective storytelling compels the audience to acknowledge its bias, its invention, its fiction, what black feminist scholar Audre Lorde calls the "bio-mythographical" element. Feminist bell hooks describes Lorde's notion as "a general outline of an incident", with the details often different for each of us (1989, 157-159).[24] It is "re-membering" as a piecing together, a textured re-telling meant to capture spirit rather than accurate detail. This kind of storying process does not aim at "a truth", but rather at *truths*, acknowledging the fiction in narration. There are many "truth-fictions" in Marasela's masquerading works: the truth of Marasela's own body being used as a vehicle for re-membering, the "true" stories of her mum pictured through the eyes of little Marasela and now enacted as a grown up (a mother herself), but also the "truths" of other women-of-colour who can relate to this narrative. Similarly, for Sibande, part of the commercial success of, and interest in, Sophie is that she haunts South African consciousness every day: Sophie is everywhere (Sibande, 2013). She's your mother, friend, a domestic worker in your house or workplace. In her dreams, failures and fears, she is someone that "everybody" can relate to, and, yet, she is the person nobody wants to be.

Sibande and Marasela's works refuse to denigrate the "imperfect" women in their lives—whether they worked as domestic workers trying to be "good Blacks" for their White employers[25] or whether they were mentally ill—these women's experiences have shaped the artists' own lives, the lives of their families and their communities. Both artists acknowledge flaws without judging the older generation of women, and instead locate agency in their mothers' actions, in their recollections, and even in their silences, understanding that this doesn't imply voicelessness, inactivity or lack of agency. Sibande affirms that her own trajectory in life would not have been possible without women such as these: "I come from these women, they build what I am right now. Actually it's their construction, it's their doing and I feel like that shadow will always follow me" (2013). Their works attempt to situate the "ordinary" on a larger visual mapping of South Africa, making us note the complex and the contradictory in the everyday "I."

Fictive emotional lives and critical play/pleasure

In these artists' works, the seduction of lens-based voyeurism (what feminist scholar Laura Mulvey calls "to-be-looked-at-ness"),[26] and its corresponding desiring fictions, are harnessed by these women-of-colour artists. Sibande forces you inside the private wishes of a Black woman oppressed by the laws of apartheid, implicating you in the spectacle and tensions of her private fantasies and the enjoyment of her defiance, mimetic gestures and flirtations with the excess she is denied in her everyday life. We can critique Sophie for her seemingly Westernised capitalistic longings, but her position as a strongly desiring Subject breaks the mere projections of one's own desires and repressions on her body, rendering her a relatable person. Theodorah remains a stranger, as her back is always turned to us. Like her daughter, Marasela, who went on these imaginary sojourns, the viewer is forced on these silent journeys. The voyeurism is not a pleasurable or easy one—we are made to identify with Theodorah, to walk in her shoes, comforted only by the objectifying distance created by the lens. We never get to see her emotions and never get to feel we *know her*. We are, instead, forced to feel with her, for her, to gauge our own emotions in relation to a cityscape that is not particularly attractive. Both artists' works differ in their masquerading excesses—the staged beauty of Sophie seduces in its aesthetically composed excesses, while it is the lack of excess that frustrates in Marasela's work.

There is little to seduce you in this display of Black womenhood (particularly in the way one is accustomed to viewing African ethnographic or popular culture "affirmative" images), as they are not externally beautiful women or sexual freaks. The narcissism on display invites even as it resists, because it is "taken"/preoccupied by itself and offers little "feminine" seduction for the voyeur.

Such masqueradings evidence the potential of performative gesturing. hooks regards performance practice as an essential critical intervention in the politicisation of historical memory and a pedagogical tool, which provides the means for varied, diverse explorations of black experience (1995b, 218). Cultural theorist Efrat Tseëlon in *Masquerade and Identities* finds that masquerading "through a dialectic of concealing and revealing… serves a critical function" in its overstating, and is a statement about the wearer (2001, 3). Masquerading can thus be revelatory—it reveals moments of reflexivity "about the otherness within and beyond ourselves" (Kaiser 2001, xiv) and, through its excessive caricaturing, provides a vehicle for a "politics of desire."[27] Thus, postcolonial masquerading is not just a conceptual tool that evidences the "constructedness" of social categories that work on and affect/effect the body and identity, but it is also a visual strategy that uses the constructedness of the arts to envision a politicisation of aesthetics, representation and the structures that create them.

A further appeal, I propose, of visual arts masquerading is its ability to provide a measure of playfulness, challenge and pleasure for *both producers and viewers* in its ambivalences and ability of double-coding. hooks, taking cue from Cornel West and his idea that public performance can result in self-critical examination and artistic pleasure, reminds us of this disruptive, transformative experience of performativity: "African-American performance has always been a space where folks come together and experience the fusion of *pleasure and critical pedagogies*, a space that aims to subvert and challenge white supremacy as a system of institutionalised domination, along with class elitism, and more lately, sexism" (1995b, 218-219; emphasis added). The fact that masquerading has become such a popular post-apartheid visual arts performative strategy indicates that it provides such a space for artists to enjoy fictive theatricality and role-playing, which perhaps also gives them the opportunity to work out their own idiosyncrasies and fantasies through the visual medium. Dressing up and playing between fictional and personal truths helps producers—and their audiences—to attend, in a manner, to the welfare of their fictive emotional lives.[28] I mean this both in the sense of artistic producers, themselves, enjoying the power to create the characters in their performances, to take them on journeys, to aid in a kind of personal catharsis, and even violate them as their non-Selves/fictional versions of their Selves, but also in the audience willingly participating in the voyeurism of their narratives and investing in the characters on display, and the stories being told.

This is perhaps not unlike the way we invest in fictional characters in literature, theatre, TV and films. Philosopher Richard Moran in his article "The Expression of Feeling in Imagination" (1994) claims that people have a vast range of emotional responses in both their investment in, or dis-identifications with, fictional characters, which has not been sufficiently accounted for. While some people are definitely drawn into a narrative by shared identification with the characters or plots, Moran interestingly argues that people's investment in fictional characters is not wholly dependent on them being able to directly identify with the characters or experiences in an illusion of reality, but rather that the kinds of excessiveness of "truths," narrative and technique aid in the audience being able to connect with characters or story:

> The outlandish character of some of the comparisons, the rhythm of the relentless piling up of image upon image, like an obsessive thought, the very unreality of it – these things are *directly* productive of feeling on the part of the audience, and not through their role, if any, in make-believe. It is undeniable that the emotions are engaged by something we call imagination here, but it would be forcing things to construe the imagination relevant here as make-believe that some set of propositions is fictionally true (85-86).

Thus, part of masquerade's popularity may be its ability to create an excessiveness and an unreality that seduces people and allows them to enjoy their "voyeurism", which masquerading artists harness to their own (creative, political) ends.

Moran believes that it reveals more about a person in their ability to imagine with others and to understand situations different from theirs, in their willingness to "try on" other points of view and "determine what it is like to inhabit it," than in circumstances of "ordinary counterfactual reasoning" (105).[29] This kind of imaginative play becomes unsettling "in-between spaces," sites which are fertile grounds for the unknown realms where our fetishistic desires lurk, and are sometimes allowed to surface, but which can be harnessed into possible points of connection between people, into wider readings of artworks. Art critic Jean Fisher argues for ambivalence in creative practice: "This slippage into the regenerative space-time of becoming other is how I should like to think about the viewer's experience of a resistant artistic practice—not the closure of academicism or the propagandist message, but the uncertain terrain of the open work" (2002, 68).

Viewing artworks as pleasurable creative critical pedagogical tools refuses to instrumentalise or functionalise them, but regards them as starting points for creative theorisation, the beginnings of conversations and not end products of knowledge. One could argue that audiences, however, will consume artworks as they want to—thus Sibande's Sophie can easily be sentimentalised and purchased by the very people who exploit and denigrate domestics. While this is true, artists from oppressed communities cannot always be concerned solely with how those with hegemonic power will consume our works. When artworks are created for one's community, which interrogate the complexities of that community, that is the audience one must be concerned for and about, with the imperative as bell hooks states, to decolonise our own selves: "Whenever we choose performance as a site to build communities of resistance we must be able to shift paradigms and styles of performance in a manner that centralises the decolonisation of black minds and imaginations, even if we include everyone else in that process" (hooks, 1995b, 218).

The process of validating and supporting ourselves, as women-of-colour, cannot be taken for granted in the here-and-now. The rise of young women-of-colour in the visual arts field, but also in the many different current movements in South Africa, has meant that we have varied narratives of cross-generational women-of-colour Subjecthood being visualised, even if theorisation of these works is often lagging. Their work is going some way towards voicing and validating the many unspectacular, ordinary, everyday experiences of women-of-colour. Despite criticisms from patriarchy on how boring or narcissistic this may appear, this is important recuperative and authorising work that needs to be done for many years to come. On the last day of a conference at the end of 2016, when I was exhausted and was leaving the event, a young Black woman writer, whom I'd never met, but whose public work I follow, came to talk to me, and through tears said, "Thank you for telling us we're okay." I was stunned—why would brilliant beautiful women like these need to be told they're okay? Because 400 years of colonialization told us otherwise. This period, and the cultural productions coming out of it, can be reduced to women-of-colour telling each other, and those that came before and those that will come thereafter, that they are okay. And that, too, is okay.

Bibliography

Abrahams, Yvette. "The great long national insult: 'science', sexuality and the Khoisan in the 18th and early 19th century." *Agenda*, 13.32, 1997, pp. 34-48.

—"Learning by doing. Notes towards the practice of womanist principles in the 'new' South Africa." *Agenda*, 16.50, 2001, pp. 71-76.

—"Colonialism, dysfunction and dysjuncture: the historiography of Sarah Bartmann (Remix)." *Agenda*, 17.58, 2003, pp. 12-26.

Ahmed, Sara. *Strange encounters: Embodied others in post-coloniality.* New York, Routledge, 2013.

Ashcroft, Bill, Gareth Griffiths, and Helen Tiffin. *Key concepts in post-colonial studies.* London, Psychology Press, 1998.

Bannerji, Himani. *Thinking through: Essays on Feminism, Marxism, and Anti-Racism.* Toronto, Women's Press, 1995.

Bhabha, Homi. *The Location of Culture.* London and New York, Routledge, 1994.

Collins, Patricia Hills. *Black Feminist Thought: Knowledge, Consciousness, and Politics of Empowerment.* New York and London, Routledge, 2000/2009.

Dawes, Nick. "Authentic/Ex-centric at the Venice Biennale." *ArtThrob*, 49, September 2001. http://artthrob.co.za/01sept/reviews/venice.html.

Derrida, Jacques. "Racisms Last Word." Translated by P. Kamuf. *Critical Inquiry*, 12.1, 1983/1985, pp. 290-299. http://www.jstor.org/stable/134372.

Fisher, Jean. "Toward a metaphysics of shit." H. Aner, N. Rottner documenta und Museum Fridericianum, Verantstatlungs-GmbH, eds. *Documenta11_Platform5: Exhibition Catalogue*, Catalogue (produced for the exhibition of the same name in Kassel, Germany), Ostfildern-Ruit, Hatje Cantz Publishers, September 2002, pp. 63-70.

Gqola, Pumla Dineo. "Ufanele uqavile: Blackwomen, feminisms and postcoloniality in Africa." *Agenda*, 16.50, 2001, pp. 11-22.

—"Crafting epicentres of agency: Sarah Bartmann and African feminist literary imaginings." *Quest: An African Journal of Philosophy*, 20.2, 2008.

Hall, Stuart and Mark Sealy. *Different: A Historical Context.* London and New York, Phaidon Press, 2001.

hooks, bell. *Talking Back: Thinking Feminist, Thinking Black.* Boston, South End Press, 1989.

—*Black Looks: Race and Representation.* Boston, South End Press, 1992.

—*Art on My Mind: Visual Politics.* New York, The New Press, 1995a.

—"Performance Practice as a Site of Opposition." *Let's Get it On: The Politics of Black Performance.* C. Ugwu, ed. Seattle and London, Bay Press and ICA, 1995b, pp. 210-221.

Kaiser, Susan B. "Foreword." *Masquerade and identities: essays on gender, sexuality and marginality*. Efrat Tseëlon, ed. London and New York, Routledge, 2001, pp. xiii-xv.

Khan, Sharlene. *Postcolonial Masquerading: A Critical Analysis of Masquerading Strategies of South African Visual Artists Anton Kannenmeyer, Tracey Rose, Senzeni Marasela, Nandipha Mntambo and Mary Sibande*. Goldsmiths, University of London, London, 2015, dissertation.

Lewis, Desiree. "The Conceptual Art of Berni Searle." *Agenda*, 16.50, 2001, pp. 108-117.

Lorde, Audre. *Sister Outsider: Essays and Speeches*. Berkeley, Crossing Press, 2001.

Marasela, Senzeni. Personal communication with author, 17 April 2013.

McClintock, Anne. *Imperial Leather: Race, Gender and Sexuality in the Colonial Contest*. New York and London, Routledge, 1995.

Minh-Ha, Trinh T. *When the moon waxes red: Representation, gender and cultural politics*. New York, Routledge, 1991.

Mofokeng, Santu. *Black Family Album/Look at Me*. Eighty 35 mm Slides, Black and White slide projection, 6 mins, 40 sec, 1997.

Moran, Richard. "The expression of feeling in imagination." *The Philosophical Review*, 103.1, 1994, pp. 75-106.

Mulvey, Laura. "Visual Pleasure and Narrative Cinema." *Film and Theory: An Anthology*. Robert Stam and Toby Miller, eds. Massachusetts, Oxford, and Victoria, Blackwell Publishers, 1975, pp. 483-494.

Sampat-Patel, Niti. *Postcolonial Masquerades: Culture and Politics in Literature, Film, Video, and Photography*. New York and London, Garland Publishing, 2001.

Sibande, Mary. Personal communication with the author, April 25, 2013.

Sibande, Mary. Re: Follow-up PhD Questions, email to S. Khan (sharlenefkhan@yahoo.co.uk), August 31, 2014.

Tseëlon, Efrat, ed. "Introduction: Masquerade and Identities." *Masquerade and identities: essays on gender, sexuality and marginality*. London and New York, Routledge, 2001.

Wallace, Michelle. *Black Macho and the Myth of the Superwoman*. London, J. Calder, 1979.

LIST OF ILLUSTRATIONS

Fig.1. Sibande, Mary. (2010). *The Reign* [Mixed media installation with life size mannequin] in T. Goniwe (Ed.) (2013). *Mary Sibande: The Purple Shall Govern*, Exhibition catalogue, Standard Bank Young Artist Award 2013 traveling exhibition of the same name (pp. 25). Johannesburg: Gallery MOMO. Reproduced by permission of Mary Sibande.

Fig.2. Sibande, Mary. (2009). *I put a Spell on Me* [Digital print on cotton rag matte paper, 90cm x 60cm, edition of 10] in T. Goniwe (Ed.) (2013). *Mary Sibande: The Purple Shall Govern*, Exhibition catalogue, Standard Bank Young Artist Award 2013 traveling exhibition of the same name (pp. 21). Johannesburg: Gallery MOMO. Reproduced by permission of Mary Sibande.

Fig.3. Sibande, Mary. (2010). *Silent Symphony* [Digital archival print, 90cm x 60cm, edition of 10] in T. Goniwe (Ed.) (2013). *Mary Sibande: The Purple Shall Govern*, Exhibition catalogue, Standard Bank Young Artist Award 2013 traveling exhibition of the same name (pp. 10-11). Johannesburg: Gallery MOMO. Reproduced by permission of Mary Sibande.

Fig.4. Sibande, Mary. (2009). *They don't make them like they used to* [Digital print on cotton rag matte paper, 90cm x 60cm, edition of 10] in T. Goniwe (Ed.) (2013). *Mary Sibande: The Purple Shall Govern*, Exhibition catalogue, Standard Bank Young Artist Award 2013 traveling exhibition of the same name (pp. 6). Johannesburg: Gallery MOMO. Reproduced by permission of Mary Sibande.

Fig.5. Sibande, Mary. (2009). *I'm a Lady* [Digital print on cotton rag matte paper, 90cm x 60cm, edition of 10] in T. Goniwe (Ed.) (2013). *Mary Sibande: The Purple Shall Govern*, Exhibition catalogue, Standard Bank Young Artist Award 2013 traveling exhibition of the same name (pp. 22). Johannesburg: Gallery MOMO. Reproduced by permission of Mary Sibande.

Fig.6. Marasela, Senzeni. (2004). *Theodorah Comes to Johannesburg (Hector Pietersen Memorial, Soweto)* [Digital print in pigment ink on cotton rag, 50cm x 75cm]. Reproduced by permission of Senzeni Marasela.

Fig.7. Marasela, Senzeni. (2004). *Theodorah Comes to Johannesburg (Diagonal Street)* [Digital print in pigment ink on cotton rag, 50cm x 75cm]. Reproduced by permission of Senzeni Marasela.

Fig.8. Marasela, Senzeni. (2004). *Theodorah Comes to Johannesburg (Zoo Lake)* [Digital print in pigment ink on cotton rag, 50cm x 75cm]. Reproduced by permission of Senzeni Marasela.

Fig.9. Marasela, Senzeni. (2011). *Covering Sarah IV* [Cotton thread on fabric, 34cm X120cm]. Reproduced by permission of Senzeni Marasela.

Fig.10. Marasela, Senzeni. (2011). *Visit to Joburg IV* [Cotton thread on fabric, 42.8cm X44.3cm]. Reproduced by permission of Senzeni Marasela.

Endnotes

1   This chapter was made possible by an NRF Thuthuka Research Fund and an African Humanities Post-Doctoral Fellowship.
2   *When the moon waxes red*, p. 136.
3   This research utilises official South African racial categories (and visually presented in capitals) as established in apartheid and their continued usage post-apartheid: "White" (persons of white European descent), "Black" (local indigenous Black South Africans), "Coloured" (persons of mixed race and descendants of Malaya/Indian/Mozambican slaves and prisoners), "Indian" (persons of South Asian descent that arrived as slaves in Cape Town in the 17th century and, in the second half of the 19th century, first as British indentured labourers and then as merchants), "Asian" (at one time it included Indian and Chinese but later primarily addressed people of Chinese descent, as well as 'new' post-democracy Chinese, Pakistani, Indian and Sri Lankan migrants). Where the term "black" (lower case "b") is used (as is the term "people-of-colour"), it is strategically used in preference of "non-White", and includes Black, Coloured and Indian South Africans also grouped under the term "previously disadvantaged" (which recently constitutionally includes Chinese South Africans). The terms black and people-of-colour, along with "women-of-colour", are also used to denote identification with blackness as a politically self-affirmative project and stance. Generally, quotes and discussions follow the capitalisation and usage of specific authors in their contexts with regard to racial terms such as "white," "black," or "coloured," as well as the US/UK spelling employed by authors when quoting them.
4   Emphasis added.
5   This chapter employs the terms "post-colonial" and "postcolonial"—the former is meant to refer to a historico-political period after the formal end of colonisation in various countries, whereas the latter refers to "postcolonialism" as a conceptual framework that developed out of the scholarship that came to be known as postcolonial studies, which examines the historical, economic, political, social, and cultural dimensions of colonialism, as well as new forms of cultural and economic imperialism (neo-colonialisms).
6   p. 56.
7   For histories of black feminist thought see hooks (1982, 1984/2000), de la Rey (1997), Collins (2000/2009), Kiguwa (2004), Abrahams (2001), Lewis (2001a, 2002, 2004, 2010) and Arnfred (2009). It should be noted that although many of these women are regarded as important contributors to black feminist discourse, they may have ideological contestations with calling themselves "black feminists" or indeed "feminists" (Collins 1999). South African black-African feminists Pumla Gqola, Yvette Abrahams and Desiree Lewis often draw on black/African/postcolonial feminisms as

intersectional terms to foreground a particular allegiance or positionality in different discussions. Key proponents of postcolonial feminisms include Chandra Talpade Mohanty, Gloria Anzaldúa, Uma Narayan, Sara Suleri, Gayatri Spivak, Ania Loomba, etc., who highlight colonial/post-colonial/neo-colonial oppressions and realities for women both outside and within Western centres.

8   "Self" and "Subject" with capitalisation is used to denote a psychoanalytic sense of Subjective and agentic Self, which creates knowledge in relationality to its own sense of being and doing. Capitalised "Other" is used in the Lacanian sense of the Symbolic Other "in whose gaze the subject gains identity" (Ashcroft, Griffiths & Tiffin, 1998, 169-170), and in the ways in which Edward Said and Gayatri Spivak use the term "othering" to denote the processes by which colonial discourse created "others" (and inadvertently Self).

9   "Experience" is not, however, used as justification in itself, but rather as 'useful embodied interrogation' to assess and understand more abstract arguments (Collins 2000/2009, p. 277).

10   This article is a starting point on my proposals around black feminist creative theorisation, and many of the theorists-creatives I mention here are mere introductions to ideas I hope to develop more extensively in further writings.

11   For explication of this point in a transnational and colonial context, see Zine Magubane's *Bringing the Empire Home: Race, Class, and Gender in Britain and Colonial South Africa*. University of Chicago Press, 2004.

12   McClintock states: "The fetish for clean clothes was eloquent of a systematic attempt to erase from view any visible trace of domestic work" (1995, 163).

13   The Bantu Education Act of 1953 segregated all educational institutions in the country with a sliding scale of finances spent on the four racial groups, with Black education receiving the lowest funding possible for an education that focused on unskilled manual labour.

14   bell hooks (1992) argues that that such positivism does little for critical representation of black womenhood. See also Wallace (1979) and Collins (2000/2009).

15   Collins (2000/2009, 192) defines "othermothers" as "women who assist bloodmothers by sharing mothering responsibilities", and this kind of relationship has been an important structural support for black mothers. These include grandmothers, aunts, sisters, cousins, friends and even "fictive kin".

16   Readers will benefit from thinking with scholarship and evidence made clearer by our current moment of Mothers of the Movement and other Black Lives Matter and Movement for Black Lives writing on how this "standing by" also includes armed self-defense; it is a loyalty to and beyond death.

17   See for instance the photography and drawings of South African White women documentarians Killie Campbell and Barbara Tyrell.

18   This site commemorates the 1976 Soweto riots in which Black children were gunned down by policemen in Soweto protesting against the apartheid government's attempt to enforce Afrikaans as the main medium of instruction.

19   This museum details the rise and fall of colonialism and apartheid in South Africa.

20   The Turbine Hall was home to a number of squatters in the 2000's and was emptied out when Marasela took her picture. It is now the headquarters for the multinational mining company AshantiGold, which also contains a conference venue.

21   Johannesburg is colloquially known as "Joburg" or "Jozie."

22   There is a long history of women's creative productions across the world that involve sewing and needlework, and one finds a number of South African visual artists working with these media.

23   Collins (2000/2009) proposes that a sense of "both/and" captures plurality, complexities,

hybridity and ambiguities which are "truer" to black women's lives than the either/or dualisms of Western discourse.

24   hooks (1995a, 64) reminds us that, as people that have endured disrupted traumatic histories, part of our identity process is to re-member: "The word *remember* (*re-member*) evokes the coming together of severed parts, fragments becoming a whole."

25   Sibande 2013.

26   Mulvey 1975/2000, 487.

27   Hall and Sealy 2001, 38.

28   This idea was inspired by a 2013 talk between Melissa Harris-Perry and bell hooks at The New School entitled "Black Female Voices: Who is Listening – A public dialogue between bell hooks + Melissa Harris-Perry."

29   "Trying on" racial difference can produce very problematic "understandings" of race as an embodied lived experience as Sara Ahmed (2000) demonstrates in her reading of John Griffin's *Black like Me* (1970) project where a white American man masquerades as an African-American man in order to "understand what it is like to be black," reducing racial-gender-class oppression to merely external signals of racial difference.

2

Negotiating the terms of staying:
Rape, shame and guilt in a post-apartheid film, the case of *Disgrace*

Derilene (Dee) Marco

Rape culture renders rape acceptable.

Pumla Gqola[1]

She lay back and laughed, drawing her skirt up. This was how they liked it, filthy and stinking. He should know that, superintendent of cleanliness and order. The naai maintje was here. Yes, he should know who and what this place had made of her all these years she had been forgotten.

Yvette Christiaanse[2]

In *Rape, A South Africa Nightmare*, Pumla Gqola unpacks the grave consequences and what it means for South Africans to live in a country where rape has been 'normalised', not condoned but heard about all too often. Alongside this, Gqola is interested in asking how and why it remains the rape victims who are questioned and vilified. Rape continues to be part of a system of violence and a pressing measure of the state of the post-apartheid nation for a number of reasons. In the first instance, with South Africa's high rape statistics, rape continues to occupy our imaginations as, according to Gqola's speech at one of the book's launches at Rhodes University in Grahamstown, something that is enacted by Martians, in other words, not something done by 'regular' people.[3] Secondly, explains Gqola, rape remains

51

a highly racialised topic, both in terms of victims and perpetrators. Both sets of people, almost always women, are stereotyped and are very particularly moulded to form part of or to be completely erased from our national and collective consciousness and consciences.

Keeping in mind this consideration of rape as a duplicitous enactment of power that this chapter turns to its primary focus: a consideration of the characters and context of rape(s) in the 2008 film, *Disgrace*. The opening quotation for this chapter is from the novel *Unconfessed* and expresses the ongoing violence against and entrapment of women's bodies as subjects belonging to colonisers. Gqola notes the relationship between war and rape as borne of "a specific idiom, from the colonial archive. It is a deliberate investment in using sexual violence as part of conquest" (48).

Disgrace is based on a novel of the same title by J.M. Coetzee. It is a complex narrative in that it was released in 1999, just as tropes of new nation and 'Rainbow nation' began to gain ground in more practical terms. In other words, *Disgrace* came at a time when the ululation of the end of apartheid had ended and many who had been previously disadvantaged became aware that they were still in positions of hardship and difficulty. In other words, the cracks in the African National Congress' Rainbow nation were coming into view. *Disgrace* also came at a time that two other major happenings were on the go: the first being the restorative justice Truth and Reconciliation Commission and the second, related, the panic and resultant flight of white South Africans who were in possession of foreign passports. This essay does not intend to explore the themes of *Disgrace*, the novel. Instead, this essay marshals the close adaptation of the novel to a feature film to explore the ways in which some of these iterations of post-apartheid come to be represented through rape victims and perpetrators in the film. This essay does not embark on a comparative analysis between Lucy's rape in the film and the novel. Instead my attention is on white female victimhood, the figuration of the men who raped Lucy as aliens (albeit with bodies that are raced in familiar ways), the normalization of David Lurie's sexual coercion of young Black women, and the ideas of shame through which all these scenarios are arranged.

In her piece that explores shame and the female body of Sarah Baartman, Zoe Wicomb writes the following: "We do not speak about miscegenation; it is after all the very nature of shame to stifle its own discourse" (1998, 92). Wicomb describes Baartman's body as a body bound up in the politics of location, relating both to her historical home, South Africa as well as her remains that were on show in France. Wicomb also writes that Baartman's body and her narrative were tied up with the project of nation building in the new South Africa. In the opening scene of *Disgrace* we are introduced to the main protagonist, David Lurie, and Soraya, the sex worker without a surname, who Lurie meets once a week. The film briefly glosses over their ongoing relations and quickly summarises what the book spends significant time setting up and developing. The film is more swiftly able to convey the idea that Lurie and Soraya have not just met, when he places a gift box on a bedside pedestal after their weekly encounter. The sex scene offers a drawling pan shot of the two bodies writhing, with Soraya's brown flesh beneath Lurie's.

The development of the film comes to show Lurie's pursuit of a young Black student (like Soraya, Melanie is also a 'coloured' student) who takes his Romantic Poetry class. As Melanie, an undergraduate student, stumbles as she climbs a set of stairs, Lurie, coincidentally passing by, helps her up. This is their first encounter that leads to an invitation to Lurie's home later that same day. Melanie has consensual sex with Lurie a number of times. On each occasion, we bear witness to Melanie's expression and temperament, which often conveys the sense that she does not enjoy the engagement. On the first occasion, the camera offers a reminiscent pan of writhing bodies, only this time it is not Soraya beneath Lurie but rather the young Melanie. The room is dark, and the camera frames the pair in a high angle shot. A tilt brings us closer to the action of the bodies. Most noticeable is the way Melanie's head is turned away from Lurie's. It is clear that the young woman is not interested, but more than that, appears visibly repulsed. The next time we see Lurie and Melanie together is in a scene in her home. After he forcefully enters the front door, the scene cuts to Melanie's bedroom where an eager Lurie waits in bed for the reluctant Melanie. The camera focuses on the young woman before she gets into bed with Lurie; her bodily gestures comprised of long pauses and staring away from Lurie indicates her lack of desire. Although Lurie does not force himself on her in the way we understand rape, the sex is nevertheless very clearly not quite desired on Melanie's part. Melanie's inaudible, but visible sigh, for example, before she gets into bed with a lecherous Lurie, shows that the young woman is participating in something other than consensual sex.

Wicomb's note on Baartman and the history of miscegenation is fitting. Both Soraya and Melanie are 'coloured', descendants of and the historical embodiment of colonial patriarchal sexual relations. Additionally, so is Gqola's comment on the relationship between rape and war and the notion of conquering. This theme re-occurs, yet the film offers no distinctive sense on these relations, something that appears to be a very distinct choice by director Steve Jacobs to adhere to a close adaptation of the book. This distinct comment on racial categories and categorisation created by apartheid is never developed. Although never mentioned, it is striking that every time Lurie and Melanie are on screen, Melanie is not interested while Lurie proceeds and most certainly, climaxes and thus attains his pleasure from the situation.

Witnessing the unseen

The pinnacle of *Disgrace* is Lucy's unseen rape. We only know it takes place because of the events around it and because of David's torture in that scene. The narrative set up for the rape is David Lurie's decision to leave Cape Town after the inquest. The shift in the setting of the film, from the city to the farm, introduces several new characters, particularly Petrus, Lucy's Black co-proprietor, the young male rapists and the dogs, Lucy's companions.

Lucy and her father have a strange relationship in which she offers him little respect but much generosity. It is a relationship that seems always tinged heavily with past disappointments, misunderstandings and disagreements. For example, David does not seem to be particularly fond of his daughter's lifestyle choices, one of them being her choice to live on a remote farm in the Eastern Cape. The idea that this is a dangerous choice is implicit from David's arrival. The scene leading up to the rape is, in direct contrast, very calm and enjoyable. In it, David and Lucy decide to take some of the dogs for a walk through the surrounding farmland. Although the content of their discussion is tinged with difficulty, the slow meander in nature suggests a sense of enjoyment. On their return to the farmhouse, Lucy and David hear the barking of the dogs still in the kennels. On seeing three young Black men David glances at Lucy and asks her whether they should be nervous.[4] The camera cuts to a close up of one of the young men hissing at and teasing the dogs through the cages.

As Lucy and David approach the boys, Lucy calls for Petrus and then shouts "hamba." The dishevelled boys are dressed in broken t-shirts and boots that are too big for them. The sense conveyed through their exterior is that they are poor. They appear shy when confronted by Lucy, only briefly glancing up at her after she begins to enquire about their presence. They generally have their heads cast down with eyes lowered, referencing a familiar historical interaction in which power is perceived between a white farmer and Black people who work on farms. Petrus is the personification of the new Black South African in the film and on the farm, and power between him and Lucy, as well as between him and David, is thus displayed in a different register to how power is shown in the scene with the young men.[5] The incessant barking serves to build tension between Lucy and David as well as between Lucy and the young men.

Through the use of shot-reverse-shots between Lucy and David as a team, and the three young men as another, the reason for their presence becomes known: "an accident […] a baby", one of them says. They need to telephone, indicates one of the three. When Lucy presses them for why they have not gone to a public phone, they do not answer and continue their coy act. David hovers protectively behind Lucy while he holds onto the leash of the golden retriever. Having made up her mind to let one of them into the house to use the telephone, Lucy puts the three dogs that she has been walking in a kennel before standing back and choosing what can only be assumed as the least threatening young man to let in. The novel is more explicit and states that Lucy lets in the most attractive of the three. David tries to interject but Lucy dismisses him and continues towards her house. The interaction from the time that Lucy and David arrive at the kennels is shot in a medium long-shot interspersed with the shot-reverse-shots when Lucy interrogates the three. The use of the long shot however distances the viewer from the unfolding scene as though wanting to shift the viewer into a witness position from the time Lucy and David arrive back at the farm.

Watching from David's point of view we see Lucy fishing the key from under a pot plant and unlocking the door. Once Lucy and one of the young men have entered the house, the camera shifts back to a shot of David nervously watching the remaining two. Their eyes are on the door and as soon as Lucy is inside a drumming sound takes over the soundtrack. It matches the change in energy from the boys' sheepish performance moments before to the decisive plan and resultant actions seen in their movements. As David watches the open door to the house, the fast drum rhythm puts the other two boys into action with one running ahead, whipping up dust as he does so and the other momentarily slowed down by the only dog who remains outside, the golden retriever that David was holding. As the second boy closes the door behind him, the camera zooms in for a close-up of his face and the shot is slowed down to show his expression, a complex fusion of achievement and guile. David manages to enter the house by kicking in the door but his gallant attempts are quickly stopped before he's able to do anything as he is hit on the head, a blow which knocks him out.

A fade to black, a pause and fade-in that shows David coming to, presents a significant point: we do not see Lucy in her moment of crisis but instead, we see and witness *his* moment of distress in relation to Lucy. The music plays an important role in heightening the tension at the outset of the attack. The way the camera frames the two groups on opposite sides of the screen separated by the dogs in the kennels further complicates the already evident racist suggestions made in the film, one being that David is nervous because they look like poor Black boys and so he assumes that they might be dangerous. One of the strengths of *Disgrace* is showing up the inadequacies of conventional morality with reference to right and wrong in a place such as South Africa. Samantha Vice's argument for a relevant moral action of silence for white South Africans seems inadequate because it does not make room for the messiness of post-apartheid as presented in this scene and film.[6] In some ways Vice reinsribes Lucy's point of view about her place in the country, which is around moral action (or inaction): that whites should accept whatever happens to them because of the past. Lucy also expresses as much when she tells David that perhaps this is what it means to live in post-apartheid South Africa. She references her own rape as collateral damage of sorts, for choosing to stay.

In such a construction, Lucy, and Vice, imply that while there should be a place for whites in South Africa, the terms of staying and belonging cannot be mediated, negotiated or endorsed by white people. While David struggles with that reality, Lucy accepts it in this dire context, as a lot which she *can* and *must* bear, for herself and to pay for the sins of previous generations.

It is unclear to the viewer and to David himself how much time passes before David wakes up in a small green bathroom with only a toilet in it. His body is sprawled out across the screen. He tries to open the door but it is locked. First he whispers Lucy's name, then he begins to shout louder and with desperation. He hears the men outside the small window of the toilet and tries to see what they are doing. Two of them joke around as they put some stolen goods into the boot of David's car. Among the stolen wares is the 'protective' rifle that Lucy referenced when David first arrived. David is left to deal with the failure that already washes over him: he knows that the rape is now over, and he knows that he failed to save his daughter. The robbers see Lurie through the small toilet window he looks out of. As one of them picks up the rifle, David, alarmed and shocked, scurries down in an animal like fashion and sits in the small confined space between the wall and the toilet seat. The look of terror on David's face indicates that he believes they will kill him but instead, they shoot the dogs in the kennels.

Although we do not see the act of shooting the dogs, we again experience violence and torture of others from David's point of view. The film restricts us here, just as David and Lucy are restrained; we are not granted the space to see, and as it is a film, this is the primary sense necessary. Instead, we are forced to listen and hear each gunshot followed by each dog's whimpering in pain. Only later, once the wounded and injured Lucy and David are permitted outside again, are we also privy to the dogs' injured, and in the case of all but one, dying bodies.

David himself is also not off the hook—two of the three men open the door to the toilet that he has been confined to. As he tries to escape, repeatedly screaming "Lucy," the robbers trip him, and then douse him in a flammable liquid. He falls back into the confines of the toilet once more, this time taking in the shock of what they are doing. The sounds coming from David now emulate the sounds of the dogs after they were shot. The camera follows a lit match in slow motion as it travels from one of the grinning young men to its landing place, David's shirt. David's flailing arms and animal-like screams break the slow motion sequence. The slow motion shot ends at the same time as the lit match hits David. Along with David's flailing arms and animal-like screams, the colour and movement of the flames emphasise that he has nowhere to go in the restricted toilet. David's imposed confinement here serves as an explicit presentation of an array of emotions that we have not seen in the character. Some of these emotions are desperation, loss and fear. Each of these are expressed in different moments in this scene, brought to light by these young boys who come to take whatever they want, including his daughter's body.

The scene ends with a shot of an exasperated David on the toilet floor. He is breathing heavily after having managed to put out the flames on his body and head by immersing his head in the toilet bowl. This paused image of David also provides a chance to take in what has just occurred. The moment is broken when Lucy unlocks the door. From David's point of view we watch Lucy walk away from David and the toilet. She is barefoot, dressed in a white robe and her hair is wet, an indication that she has washed herself. The way in which Lucy is portrayed in this brief moment is the only direct access given to Lucy's rape from Lucy. As she is framed in a long shot from David's point of view, not only she but also her home is reestablished. The kitchen is in complete disarray with broken furniture and Lucy's things all over. Lucy herself stands in the midst of it as she pours herself a glass of water. The use of slow motion in the two places it is used in this scene serves to highlight *David's* helplessness, again focalising our attention on him and on the violence of the scene through him.

The description about what happens between Lucy and David's arrival back on the farm until the point when Lucy pours herself water is about an attack on Lucy. However, although the ultimate emphasis is Lucy's rape, the information and how the film chooses to set up the rape is really about David Lurie. This is intentional and highlights the film's investment in Lucy's rape as an event which reveals something about the complexities of post-apartheid identity and belonging. The lack of focus on Lucy in the rape scene places emphasis on the unspeakable. For Lucy, the unspeakable repercussions of the rape and of her emphatic choice not to report it, is a distinct comment on her place as a young white post-apartheid South African. For the 'boys', as perceived through David's white masculinity, there are no repercussions for bad behaviour because, as the film seems to comment, the power of the 'Rainbow Nation' is primarily embodied in post-apartheid Black masculinity. While we are invited to see two versions of post-apartheid Black masculinity, the film comments, once again through David, that both versions are primitively beast-like, vengeful and crass; these are explicit representations of violent taking (the rapists) or conspicuous consumption (Petrus). Neither of these caricatures of Black masculinity has anything to do with Madiba's democractic Rainbow Nation.

This scene also emphasises David's inadequacies. He was unable to protect his daughter and her land. His shame and guilt, already present in the character, become even more apparent after the rape scene. David comes to realise that his own (intellectual and philosophical) position of referencing back to the Romantic poets Wordsworth and Byron, and his white imperialist outlook, has no place in post-apartheid (Beard 2007, 59-77). The scene and its repercussion also seem to make the pressing issues of identity already alluded to in the film even more apparent and convoluted. When Lucy's farmhouse is first represented in *Disgrace,* it and she are read as metaphors of safe and complementary change in the new South Africa—in other words, Lucy had done everything right to be part of the landscape and she in essence personifies what Vice argues for all white South Africans to be—quiet and appreciative for a little space in South Africa. This shifts after the attack.

A number of other matters arise from the rape scene; most perplexing, Lucy's silence about the rape and her vehemence about staying on the farm after the attack. Lucy continuously refuses to go to Amsterdam to be with her mother, emphatic that there are things that David does not understand. Lucy is caught in the difficult place of accepting the new South Africa to be unequal and unfair but also wanting to remain liberal and open, unlike, for example Ettinger, a neighbouring farmer who drives Lucy and David to the police station after the attack. Ettinger, a staunch Afrikaner, comments on the differences between "then" and "now" in reference to how the police won't protect you anymore, referencing post-apartheid law and order. Lucy's generational guilt becomes even more apparent in light of the hyper masculinities of Ettinger and David.

This generational separation becomes clearer after the rape scene and is indicative of lost power (seen in the white men) but also, indicative of something as yet unseen: that Lucy is representative of an emergent post-apartheid sensibility. What is troubling is how the film consistently shows Lucy's position as different and more progressive than her father's, but it affords the young men very little texture. This raises some questions around what a post-apartheid emergent sensibility might be. Even if this is a new white emergent sensibility, which I do not think it is, it makes white people vulnerable and weak and humiliated in a way that we know is not the case politically or economically. So why is this myth being told? It is as mythical as the one that says Black youths have no post-apartheid emergent sensibility. *Disgrace* persists in its reliance on the racial binaries of apartheid to show how white youths are dealing with their post-apartheid identities but offers little positive outcome for Black youths dealing with their new identities. The differences between Lucy and the older white men also points to a residual apartheid structure of feeling.[7] *Disgrace* thus employs a rape scene in a twisted fashion to bring three generations of South Africans into its narrative: David, representative of residual apartheid sensibilities and who cannot quite make sense of his own new place or identity; Lucy, who accepts her white post-apartheid fate, takes on David's guilt, and who is forced to deal with the repercussion of the rape; and a third generation, mixed in as yet unknowable ways, beyond only race, class and the various effects of historicity(ies)—a tarnished 'baby'.

Unlikely union through the 'Rainbow Womb'

The above section of this chapter was concerned with the rape scene in *Disgrace* and the representations (or lack thereof) of the act of rape by the young Black boys as well as the way in which we, as viewers, perceive it through David. This section is more concerned with the aftermath of the rape, which leads to Lucy's realisation that she is pregnant and her decision to keep the child. *Disgrace* ends on a melancholic note when Lucy asks her father to accept Petrus' proposal for marriage. Part of the negotiation that she offers is that Petrus can have the land but that she wants the farmhouse for herself. Lucy's offer, like the conception of the baby, is a dark twist on rituals (such as lobola and marriage—different iterations of it but conceived of as union and ownership) which, in other contexts, are enacted differently.[8] Meg Samuelson's discussion of Lucy's rape in the context of the novel uses the term "rainbow womb" with reference to the post-apartheid terminology 'Rainbow Nation'. In using such a description, Samuelson describes the white womb as a boundary of race, noting that "as a white woman, Lucy has no future until her womb has been 'soiled' and 'darkened'" (2002, p. 93). In this now impure form, Lucy must (and almost can) assimilate in a way she could not before. Although still an outsider, Lucy's soiled womb, and attendant pain, is likened to the Black woman 'naai mandjie' in Christiaanse's novel. In a dangerous twist, we are forced to experience the failure of the Rainbow Nation through Lucy, a white female body, not through any of the Black characters in the film.

Before David leaves the farm, and after Petrus' return after the break-in and the rape, Petrus comes to Lucy's house looking for David to assist him with pipefitting. The scene takes place as David and Petrus crouch down opposite each other to join pipes under the ground one by one. These pipes will provide running water to Petrus' new house that he builds throughout the film. A conversation ensues about what happened when Petrus was gone. Petrus knows the boy Pollux who is back after the incident, a young boy who was identified as one of the rapists by David and Lucy and who was present at Petrus' party. Petrus does not admit that Pollux is family but instead confidently assures David that "now, everything is alright" and that Lucy is "forward-looking, not backward-looking." Petrus' emphasis on "forward-looking" is interesting because he insinuates that Lucy's approach is the best one in this new context. He also insinuates that David, in his insistence to know about the boy, is "backward-looking" which is not good. The sentiment conveyed by Petrus is that being too engrossed in what is past, what has already happened, is not good. This scene between Petrus and David sets up the focus of this section: an analysis of the makeshift lobola negotiation that takes place between David and Petrus about Lucy, the baby and Lucy's place on the farm (and in South Africa).

The B(b)lack 'boys' who rape Lucy are stereotypes of young Black men in South Africa. Gqola's *Rape: A South African Nightmare* contextualises the employment of this stereotype and traces its historical place in South Africa when she writes that stereotypical representations of Black males as rapists of white women has played a major role in the rise of racism. Gqola cautions that this is "not a small matter, and constructions of 'black peril', or what was termed '*swartgevaar*' (*black danger*) in colonial and apartheid South Africa, depended heavily on this idea of the sexually and otherwise violent Black man" (2015, 4). What I intend to show in this brief analysis is that the union between Petrus and Lucy is a complex negotiation of what Gqola describes as the "constructions of 'black peril'" and however shameful and heavily laden, possibilities for new (and productive) unions.

Lucy tells David of the pregnancy when he returns to visit her under the pretext that he is on his way to a job interview. The two are seated opposite each other at the kitchen table when Lucy tells him that she is pregnant. The short scene incorporates a shot-reverse-shot pattern between Lucy and her father. They are both framed in medium close-ups as Lucy explains that she will have the child, that she is a woman and will not hate a child because of who its father is. The scene ends when David excuses himself, tea untouched, to go for a walk. A medium close-up of Lucy's face is held before a cut to David, who stands outside facing a wall. Overcome by the humiliation and grief of the situation, David is crying, first slightly bent over and then, more violently, as though he might collapse. With the pregnancy as a new challenge to the experience of living on the farm, Lucy has to make certain choices about her future. Her growing belly poses imminence and urgency, just like the end of apartheid, asking: what will happen next, what will it look like and is it possible to love this child born of such a violent experience?

Although Petrus expresses that he will look out for Lucy, he also points out that while David protects his child, Petrus too must protect Pollux, who is his family. The conversation takes place while David, hands in pockets, watches Petrus lay concrete for a house that will soon be his own property. Different to the conversations between Lucy and her father, where they are often both in the same eye level position making shot-reverse-shots appear natural and equal, dialogues between Petrus and David always take place with one or the other positioned higher or lower than the other, a subtle indication of power and the presence of a battle for it. It is ironic that in this 'building' scene it is Petrus who looks up at David from a low angle shot, when it is Petrus who is in fact in power. Even so, in this apparent play of power, Petrus is as much as a hollow plot device as the boy rapists. His advice to David is about how white people should be—it is not about Petrus's own emergent sensibility. Still, David has a hard time accepting a second defeat when Petrus makes a pragmatic suggestion to marry Lucy. Although Lucy is able to see and acknowledge the suggestion as a gesture of protection, specifically in relation to how white people ought to behave, David is not.

There are, however two expectant women in *Disgrace*: one is Lucy and the other is Petrus' wife. Writing about the novel, Samuelson notes that Petrus' "'pure' race child will be born in the spring with all its suggestions of renewal and growth, while Lucy's expected only in late May, will be born into the frosts of an early Eastern Cape winter" (2002, 93). The building, as with the pipes and running water, is indicative of another new present, one in which the formerly disadvantaged have access to the satisfaction of basic needs. The culmination of the conversation between Petrus and David is a suggestion that Petrus will marry Lucy because Pollux is still a child. While David thinks that the idea is preposterous, Lucy immediately sees its value. She perceives it as an acknowledgement of her presence in the new South Africa and a justification and legitimation of her stay and white presence. Lucy's awareness about the union invites us to see Lucy's controversial pregnancy in a different way, one where *she acquiesces in power for her greater good and protection through the baby*. Although unwanted, the child serves a purpose and invites possibilities for Lucy where they did not exist before: her presence will be tolerated through this rather crude interpellation. The scene in which Lucy and David discuss the possibility of a union between Lucy and Petrus is illuminative in showing how her pregnancy is conceived of differently after an unexpected proposal which holds unexpected promises, just like the 'Rainbow nation'.

The scene opens with a medium close-up of David as he expresses his feeling about Petrus' proposal. A shot-reverse-shot pattern ensues between the two through which we get the distinct impression that David is angry with Lucy for not dealing with the situation in the way he sees fit. The setting is Lucy's front garden, now filled with flowers, vegetables, and plants which she tends to. Lucy disagrees with David's position and clarifies that Petrus' proposal is not a traditional marriage but "an alliance, a deal," a failure that like the new South Africa can somehow still be celebrated. Lucy's point of view is of David and in the background Petrus' house (and Petrus building the house) is visible in the shot. Still beyond that is the landscape of the Eastern Cape. From David's point of view we see Lucy in her garden. These background choices are important because for David and generations before him, white men controlled the land. The film comments on this intricate racial and economic power battle of and around the land, often, shown through the pursuit of exoticised womens' bodies and Lucy's rape juxtaposed with Petrus' new material acquisitions, land and the house that he builds throughout the film. These interracial narratives are consistently bound up in time and space and burdened by history and memory.

For Lucy's generation, there is a dangerously pressing need to negotiate the terms of staying in post-apartheid South Africa. David is about to return to Petrus with a rejection of his proposal when Lucy jumps up. A full-length shot makes the importance of her following lines even more compelling. She offers her terms of the negotiation: that she will accept the marriage as protection on the condition that the child is Petrus' too and thus part of his family. She will sign over all the land to him but she wants to keep the house and the kennels, which nobody, not even Petrus is permitted to enter without her permission. These are the terms of Lucy's agreement to marrying Petrus. When David tells her that it is not "workable," Lucy, in a medium close-up, exclaims, "I am not leaving, David!" Before David leaves to tell Petrus the terms of the agreement he resignedly tells Lucy how humiliating to end like this, "like a dog." Lucy agrees before David turns towards Petrus who is still building.

[Figure 1] David looks at Petrus in the distance as Petrus continues the building of his house (Included here with permission from See-Saw Films Pty Limited/ Wild Strawberries Pty Limited.)

What takes place in this scene is an unconventional lobola, a negotiation of the terms of marriage, even without a bride, as well as a play on concerns around permission: permission for Lucy (and other whites) to remain in this country, permission for the baby (and other babies and futures) to be truly 'free', permission for the land to be lived on. Even though Petrus does not call it this, Lucy understands that his suggestion to marry is about making an untenable situation work in the best possible ways, a situation so much akin to the new South Africa. The actual lobola and the union may appear unconventional but two primary characteristics stand out: One is that the 'negotiation' still takes place between male elders about a woman, Lucy's father and Petrus, who is Pollux's elder. Secondly, Lucy carries the ultimate offence in 'damages' (lowering of the bride price) in lobola negotiations, which is a pregnancy before marriage. Although it appears as though it is Lucy who articulates the terms of the agreement, it is really Petrus who steers the arrangement, as he knows it will benefit him. Both Petrus and Lucy also know that Lucy's pregnancy by rape is not the only damage she carries in her "soiled womb." Lucy is also a white woman in post-apartheid South Africa and thus carries generational guilt.

The contrast between Lucy and David's understanding of the realities of her situation provides an illustration of a pressing emergent but inarticulate sensibility—Lucy's—emerging against the residual dominance of her father's. At the same time, the young men rapists are allowed no room for such and their fate, left to the audience, seems to be a forgone conclusion.

Conclusion

A whole range of pre-emergent sensibilities are featured in the film version of *Disgrace* which is ultimately a cautionary tale about rape, and the meanings to be gleaned from it, conative of the founding violence of post-apartheid South Africa. These peaceable and submissive emergent sensibilities however still dwell on the inner life of white men and white women as victims, and their decisions about the dispensation of property. Rapists are figured as out of this world characters—young and unprosecutable— and sexual predators in positions of authority are depicted as cavorting and promiscuous and protected. As an important account of the present, the film has received critical attention, both acclaim and derision.

The paper also briefly considers the choices made around the difference between David Lurie's exotic promiscuity in his cavorting with young Black women in relation to the explicit gang rape which becomes a focal point of the narrative. The fact that even when Melanie, the young student is shown to be overtly uncomfortable with Lurie's sexual coercion, it is certainly never called assault or rape, and both novel and film make it clear that that matter is dealt with 'on the inside', through the process of disciplinary action *within* the university structure. Shame and a humbled emergent white sensibility unite these different episodes of violence. This structure and the attending systemic violence that is publicly named in post-apartheid South African universities through *Fees Must Fall* (2016, 2017) and *Rhodes Must Fall* (2015), places a 'new' gaze on men like Lurie and their lurid and ugly yet all to normalized relationships to (young) women in South African universities. Shame and a humbled emergent white sensibility unite these different episodes of violence.

By depicting white people as the vulnerable, the weak and the humiliated—and insisting that Black people are in power— in a way that we know is not the case politically or economically *Disgrace* uses visual technology to tell many powerful cinematic myths—myths that are lethal both to Black people's lives and lethal to the possibility of ever getting to the power that has exercised force to guarantee that rape remains normalized. Shame and ideas around it ties these different incidents of violence together

Bibliography

Beard, Margot. "Lessons from the Dead Masters: Wordsworth and Byron in J.M. Coetzee's *Disgrace*." *English In Africa*, 34,.1, May 2007, pp. 59-77.

Christianse, Yvette. *Unconfessed: A Novel*. New York, Other Press, 2006.

Gqola, Pumla. Talk at UHURU. Rhodes University, February 18, 2016. https://www.youtube.com/watch?v=7dWkNBykP5s. Accessed May 10, 2017.

—*Rape: A South African Nightmare*. Johannesburg, Jacana Media, 2016.

Mupotsa, Danai. PhD Thesis. *White Weddings*. Wits University, 2014.

Samuelson, Meg. "The Rainbow Womb: Rape and Race in South African Fiction of the Transition." *Kunapipi*, XXIV, 1.2, 2002.

Vice, Samantha. "How Do I Live in This Strange Place?" *Journal of Social Philosophy*, 41.3, 2010, pp. 323-342.

Wicomb, Zoe. "Shame and Identity: The case of the coloured in South Africa." *Writing South Africa: Literature, Apartheid and Democracy 1976-1995*. Rosemary Jolly and Derek Attridge, eds. Cambridge University Press, 1998, pp. 91-107.

Williams, Raymond. *Marxism And Literature*. Oxford University Press, 1977.

Endnotes

1   2015, 12.

2   2006, 2.

3   Pumla Gqola book discussion at UHURU, Rhodes University (UCKAR). February 18, 2016. https://www.youtube.com/watch?v=7dWkNBykP5s. Accessed May 10, 2017.

4   The use of the term Black, with a capital B, is intentional and in line with an understanding of blackness according the Black Consciousness Movement (BCM) and attached sensibilities which were present during apartheid. The term is thus not only about the categorizations and characterizations of race (black African, coloured, Indian) as experienced in apartheid parlance, but invites a criticality to thinking about Blackness in its historical and contemporary formations. In the context of this article, using the term Black for the boys who rape Lucy and for Soraya and Melanie, complexifies notions around how rape works and functions as a highly racialised, masculine act in this film, and it certainly poses questions about the larger cultural and socio-political context of post-apartheid South Africa.

5   I sometimes use the term 'boys' in reference to the young men because of the way that they are infantilised to this status, in line with apartheid descriptions through naming Black men 'boys'.

6   Samantha Vice's "How Do I Live in This Strange Place?" appeared in *Journal of Social Philosophy,* 41.3, 2010, 323-342. Vice's polemic implores white South Africans to have a retributive stance towards the politics and the quotidian of South Africa. However, more than this stance, Vice's piece suggested that white South Africans take a particular position in relation to black South Africans making decisions about the country.

7   I use the terms "emergent," "residual," and "dominant" sensibilities in line with Raymond Williams' theorization of these concepts. Although not previously applied to a post-apartheid context in this way, I find it a productive way of thinking through this society and post-apartheid screen representations.

8   Danai Mupotsa's PhD dissertation (2014) on marriage and rituals of and around lobola is illuminating.

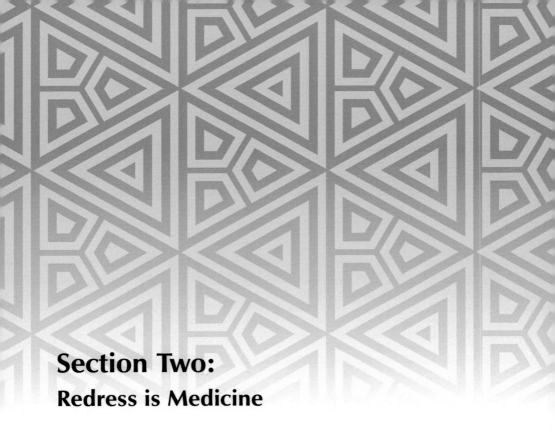

Section Two:

Redress is Medicine

3

Healing Perspectives of a Black womxn poet:
Writing the unborn and the dead

Natalia Molebatsi[1]

I.

Poetry as memory in the journey towards healing

Memory lives in our bodies, memory is alive *on* our bodies. Memory is passed on from one body to the next, one dream at a time, and through our perceptions of the world and its systems around us. McCoy-Wilson (2007, 14) asks "do bodies remember?" Like hers, my answer is "yes," bodies carry memories, and it is up to us how we hold this re-membering (of both the dead and the living) as well as how we choose to usher in the unborn with the information carried by the memories of our bodies. In a world where oppression marks the lives of most women, Black women in particular, the power of memory, wishing, and dreaming, opens a window through which a grandchild can learn from their ancestor grandmother, and where a mother can imagine and *will* a better life for their unborn child—not prison, not premature death, not life in a squatter camp, not a job as a domestic worker, not a life of domestic abuse or rape.

In the *Art of Memories*, Derrida writes:

> Memory is the name of what is no longer only a mental "capacity" oriented toward one of the three modes of the present, the past present, which could be dissociated from the present and the future present. Memory projects itself toward the future, and it constitutes the presence of the present (1989, 6).

The statement above plays a powerful connecting medium between poetry, the body from which the poetry is produced (in the now), the absent-present ancestry of my grandmother, as well as the present-future that is represented by the unborn baby. Together with this notion of memory, an Afro-centric perspective is threaded throughout this chapter to encourage the exploration of African roots and values, from politics to aesthetics, to spirituality and ancestral knowledges. According to Nkulu-N'Sengha "African epistemology is the African theory of knowledge, which includes the African conception of the nature of knowledge, the means used to gain knowledge, the criteria for the assessment of the validity of knowledge, the purpose of the pursuit of knowledge" (2005, 40).

Dreams for example, are an important part of the Afrocentric epistemology because the ancestors deliver messages (and poems) through dreams. The dreams too, through expert interpretation can contribute to a healing narrative of a wounded community or individual. The "wounded" I am referring to includes the often ignored post-traumatic disorders caused by Apartheid and other forms of racial and gender oppressions experienced by Black women especially. Asante asserts that Africans should reconstruct how they see themselves, as well as how they negotiate their existence within the globalising world, a world that comes from slavery, colonialism and racial inequality (1998).

"Afrocentricity," highlights that Africans be viewed as subjects rather than objects (Asante, 1980). In this world-view Africans can gain a better understanding of how to interpret issues affecting their communities, their histories and their futures. In African culture, for instance, the invocation of ancestral spirits (of both the dead and the unborn) is an important aspect of life and of healing. It is through the spirits of the dead and the unborn that the two poems analysed here were created. Engaging an array of scholars who explore poetry as a tool of healing, memory and the body, and indulging the dead as part of memory and of healing, this chapter pursues how poetry operates to unite the living and the dead.

The main scholarship on memory that has been most meaningful for my own research includes an article by Alberto Sandoval-Sanchez[2] The writer states that:

> There is no way I can draw a line between my body and my scholarship: my body always pushes me to the limits, my writing always makes me put into practice the interdependency between body and mind (2005, 543).

Sandoval-Sanchez (a poet himself) writes about his memory of AIDS, migration, love and sex. Although his work does not necessarily highlight the intergenerational memory between Black women, his work is important in how we can think and theorise about memory itself, and how the body walks with the dead, or how the body thinks about and creates new things from loss. It is this idea that I weave into my work—that of the body that remembers, mourns, honors, dreams and creates words to connect the unborn to the dead. This important work on the body and memory coupled with Toni Morrison's use of fiction and biography as spaces of re-membering (especially in the era during and post-enslavement of Black bodies and minds in the African diaspora) have drawn me into an analysis of writing as power, writing as the body's personal experience, and writing as representation of the self. Morrison also reminds readers however, that "In shaping the experience to make it palatable to those who were in a position to alleviate it, they [the writers] were silent about many things, and they 'forgot' many other things. There was a careful selection of the instances that they would record and a careful rendering of those that they chose to describe" (1995, 91). This is to say, certain experiences will be remembered, and understood, only by the body. From this lesson, taking the teachings of the body seriously has been central to my work.

This chapter provides perspectives from two examples of my poetic works, a poem named "Listen up child" (from my book of poetry entitled *Sardo Dance* published by Ge'ko publishers, 2007), and another named "Summers at your feet" (from a forthcoming publication, 2010). I have convened hundreds of writers workshops on poetry; nurtured hundreds of young poets; been nurtured by an unbroken community of poets in South Africa and around the world. My teachers include writers and poets such as South African poet and storyteller extraordinaire Dr. Gcina Mhlophe (b. 1958), the late South African poet laureate Prof Keorapetse "Bra Willie" Kgositsile (1938-2018), and Kenyan writer, philosopher, and cultural activist Prof Ngugi wa Thiong'o (b. 1938),[3] among others. It is through the work I have done already with other contemporary poets and mentors that the explorations of this chapter are presented as necessary and sufficient tools for analysis.

A central part of my work has been to document these poetic communities from the insider perspective of a person who knows them well and has authority to speak about how these poetic communities and their creative labors should be understood. In my view, poems are essentially born from the experiences of our bodies, and such poems should not be viewed as separate entities—alienated from the sites of their creation. In addition, the body (and the work that it crafts from experience) cannot be divorced from its spiritual world, as Sandoval-Sanchez explains (2005).

The two poems presented here represent a distinctive theme in my work—the connection between the cycle of life, death and the spiritual world. These poems provide an opportunity to reimagine intergenerational memory and conversations about healing between women. By healing, I am asserting that the dead and the unborn have a hold on us that exists in the here and now. Not only do they have a hold on us, but they also communicate with each other through us and our perceptions of them.

Poetry has been essential as a tool for healing in my creative life and work. These specific poems, in particular, provide me an opportunity to speak to the dead and to the unborn. To speak these poems through my body, is to dream, to wish, and to honor—three very necessary elements of life that are desired by most people within contemporary South African poetry communities in order to heal the arbitrary and mythical breaches that systems of power insist on imposing upon us.

Time and certain conceptions of temporality that insist that the dead and the unborn cannot exist together through the living is one of the most damaging systems of power. And this concept of time does much harm, creates many injuries, and imposes value systems that devalue the human desire to heal. In my poetry I have defined the present as that set of moments during which our capacity to meditate alongside, to learn with, and to be in the service of the dead and the unborn—is a primary dictate of ancient African tradition and culture. As Willoughby-Herard proposes, following Nomboniso Gasa, "there is an uninterrupted nature [to] gendered black consciousness, [a] continuous undercarriage of activities, institutions, and relationships that subverted the influence of post-apartheid nation-building domestically, globally, and throughout Southern Africa."[4] To the extent that we focus on our dead and our unborn, we make ourselves *unavailable to being slaves of the state* and society (Quan, 2013). These poems are also about acknowledging the existence and play of oppression on the lives of Black women and girls but also to celebrate "the power that Black women have over their own lives and their high levels of self esteem"—as pointed out by research psychologist Kelly Patterson (2004, 322). And with this power I have chosen to use my poetic work to dream, to wish, and to honor.

Thus, these poems raise many ethical questions about the ways that societies like our own in the past twenty years have governed and organised itself. When we follow what we learn from these poems from the dead and the unborn, we understand our history and our obligations to those other generations much differently. This is for me how we must begin to understand healing. Poetry's greatest power is to heal. Christian J. Collier, in his 2016 TEDx Chattanooga talk reminds that "poetry has served as a tool to help us make sense of the world around us" adding that:

> words have the ability to hurt, to empower, to start and end wars... to yield understanding. The act of writing and manifesting words is much like prayer, like meditation.

I use poetry much like Collier's explanation, in order to understand what is happening as well as to reflect upon the relationships that form part of my experiences in the world.

II

Writing to the unborn

I wrote this poem when I was 7-months pregnant with my only child, Atisa, in 2007. I didn't know what gender she would be but had the spiritual awareness (or a strong hunch that only the body can know[5]) that my body was carrying a Black girl. I felt like I was carrying an opportunity to heal my childhood wounds, to raise another girl, to keep her safe from a dangerous world and from toxic relationships that take from us without ever giving opportunities to replenish. The poem is also a teacher-learner experience whereby both mother and child are learning from one another regardless of generational differences, and that one is not yet born. Once the poem was complete, the mother reads it to her unborn child over and over, as a comforting and affirming gesture. This poem was my child's first lullaby and how she came to know my voice after she was born and lived outside of my body. Like her, the poem was conceived inside my body.

III

listen up child

i'm raising you to wake up
and take a ride to any universe
be the beauty of soul sound and energy
create my child like you the created
earn the language of moulding
seeds into fruitful beings
i'm raising you so you too can raise me
infant of my skin
reveal chapters the two of us are yet to learn
and believe me child some of the rules
i have run into can save your soul,
so listen up child
be yourself or don't wake at all
life is not for the feeble
are you ready for the fires of time
that only life alone can extend

her long arms to light up?
If so clothe yourself with ancient selves
who knew before we did that you, the future
will be born into this crazy but jazzy
scene called living
rise and let the world know
you are here to claim no sense
nor sin but only the waking and dream-dripping
sun of each dawn
never wait for time's breath to blow
into your lungs rather bloom
from the dust we rose from like mystics
to grow your own wings
and be sure to ask for strength
between these wings
so they don't split into pieces and halves cause child,
i'm raising you to be whole
paint your life's everyday in ways not forced on you
but reflections felt by you cause none but ourselves
can blow up a true self that is everything there is to be
raise your story's voice to go beyond any beyond
and beat any ghost that could suck
out your way up to clouds of choice
have sacred communion with the past
that knotted to you your present
cause child, any presence that
lacks a past is part of the lost so listen up child
listen close child cause you're a sister, and i'm a sister
remove your walk from exhausting
arms of men-talities who can't take a strong sister
and white supremacies who still believe
we're strong enough only for taking instructions
and child, i'm still tasting the bitter truth i'm learning
that not every woman is a sister
so, listen up gal
listen up, bloom of my belly
infant of my skin never step into boxes
these aren't enough to hold our stories alive
rise to the knowledge that our people
and theirs are tapestries
sown long and wide enough to hold you up
till you can uphold yourself

never forbid your truth in spaces that strangle our realities
rise child your vision is our voice
i have laboured to challenge convention
beat conviction on my soul, scrubbed the floors of my heart
tended the soil of my womb so the fruits of my garden
would be like you child of mine beautiful beyond magic herself
i stood guard at the entrance to your ride
to usher you into these arms bosom and back
that i'm raising you to fly beyond
so listen up child
i'm raising you within the rain you were made of
walk to the knowledge that you are everything that is musical…

The poem has numerous movements and thematics, including instructions and calls to action from the mother to the child. But another thematic that is developed with even more urgency and that undergirds the first is the concept that the unborn child is a teacher in an infant skin, that the infant is a creator of its ownself. Not only this, but the poem insists that unless the baby can be itself it should not continue on its quickening journey at all. Drawing such a stark contrast between being alive and not being alive, the poem invites the child to come into the world ready. The baby plays the role of connecting medium between the human and the cosmic-ancestral world. The writer sees the importance of 'being yourself' from the onset as healing generational wounds and acknowledging the wounds of our past. The mother instructs the child to have sacred communion with the past. In this way, the child is being taught about the importance of a history of a people from which she comes. To learn about the dead (people of the past) is to know that the present is because of its past. The poet calls the child and hails her as having been made by rain and music and by something beyond magic and confides that conviction has not been easily attained in the land of the living. The poet mother also warns the unborn baby against patriarchy and white supremacy and that both these forces carry a fundamental hatred for strong Black women.

IV

Conversations with the dead

The various ways that I keep my grandmother alive are through how I choose to remember her, how she shows up in photographs, in dreams, and on the pages of my work. I wrote *Summers at your feet* after my grandmother died (at the end of 2009), as closure and as a way to heal from the pain and void caused by her death. The poem goes beyond keeping her alive, it also invokes her spirit in how I re-imagine her life of struggle. It is also to perform an inventory of her life, and try to fix her [body's] wounds with words. In the poem I ask her about her childhood and her children, her worries and her desires. I ask her Black girlhood questions that I would never have otherwise had the courage to ask—about sex, depression, rape and the pain of childbirth. Morrison indulges the reader about death (1995). She, for instance, states that "I can't tell you how I felt when my father died. But I was able to write *Song of Solomon* and imagine, not him, and not his specific interior life, but the world that he inhabited and the private or interior life of the people in it" (1995, 93). Therefore in writing about the dead I agree with Morrison and James Baldwin that this writing is about filling the blanks or filling empty bottles with text. In James Baldwin's words:

> All of my father's Biblical texts and songs, which I had decided were meaningless, were ranged before me at his death like empty bottles, waiting to hold the meaning which life would give them for me (1984, 111.)

In this chapter, I am attempting to fill my grandmother's "empty bottles" with poems, with memories, with imaginings. Experiences and beliefs of hers I did not understand, are now standing before me like Baldwin's "empty bottles" needing new meaning, deserving of a legacy. Baldwin's example alludes to how and where memories are kept [safe]. It is almost as if, when death finally takes over the body and its memories and experiences, there is fear that they will somehow be lost when the body is no longer their home. Baldwin uses the metaphor of "empty bottles" as something awaiting to be provided its rightful place, to be filled with its own meaning or a reimagined one. It is the *meaning* that continues the journey of the dead for the living when the body can no longer do so. It is the living who have the responsibility to make sense of what they collect as memories of the dead. "All of my father's Biblical texts and songs" become the connecting medium or the memory that links the living with the dead.

When I speak to my grandmother in the poem about being *forced to grow, and living loving and lying awake at night,* I am using Sindiwe Magona's words from the titles of her books *Forced to Grow* (1992) and *Living Loving and Lying Awake at Night* (1991). Magona is another Black woman writer acclaimed for using her words to heal the wounds of Black girlhood, to bridge the gaps between generations of Black women and girls whose lives continue to be sites of struggle through racism, patriarchy and institutional doors that refuse to open to them. I therefore imagine and wish for simple but vital images of living ... loving... and lying awake at night. As Magona herself is preoccupied with the experiences of Black women in South Africa, her work is echoed by the poems being analysed here.

For example, *Forced to Grow* is about a 23 year-old young woman who is deserted by her husband and forced to raise small children by herself under Apartheid laws. Her determination to take herself through school and college and to be a present and loving mother is evident throughout the book and is one of the references for the two poems I analyse here, especially "Summers at your Feet." This is another scale of analysis and understanding about the losses that we carry from the violence of Apartheid. That we can commune with the dead in a concrete and yet deeply satisfying immaterial fashion suggests much about the stakes of what is being killed when the Apartheid state, society, and its structures deal death on us now and when these forces deemed us "deathworthy" in the the past (Eberhardt, et al, 2006). In my poetic work I have centered a refusal to be separated from the dead and the unborn. Rather I have invested time in my conversations with them as a way to make sense of the tangible everyday violence that constitutes contemporary South Africa—and my own capacities to face this violence and not be ruined by the value systems on which the violence stands. To be present, then, is to do a kind of vital work of refusing to be made absent and stitching the worlds of the ancestors together in the face of worlds that suppose that the unborn, the dead, and even the living Black woman poet does not and should not exist.

Living Loving and Lying Awake at Night is also a symbolic piece of work which brings the lives of Black women working in White people's homes (under undesirable conditions) to light. The women in the book are my own grandmother and other women who are ancestors in a spirit world that is often not enough for 'academic knowledge.'

Living—the life of a Black South African woman born in the 1920s is both promising and breaking. The 20s were highly interesting times for Black people in South Africa—Brakpan in this regard (an urban coal and gold mining town). We were not always confined to rural villages (not that villages are not part of our beautiful and complex realities). We were city people, too, we were business folk, working class people, teachers, artists, intellectuals. My grandmother was born in those years, over two decades before the official start of Apartheid, to a father who was a teacher and a preacher, and a mother who was a motivational speaker. White rule and domination during this period, was met (as always) with harsh resistance from Black people. How then does she reconcile her life as a 20 something year old woman who finds herself forcefully removed off her father's land, working the kitchens of White people—even after witnessing the possibilities her parents' lives bore. Even after seeing how possible it was for her own Mother to be a Blackwoman with a mouth, and words falling out of that mouth in the name of healing others through her motivational talks. Such is living.

Loving—in the midst of a dying world, my grandmother, and many other women of her era were still lovers, and were loved. Even with dreams left under a rubble in the place where a home, a family, and a future used to be.

Lying awake at night—is imagined as a constant feature in my grandmother's life. A dead husband, six mouths to feed, and years later, sons in prison. How does one sleep at night?

In this poem I speak without self-censorship about desire for example. I am imagining how this woman seduced her partner and how her body held its desires, and how she wanted to be loved during intimacy, in the confines of being a *proper woman.*[6] This poem is intentional about the power of memory and imagination to weave a healing narrative. Beyond her sexual desires, I also imagine the kind of disappointments the poem's subject has had to chew, such as the story she always told me about how she had dreamt of being a pianist. I link that thought with how today, I insist that my daughter plays the piano, and luckily she loves it. This is intergenerational healing that neither my daughter, nor my dead grandmother may be aware of. The one woman dreamt of being a pianist but her circumstances proved it impossible, while two generations down the line a young girl's fingers are being honed to become her ancestors' wildest dreams. "The act of imagination is bound up with memory," says Morrison (1995, 98). Today I lie awake at night crafting these poems with the intention to soothe other aching bodies and hearts, beyond my own. I listen to and witness how these healing words are being birthed by my body and how they are interlinked - the body, the poetry, the scholarship, the dreams, the spirits, the wishings, the memories, the futures.

V

Summers at your feet

i want to be you in your youth
i want to be the children laughing
in the garden of your dreams
the learning mother
and the wise old women who soothe your esteem
when life disappoints you on so many occasions but most times,
i want to taste your laughter…
be the colour and slope of your gums
your giggles and lie awake on the land of your tongue
in contemplation so that when I have rested enough
i can begin to fall like speech from the unfolding margins of your existence

Let me share one life…
at least one night at the edge of your feet
and walk the gentle summers your prints have footed
i want to go back into time
way back into the unknown
And erase all your pain
i want to hold on to all that ever made you laugh
Let me hear your whispers aloud in the secret of your lonely being
i want to be you, a choice and love poem,
speaking in the dialect of our desires
i want to drink from the thread-like blood of your song
and be the breeze that came to those who heard
and listened to you sing so let me walk with you
let me walk you
Let me scroll you from beginning to no end
Let me climb you like a song of survival

i want to be seven and under the skin below your dress
i want to touch the smooth of your baby thighs
and wrap them with bandages to seal the untold pain

i want to be 17 and play guard at the entrance to your innocence.
sing hymns to your hymen and protect it against painful raptures
i want to comfort her, tell her not to be afraid of rapists
and men seeking to conquer the sweet at our rivers
so let me walk with you, let me walk you
Let me scroll you from beginning to no end
Let me climb you like a song of survival

i want to dance and play tap scotch on the keys
of the piano you so wanted to play
roll myself in the flavor of your moves
At the assembly of your heart
i want to mumble sweet lil' nothings to the air that makes it beat
Knowing that even the absence of your physicality
Will bring you closer to everything that I touch and breath
Everything that I see is smeared with your gaze
So let me dip my wings in your aura
Before I am forced to grow
Before I am called to wake up and lead
i want to be you living loving and lying awake at night
i want to be the fire in your eyes

i want to read your signs of life
All over again
Speak with all your trusted saints and demons
In hushed tones
So that they can calm down
When I am in conversation with your sonnets
So let me walk with you
Let me walk you
Allow me to walk by you
So i can learn to tell my people's stories

My grandmother had a sweet singing voice, and I know that she used her singing to lift the heavy load off her shoulders. Today my daughter sings, unaware that her ancestor is humming along. My grandmother had many other gifts too that were for the healing of her community, such as her knowledge and use of indigenous plants to heal babies' and children's ailments. I use this poem also to acknowledge her own 'untold pains'. The poem acknowledges that she, like many Black women of her generation took to their graves personal and political injustices, shame endured by their bodies and secrets that caused their bodies discomfort, and disease. In a way, some of these stories are known by the body, as witnessed by Morrison in how retelling and remembering was always selective (1995). This is in acknowledging how some stories of trauma might have been too painful, too hurtful to share or reveal. In this way, the poem declares that Black women, especially those of my "grandmother's generation" were, and are "wounded healers", warriors in battle, who regardless of their injuries and fatigue continued to fight. It is not to say that they could not feel their pain and disease. Perhaps it is because they knew that their fighting would lessen the battle for the generations after them. Thus this poem is a healer of untold pains, as much like what Terzieva-Artemis describes as a "history of survival-in-suffering." In addition "the second level is the level of depiction of survival in the history-of-suffering" (2004, 128) that Terzierva-Artemis addresses in Toni Morrison's *Beloved*. This account of survival-in-suffering and the history-of suffering is applicable to the two poems addressed here, especially "Summers at your feet" because of the attempt to re-member and hold space for traumatic experiences endured by Black bodies. Morrison's *Beloved*, as articulated and analysed by Terzieva-Artemis (2004), performs the "psychic history" of slavery.

In his poem "Requiem for my Mother," Kgositsile (1995) invokes his late mother's spirit in another way that "fills empty bottles." Through reading the poem, one understands that the subject has died. In the poem, which is more of a lament, or a longing for his Mother, the poet writes "as for me/

the roads to you/ lead from any place" (1995, 45). These lines demonstrate the invocation of spirit and a conversation with ancestry. Kgositsile wrote the poem while in exile in the USA (or some place else in the world), and could not bury his own Mother due to having been banned from the country of his birth by the Apartheid government of South Africa. Through this poem Kgositsile makes amends with the loss of his Mother, and speaks to her beyond the grave, beyond the geography of exile, about what he imagined her last words to have been, and what her last gasps might have felt like. The words of his poem are a connecting medium and provide healing and closure to both him (the living) and his Mother (the dead). His poem thus becomes an example of a memory collected, and acknowledged. In the following excerpt, the poet connects to his late mother in this way:

> I do not know if you hollored in delirium
> Like an incontinent dotard
> I do not know if you gasped
> For the next breath, gagging
> Fighting to hold your life in
> I do not know if you took
> Your last breath with slow resignation
> But this I know (1995, 45)

The poem continues to go back in to time, and through the poem, the writer recollects the sadness and the smile on his mother's face:

> As for me I will
> Never again see the slow
> Sadness of your eye
> Though it remains
> Fixed and talks
> Through a grave I do not know (1995, 46)

Like Kgositsile's (1995, 45) laments about missing the "the morning odor of your anxious breath" and though "I will never again see the slow sadness of your smile under the sun" (1995, 47) he knows that "the roads to you lead from any place" (1995, 46). This line lends the poem the power to communicate with the subject (the Mother) beyond the grave, beyond the geography of exile.

There are many things we do not know but through the type of poetry presented here we are afforded the opportunity to connect the living, the dead and the unborn, through words that transcend geography, time and distance. I too do not know if my grandmother ever had to go through and or survive rape, for example. However, judging by the harsh lives endured by Black women's bodies under Apartheid and patriarchy—where both White colonial men and Black men had convictions that Black women's bodies belonged and belong to them—I make provision for the unfortunate possibility of that ordeal in "Summers at your feet." The poem continues to go back into time to perform the work of protector and healer with words where poetry is standing in for the 7-year old and the 17-year old Black girlhood against rape and against the conquest of men over Black girls' bodies. Like Kgositsile's "Requiem for my Mother," where he indulges the reader with the sounds and scents of his Mother, my poem "Summers at your feet" acknowledges my grandmother as a spiritual being who navigates her conversations not only among angels but with demons too.

Through remembering my grandmother and having this conversation with her, I am learning to tell my people's stories in my own voice in the quest to find healing from the many layers of trauma endured by our people, especially women—young and old. Such poems also serve as avenues where Black women can speak to and about each others' healing from historical violence—in a world where people suffer because they are firstly, Black, secondly, women and lastly, poor.

VI

Conclusion

The work of a poet is usually to create poems, and not necessarily to analyse them. These poems are created from experience and a yearning to tell the truth about life and its people - the dead and the unborn. In this chapter, I chose to not only present two poems that treat two important subjects - my grandmother and my daughter, and how I find healing from meditating on their lives before they arrived and after they left this world. In this chapter I also analyse what lies within the poems, and what the poems try to communicate in their effort to speak healing messages about Black womanhood intergenerationally.

These two poems are examples of not only what the poet writes about in the act of engaging with Black girlhood and how Black women experience life, but are also an attempt to have uninterrupted conversations with an unborn baby on the one end and a dead grandmother on another end. It is through these poems that I attempt to celebrate the life of a wise old woman, to mend her heartaches, and to have a conversation that transcends the living in physical form. I also speak to an unborn child about what lies ahead, where the unborn can also be teachers, and healers of their own mother's wounds.

This chapter addressed the reasons for writing the two poems analysed above. These poems also attempt to link memory to healing and intergenerational conversations that attempt to write against the erasure of Black women and their memories and experiences. The chapter also privileges memory, and ancestry within an ancient Afro-centric lens. Using examples from Baldwin (1984); Magona (1991, 1992); Morrison (1995); Kgositsile (1995) and Sandoval-Sanchez (2005), I offer perspectives from these authors on how they too, indulge memory through creative work, and provide other examples on the interconnectedness of the living, the dead, and the unborn. This chapter provides a lens through which poetry can be used as a medium of communication and healing that transcends time, geography and physicality.

Bibliography

Asante, Molefi. *Afrocenticity: The Theory of Social Change.* New York, Amulefi Publishing Company, 1980.

Baldwin, James. *Notes of a Native Son.* Boston, Beacon Press, 1984.

Collier, Christian J. TEDex Talk: Chattanooga. https://www.youtube.com/watch?v=oCUKT4CIuuI

Eberhardt, Jennifer L., et al. "Looking deathworthy: Perceived stereotypicality of Black defendants predicts capital-sentencing outcomes" *Psychological science*, 17.5, 2006, pp. 383-386.

Ebila, Florence. "'A proper woman, in the African tradition': The construction of gender and nationalism in Wangari Maathai's autobiography *Unbowed.*" *Tydskrif vir letterkunde*, 52.1, 2015, pp. 144-154.

Kgositsile, Keorapetse. *To the Bitter End.* Chicago, Third World Press, 1995.

Maathai, Wangari. *Unbowed: A memoir.* New York, Anchor, 2007.

Magona, Sindiwe. *Living, Loving, and Lying Awake at Night.* Cape Town, David Philip, 1991.

—*Forced to grow.* Cape Town, New Africa Books, 1992.

McCoy-Wilson, Sonya. "In 'Rememory': Beloved and Transgenerational Ghosting in Black Female Bodies." New Voices Conference, Graduate English Association, English Department, Georgia State University, Atlanta, Georgia (September 27-29, 2007).

Molebatsi, Natalia. *Sardo Dance: Collection of Poems*, 2nd ed. Nokuthula Mazibuko, ed. Foreword by Makhosazana Xaba. Afterword by Gabeba Baderoon. Hyde Park, Johannesburg, Ge'ko Publishing, 2014.

Morrison, Toni. "The Site of Memory," *Inventing the Truth: The Art and Craft of Memoir*, 2nd ed., William Zinsser, ed. Boston, New York, Houghton Mifflin, 1995.

Nkulu-N'Sengha, Mutombo. "African Epistemology." *Encyclopedia of Black Studies*, Molefi Asante and Ama Mazama, eds. Thousand Oaks, CA, Sage Publications, 2005, pp. 39-44.

Patterson, Kelly L. "A longitudinal study of African American women and the maintenance of a healthy self-esteem." *Journal of Black Psychology*, 30.3, 2004, pp. 307-328.

Quan, H.L.T. "Emancipatory social inquiry: democratic anarchism and the Robinsonian method." *African Identities*, 11.2, 2013, pp. 117-132.

Sandoval-Sánchez, Alberto. "Politicizing abjection: in the manner of a prologue for the articulation of AIDS Latino Queer identities." *American Literary History*, 17.3, 2005, pp. 542-549.

Terzieva-Artemis, Rossitsa. "Toni Morrison's *Beloved*: Feminine Mystiques." *AnaChronisT,* 10, 2004, pp. 125-142.

Derrida, Jacques. "The Art of Memories." *Memories for Paul de Man*. New York, Columbia University Press, 1989.

Willoughby-Herard, Tiffany. "Proposal for the 2017-18 University of Western Cape Centre for Humanities Research DST-NRF Flagship on Critical Thought in African Humanities Visiting Scholar Fellowship, Migrating Violence Theme," *Unpublished Paper*, 2017.

Endnotes

1   Direct correspondence to nmolebatsi@gmail.com.

2   Alberto Sandoval-Sanchez is Professor of Spanish at Mount Holyoke College, which in 1993 produced his theatrical piece *Side Effects*, based on his personal experiences with AIDS. His present research and scholarship center on the staging of monstrosity, enfreakment, queerness, and abjection on Broadway and minority theatre. In his article Politicizing *Abjection: In the Manner of a Prologue for the Articulation of AIDS Latino Queer Identities* he writes "Memories are archipelagos of islands surfacing on the horizon waiting to be revisited. With the AIDS epidemic, my memories are anchored in floating cemeteries in an ocean of pleasure and death, remembrance and oblivion, *suspiros y cenizas*. Wherever I go I carry *mis muertos conmigo, en mis recuerdos*, a generation of Latino gay men that in a self-imposed s/exile migrated to the US from the Caribbean and Latin America in search of independence and sex, satisfaction and love" (2005, 542).

3   These three writers are instrumental in mine and many other African writers' work because they address issues around the importance of African language,

spirituality and positioning African indigenous knowledge in a position of privilege for any African artists and in relation to Western languages and modes of knowing.

4   Willoughby-Herard, Tiffany. "Proposal for the 2017-18 University of Western Cape Centre for Humanities Research DST-NRF Flagship on Critical Thought in African Humanities Visiting Scholar Fellowship, Migrating Violence Theme." Unpublished Paper, April 15, 2017.; See also Gasa, Nomboniso. "Let them build more gaols." *Basus' iimbokodo, bawel'imilambo/They Remove Boulders and Cross Rivers: Women in South African History*. Gasa, Nomboniso, ed. Pretoria, Human Sciences Research Council Press, 2007, pp. 129-152.

5   Cakata, Zethu. In Cakata's language, "the body knows its truth." Personal Conversation, April 22, 2018. "Body That Takes Pride: Celebrating LGBTQI Icons Panel." Hosted by Embassy of the Netherlands in Pretoria, University of Pretoria, and Village Verbals (a global network of culturally conscious events specialists), December 6, 2017.

6   Ebila (2015) explains the concept of the 'proper' woman in the the context of Wangari Maathai's work in the following way: A proper woman in the African tradition has always been imagined within the context of the family; she is expected to accept marriage and have children because marriage is assumed to be the end goal for most African women (Maathai 2007, 54). A proper woman puts the family interest first before even her own personal interest. A proper African woman is not concerned about trees and the environment; rather she is supposed to be concerned about her family and children. If she were to be concerned about trees, it would be in terms of firewood which she needs to provide fuel for her kitchen. To Moi (Ugandan statesman), a proper woman in the African tradition was that woman who did not talk back at men. Silence is construed here to mean respect but it is important to critically analyze what makes women silent and the implications of women's silence...

4

South Africa belongs to all who speak colonial languages

Zethu Cakata

Introduction

The current public discourse on the need to re-imagine education in general and higher education in particular, which was ignited by the university students' 2015[1] demands for a free and decolonized education, is challenging 'academia' to look at what the epistemic land it is standing on has to offer. The students' demands meant that education as a tool to define the world could no longer exist unquestioned. What the students were highlighting was the need to re-orient the tool to assert African people's definitions of the world. Thus, decolonization meant shifting the cultural orientation upon which knowledge is grounded. This requires the re-africanisation of the ways of knowing, knowledge production and dissemination. Re-Africanisation could be loosely defined as a process to make a considered and concerted effort to re-embrace African ways of life and of being. These are found in indigenous languages, indigenous ways of expressing the African essence and how Africans understand life. This is where indigenous languages become crucial as a gateway to re-africanisation of teaching and learning to ensure a cultural foregrounding that reconnects the people to their ways. This happens through reconnecting people to their essence in which lies their life definitional framework.

I argue that the usage of indigenous African languages in spaces of learning could ensure a voice and a lens to indigenous African people. In advancing this argument I use 'metaphoric language' (which is actually in African conceptology the essence-encapsulating language) in the form of a proverb to show the value of language in communicating African epistemologies. 'Figurative language' as alluded to by Maseko (2018) is the reservoir of

African knowledges. It is among the tools that help preserve African people's understanding of themselves, the world around them and others. It is one of the practical ways of illustrating underlying values, ethos and beliefs of a people's culture and their sense of humanity (Nobles 2015, 44). For Nobles, figurative use of language is a useful element in efforts to ensure cultural retention while at the same time responding to the dehuminisation meted on people of African descent by the European enslavers and colonisers. Figurative use of language in this chapter is therefore applied in lieu of a theory to argue against the dehumanizing absence of indigenous languages while advocating for the retention of the cultures these languages carry.

Drawing from a 'proverb' in isiXhosa language, "Amandla engwenya asemanzini," I aim to illustrate that indigenous languages cannot merely be add-ons to colonial languages at institutions of higher learning but could be used as accessories for transmitting the African experience and knowledge forms. Idioms and proverbs are a rich source of African wisdom and knowledge because they ensure creative ways of learning from how people experience the world. Furthermore, a critique of the representation of African ways of being in Euro-American Psychology textbooks will be offered in order to illustrate the manner in which language has been used as an oppressive tool to impose Western epistemology while undermining the epistemologies of indigenous people.

Invisibility of Indigenous African Languages in Learning Institutions

Indigenous African languages continue to be invisible in what Cress-Welsing refers to as areas of people activity which I call colonially professionalised spheres such as education, the judiciary, health, etc (1991). This is not by accident but in line with the colonial mission of Europe to dominate indigenous people in South Africa. As wa Thiong'o states, the era of brutal physical violence was followed by the age of chalk and black board to ensure that the minds and spirit of indigenous people were in line with Europe's mission (1986). Language was key in the capture of the mind and spirit hence one of the distinct features of colonial presence is the usage of the colonisers' language in lands they colonised. Their languages were introduced as languages of sophistication and civilization and their world as universal and the only valid world. Not only was language used to promote Europe and its cultures but to also distort and demonise the cultures of African people throughout the continent of Africa. According to Biko (2004) and wa Thiong'o (1986), African children were made to perceive their ways of being with a sense of backwardness, shame and defeat.

About the aforementioned invisibility, both Alexander (2005) and Prah (2006) argue that anything which is not in your language is not designed for you but addressing the needs, the concerns and the interests of the people whose language it uses. This could be interpreted to mean that the use of colonial languages ensures that the ontological orientation and the epistemic lens of the coloniser inform the country's status quo. Nobles succintly captures this point in his assertion that, fundamentally there is a clash of culture between Africans and their European invaders (2015). Thus, the manner in which Africans conceive of such phenomena as education, law, philosophy, spirituality economics etc. contrasts Western conceptualisations. By imposing their languages therefore, they were entrenching their own conceptualisations of such phenomena. Thus if, for example, the language of the judiciary is of European origins the conception of the judiciary system will be grounded in European understanding of the world and that understanding will be made to appear applicable to Africans. This notion threads well into wa Thiong'o's argument that the inferiorisation of indigenous languages which was initiated by colonialism was central in ensuring that the indigenous people of the African continent lost their sense of being in the world, thus their belonging (1986). The inferiorisation of indigenous languages served to ensure that the knowledges and experiences of African people are invalidated.[2] This has already led to indigenous people here in South Africa being merely accommodated in their land and that in turn has compelled them to assimilate the ideals of a foreign world. Even in the 'democratic' era, indigenous people in South Africa have been made to continue being what Biko called appendages of the western world despite 'post-apartheid' policy undertakings (2004).

Language policy in South Africa is informed by the undertakings of the constitution that all languages deserve equitable usage and indigenous languages should be accorded particular care because of the racist inferiorisation and marginalisation they endured in the oppression era. Regarding language in education, the Constitution states that, "everyone has the right to receive education in the official language or languages of their choice in public educational institutions where that education is reasonably practicable" (Section 29(2) of the Constitution).

Furthermore, the Constitution stipulates that the exercise of language choices in education should not be in conflict with considerations of equity and redress within the context of our shared values and aspirations as a nation. The Department of Education formulated policies that give effect to these constitutional provisions. The Language in Education Policy (1997) and the Language Policy for Higher Education (2002) were designed to promote multilingualism in the education sector. Their aim is to ensure that all South African languages are developed to their full capacity while at the same time ensuring that the existing languages of instruction (English and Afrikaans) do not serve as a barrier to access and success. What has been found to be a major flaw of language policy success is the obvious lack of implementation. As findings by Maseko & Kaschula (2014) and Cakata (2015) suggest, the clauses of these policies are phrased in a language that can easily make the implementation avoidable. For example, practicality and affordability are some of the conditions for implementation and this has been used as an excuse for lack of implementation. The lack of success in implementing these language policies allows the education system to continue using one voice and one lens to define and understand the world. In its attempts to ensure conducive policy environment, the South African Department of Higher Education in 2017 drafted a revised language policy. This was aimed to address the shortcomings of the old policies. While I commend the Department of Education's efforts especially for being cognizant of the need to monitor and evaluate policy implementation. The policy still does not address the clause on practicality and affordability and still declares English the de facto language of Education despite research that has highlighted these as obstacles. Furthermore, the 2017 draft policy only highlights the need to treat indigenous languages as languages of epistemic access without fully elucidating what the concept entails. The policy needs to explicitly explicate what it envisages higher learning institutions do to ensure epistemic access. It should be clarified that epistemic access requires the utilization of these languages to access African epistemologies. This necessitates that the teaching in an African language should be with an aim of encompassing the culture the language carries. Therefore, indigenous languages cannot be just languages of teaching because that will reduce them to just languages that translate European epistemologies defeating the purpose of this envisioned re-Africanised education. To reduce indigenous African languages to just teaching languages will render these languages useless because the core function of the language is to project the essence of its culture. Language, therefore, demands to be used within its conceptual framework. Thusly, language is meant to communicate a worldview of its speakers and if the worldview is removed it becomes impossible for the speakers to see the cultural images which the language is designed to make them see.

Using Figurative Language to Confront the Appendage Status of Indigenous languages

In the ensuing section I apply an Isinguni "figurative expression" to confront the continuous [mis]treatment of indigenous languages as stepchildren of knowledge transmission in South African education. The figurative use of language in our efforts as scholars to recover African epistemologies has been made critical by elders such as Wade Nobles. Nobles urges us to use metaphoric memory embedded in our languages to fight against epistemic hostility with which people of African descent world over have to contend (2015). This metaphoric memory as Nobles asserts is part of the accessories that ensure cultural continuity thus ontological relevance of African people. It is for this reason I turned to amandla engwenya asemanzini as a 'metaphoric expression' to excavate memories it could be triggering about language as a mode of transmitting knowledge.

I wish to register the fact that I use the terms "proverbs," "figurative language," or "expressions" very cautiously. This is due to the fact that our proverbs, as in the nomenclature of Europeans, are not simply for linguistic aesthetics but for buttressing our deep thought which by and large captures our worldview as African people. What Europeans refer to as 'proverbs', our African cognation of the concept can be inferred in the Sesotho notion of "maele" which means words of counsel; which are the embodiment of African philosophy, the spiritual-cultural and scientific epistemies. This finds better expression in wa Thiong'o's notion of language as a mode of transmission of images as contained in the culture it carries (1986). The conception of knowledge as images further explains the utilization of nature's imagery in the form of plants, animals, the galaxies, etc., in "figurative expressions." The imagery in our figurative use of language connects us to our essence because nature is the root of our essence. Imagery is also the essence's mode of communicating to us. Essence could be defined as the very chemistry and mechanics through which one's being is defined and conveyed to life. How we define ourselves and how we live is rooted in our essence. It is thus that which makes us who we are. Even without verbal language, connection with one's essence can still be attained but language augments that connection. Language becomes the imprint of the connection because it renders the essence intelligible. Our essence is made lucid by culture. You therefore need your cultural prescripts as tools to steer your essence. This therefore means that language is the thread that connects culture and essence.

The inseparable link between language and culture is best articulated by wa Thiong'o when he argues that the deliberate elevation of the coloniser's language and the devaluing and the distortion of the colonised people's cultures were instrumental in breaking the harmony that existed between language and culture in pre-colonial times (1986). Language is an integral part of knowledge thus culture. Culture (as repeated knowledge acts that are endorsed by communities and never considered static) relies on language for transmission. This is the interconnection that Western scholarship does not explicitly acknowledge in order to blind the colonised from the transmission of a Western value system through colonial languages. Both Mignolo (2011) and Grosfoguel (2007) caution us about an education which pretends not to have cultural origins because it is numbing us into accepting their knowledge biases without question. For these two scholars all knowledge reflects its place of origin and should be presented as such. When a person communicates, it is more than language they are using. The person brings his/her world through language. As such colonial languages, which are still dominant in South African institutions of higher learning, communicate exactly what colonial education was intended to do, which is to make the colonised feel inferior. The proverb "amandla engwenya asemazini" aptly encapsulates this intention and better serves the purpose of applying metaphoric memory to rehumanise ourselves. In the section that follows, I decipher the metaphoric memory conveyed by the proverb, "amandla engwenya asemanzini." What elements of our educational ethics does the chosen proverb as metaphoric memory call us to remember?

Amandla Engwenya Asemanzini

Without indigenous languages in institutions of higher learning indigenous people are not only prevented from bringing their worldviews but are also taken out of their ways of knowing the world. This finds accurate expression in the isiXhosa proverb "amandla engwenya asemanzini" (the strength of a crocodile lies in the water) which means a person is truly powerful in her or his territory. This 'proverb' reveals the scientific content that figurative use of language nestles which was alluded to in the previous section. The proverb is rooted in African people's in depth knowledge of nature. From their repeated observations of a crocodile's behavior both in and outside of its habitat they could conclude that it would not be at its optimal outside of its habitat. They then applied this literal understanding as words of counsel to human beings to caution about the dangers of being uprooted from one's territory.

This 'proverb' communicates a powerful message about not just the impossibility but also the unethicality of universalising ways of knowing and being. It is impossible because the cultural context (the habitat) from which a people emanate, as Ani states, becomes the frame of reference that allows them to function (1994). It is this frame of reference which allows the individual to conceptualise the world in and around it and operate from a position of strength. To thus enforce the perception of a universal frame of reference is unethical because it is imposing other people's ways as the only ways of being in the world. In the process rendering those uprooted from their habitat vulnerable. They are vulnerable because not only are they forced to adjust to the demands of the imposed habitat but are also made to denounce their original habitat. This induces a dissonant way of relating to self which affects a people's psychological state. This is anchored in the assertion of Baffour Amankwatia II/Asa G. Hillard III. In a foreword to Nobles (2006) Baffour Amankwatia II/Asa G. Hillard III states that Europeans lacked the competency to treat their culture as one of numerous cultures in the world. This caused them to perceive European cultures as normative thus forcing everyone to assimilate them. This is the universalism of which the proverb is scornful. People of African descent in general always understood that you can truly be strong in your territory. We observe the display of this understanding even in the African-American metaphor, "Be who you is because to be who you aint is to be nobody." Similar to "amandla engwenya asemanzini," this metaphoric expression is scornful of the assimilation of other people's ways of being because they strip a person of her or his essence.

Crocodiles outside the water: Delanguaging African students

I use "amandla engwenya asemanzini" to argue that institutions of learning in the colonised world were used to remove indigenous people from their natural habitat thus a space where they are truly powerful. These institutions continue to strip them of their strength and introduce them to ways of knowing that separate them from their knowledge forms. They are therefore forced to be strong in the world of others. "Amandla engwenya asemanzini" illustrates the importance of one's locality or positioning as a critical element of one's essence. This proverb aids the argument that our conceptualisation of ourselves (as people in general) and the world around us is informed by our cultural positioning. We therefore lose our sense of knowing and being in the world once we are dislocated from our cultures. The cultural dislocation that colonialism has caused could be subverted by drawing from our cultural reservoirs which is language. Language could thus be allegorised as what the water is to the crocodile. It allows a people to image itself after its essence, which essence gives them impetus to seize the power to define—to ultimately be self-defining as a position of strength. Language, therefore, becomes the perpetual trademark of the awareness that makes our connection to and relationship with the habitat intelligibly meaningful. In this sense language is the strength to a people's connection to its habitat.

Being removed from their strength has prevented indigenous people of South Africa from living life within their definitional frame. The Westernised education has made indigenous people to look at their cultures with a European eye. This was done through the schooling system which only perceived African cultures using the European understanding of the world. Dubbing African cultural practices such as naming, rites of passage and other spiritual practices as backward and barbaric because they did not reflect their own understanding of the world. This, as alluded to in the introduction section, forced African children to look down on their and assimilate the European cultures. This also caused African people to look down on their languages and perceive them as tools to communicate their backwardness. The schooling system inferiorised these languages and devalued them as languages of knowledge. The exclusion of indigenous languages as languages of knowledge in education is therefore a deliberate strategy to exclude indigenous people from appreciating their production of knowledge thus from inserting their worlds and their experiences as knowers. As I argue in my doctoral thesis, by enforcing colonial languages, the colonisers were enforcing their culture (Cakata 2015).

To show that the intention of imposing Western education was to transmit western ways of knowing, even the so called historically black universities did not have indigenous languages as languages of education while institutions built for the Dutch and the English used their own languages. This serves to prove that education was aimed at making indigenous children not to learn to understand their world but the world of others so they may contribute into maintaining the colonial order. The efforts of the 'democratised' South Africa (through policy frameworks) to include indigenous languages have only yielded to the accommodation of these languages while what could be considered colonially professionalised sphere continues to be dominated by colonial languages. This makes the education system to be only about the views of the coloniser and the knowledge forms of indigenous people become only accommodated as outlier viewpoints. The danger with this domination is that colonial languages communicate a message of inferiorisation and by accepting their knowledge claims, indigenous people are internalizing the inferiority these languages imply.

Undergraduate Psychology textbooks provide a perfect example of how a world which is not western is inferiorised and merely accommodated in institutions of higher learning and how language plays a central role in that. When knowledge forms which do not have a western bias enter the discussion in these textbooks they do so as 'other cultures' or 'tribes'. This is evident in two Introduction to Psychology textbooks I reviewed which are commonly used in South African universities and their human development chapters were similar in their portrayal of theories in that it is only people with a Western socialisation who are able to relate and Africans or those who are not inclined to Western ways are either left to adapt or being left out. The curricula content in Psychology has been unapologetically Euro-American and disregarded the fact that the majority of its students are indigenous people whose worldview and experiences are different. For the sake of obtaining qualifications students, even when they do not agree with this Euro-American content are forced to accept it. This is where the call by students for a decolonial education alluded to earlier emanate. Students grew weary of the content that does not reflect their understanding of the world and their realities. For example, a human development chapter in a textbook entitled *Psychology: The Science of Mind and Behaviour* uses Western based research to explain how infants acquire traits such as attachment, morality and emotional development. What is implied by these theories is the fact that children need to have a stable nuclear family to be able to have a chance at a healthy and successful life. From this textbook there is little mention of the nation of 'Himba' in Namibia to illustrate that the need for attachment in babies could be universal. Interesting to note is the fact that the Himba nation is referred to as a 'tribe' which is an act of othering. The usage of tribe is even more problematic because it did not feature in the discussion illustrating Western knowledge. A similar description is found in another textbook entitled *Themes and Variation* where "other cultures" is used to hint to a possible different experience and again Western knowledge is not presented as a culture in the discussion, only a non-Western experience is viewed as such. The word tribe does not have an equivalent in many South African indigenous languages. For example, my home language, isiXhosa, does not have this word. The speakers of isiXhosa do not refer to themselves as such; they instead use words such as nation (isizwe sikaXhosa/umzi ka Xhosa) or a people (AmaXhosa). This is also true for Setswana and TshiVenda languages which use the words "morafe" or "setshaba" (for Setswana) and "lushaka" (for TshiVenda) to refer to themselves as either a nation or a people. The usage of the word tribe is communicating an epistemology of the Western world. Ever since its first encounters with people of the African continent, the West has made it its duty to label and define Africans without permission. Once those labels are in textbooks they become an education indigenous children of the African continent consume and use against themselves. This education causes them to self-reject, self-loathe and eventually assimilate a culture which the education system has deemed positive.

It is for this reason that Mignolo is calling scholars from the former colonised lands to reject colonial knowledge forms through a process he coined epistemic disobedience (2011). This means a rejection of epistemologies that define the reality of others and embrace our own. It is a moment to stand up and assert that indigenous people do not need new labels, they know who they are and what to call themselves. Indigenous children encounter the word tribe through a westernized education system yet it is pinned on them as if their forebears birthed it.

As Wiley argues, the term tribe has been largely used to refer only to indigenous people in regions of Africa, Asia, Canada, New Zealand and Australia (1981). Its use in academic literature is always to denote inferiority and uncivilisation. It is this kind of depiction that sends a message to African students in their first year of university that they are less than human and their experiences do not belong in academia. They are mere footnotes, 'tribes'. They do not see their upbringing in these textbooks. This has been pointed out by Biko in his assertion that African children return from school questioning their ways of life because they are invisibilised and demonized to a point where children are left with shame about who they are (2004). At the same time this depiction grants belonging to those who are of the culture of colonial languages. Their experience is prioritized turning higher education into their territory. The western experience is made to appear as the only experience which should influence knowledge production. In a western context this (the prioritization of western experience) should not be a problem as knowledge should reflect its locality. It becomes problematic in a context that is not western. Here in South Africa, it uproots indigenous people from their ways of understanding human development and behavior thus inferiorising and invisibalising these ways of knowing. This inferiorisation and invisibilisation of indigenous languages and the knowledges clearly illustrates the meaning of being strong in your territory. The education system does not only prevent indigenous people from learning from within but also denies African epistemologies their due place in the knowledge space.

Conclusion

Returning to the title, to truly belong is to self-define and that requires a language. Indigenous people of South Africa have not had self-definition since colonial interruptions and that has put them in dislocation. Education as an engineer of this dislocation has ensured that indigenous South Africans are alienated from their cultural essence. Through the content and the language of its delivery, the education system has been instrumental in granting belonging to the colonizing nations. Without self-definition indigenous South Africans have been made to live the life of others thus set up to fail because no one comes to the world to pursue an assignment that is not their own. Colonialism has made indigenous people appear as though they had no knowledge of their own on which to rely. By doing so, institutions of higher learning in South Africa have afforded the unqualified right to belong to the colonizing minority. Belonging is an existential ethic because everyone comes to the world of life on their own cultural terms.

The Europeans who invaded this country unethically imposed a cultural overhaul because their domination of indigenous people required that they removed them from their strength. The demand therefore for a re-Africanised education is a cry by indigenous people to return to their position of strength where notions of inferior and superior languages are dismantled. Indigenous

African students deserve to find their images, thoughts, and experience inside the walls of their learning spaces. In that way they will be able to see that they bring more than just their bodies to the learning process.

I am aligning myself with African scholars such as Babalwa Magoqwana and Pamela Maseko who are calling for an education system which draws from indigenous knowledges. Magoqwana gives practical meaning to the proverb inyathi ibuzwa kwabaphambili (which means that the gift of knowledge is held by those who have journeyed life before us) when she relocates the site of learning from university to the African household and centres uMakhulu (the grandmother) as an expert and the facilitator of the transmission of various indigenous knowledge forms (2018).

Magoqwana points her audience to a different site of knowledge which academia has largely ignored. The elderly in African communities are regarded as rich sources of knowledge; as such the death of an elder is likened to the burning of a library. These are the knowers the proverb is calling us to place at the centre. We see a similar disruption of colonial teachings in the work of Maseko which stresses the importance of understanding the historiography of indigenous languages and how it helps us to dispel certain myths about the culture of the speakers of isiXhosa language (2017). Language as a social institution according to Maseko needs to be used to challenge existing discourses about African life. She believes that the continued use of these western imposed concepts results in a misrepresentation of African life and experience (as shown with the use of the word tribe).

This strengthens the argument that an in-depth knowledge of indigenous languages is necessary in designing a re-Afrikanised scholarship which will affirm and empower African learners by showing them that their world has always had something to contribute to the intellectual space. A re-Afrikanised scholarship will ensure that learning institutions are not a space where African learners learn how not to be themselves and how to rebel against the knowledges of their origin.

Centering indigenous languages in higher education is a way of dispelling the myth that these languages are not appropriate for academic use. The fact that indigenous languages were used as media of instruction in the former homeland schools[3] shows that these languages are indeed languages of indigenous knowledge transmission. However, as pointed out earlier, this should not be read as a call to merely translate existing knowledge from English to indigenous languages. The exclusion of these languages as sources of knowledge should also be addressed. There is a need to start re-imagining, for example, a Psychology which uses indigenous concepts of mental health and indigenous approaches in understanding human behaviour. In this way higher learning institutions would be a true reflection of their geographical positioning. As illustrated in this chapter, many concepts in psychology are largely gazed through a western eye with Asian, Aboriginal and African experiences usually given an adhoc mention as alternative perspectives. How can that be mainstream education in a land where more than 70% of the people are not of the culture the education system regards as a norm?

Educators have a critical role to play in the proposed task of centering indigenous languages in centres of learning and their training, therefore, should be relevant to the task at hand. Resources would have to be directed toward ensuring that the un-learning of colonial ways of knowing and being which elevated English and Afrikaans to a status of superiority in South Africa is facilitated. This should be accompanied by a nurturing of a re-learning process where educators are made conscious of what languages truly mean.

Bibliography

Alexander, Neville. "Language, class and power in post-apartheid South Africa." Paper presented at Harold Wolpe Memorial Trust Open Dialogue Event, 2005.

Ani, Marimba. *Yurugu: An African Centered Critique of European Thought and Behavior*. Indianopolis, African World Press, Inc., 1994.

Baffour, Amankwatia II & Asa G. Hilliard III. "Foreword." *Seeking the Sakhu: Foundational Writings for an African Psychology*, Wade Nobles, Chicago, Third World Press, 2006.

Biko, Steve. *I write what I like*. Johannesburg, Picador Africa, 2004.

Cakata, Zethu. "In search of the absent voice: The Status of Indigenous Languages in Post-apartheid South Africa." Ph.D. diss., Pretoria, University of South Africa, 2015.

Cress-Welsing, Frances. *The Isis Papers*. Chicago, Third World Press, 1991.

Grosfoguel, Ramon. "The epistemic decolonial turn: Beyond political-economy paradigms." *Cultural Studies*, 21.2, 2007, pp. 211-223.

Kaschula, Russell H. and Pamela Maseko. "The intellectualization of African languages, multilingualism and education: A research-based approach." *Alternation Special Edition*, 3, 2014, pp. 8-35.

Magoqwana, Babalwa. "'Putting Food back on the table': Decolonising towards a Sustainable University that Feeds Us in South Africa." *International Journal of African Renaissance Studies - Multi-, Inter- and Transdisciplinarity*, 13.2, 2018, pp. 112-128. DOI: 10.1080/18186874.2018.1536421

Maseko, Pamela. "IsiXhosa does not do gender: Contesting assumptions and re-imagining women identities in Xhosa society." Paper presented at the Pre-Colonial Catalytic Conference, Port Elizabeth, South Africa, March 15-17, 2017.

Mignolo, Walter. "Geopolitics of sensing and knowing: On (de)coloniality, border thinking, and epistemic disobedience." *Postcolonial Studies*, 14.3, 2011, pp. 273-283.

Nobles, Wade. "African Consciousness as Cultural Continuity." *The SAGE Encyclopedia of African Cultural Heritage in North America*. Mwalimu J. Shujaa and Kenya J. Shujaa, eds. Thousand Oaks, Sage Publications, Inc., 2015, pp. 44-48.

Passer, Michael, et al. *Psychology: The Science of Mind and Behavior*. United Kingdom, McGraw-Hill Education, 2009.

Pewewardy, Cornel. "Ideology, Power and the Miseducation of Indigenous Peoples in the United States." *For indigenous eyes only: a decolonisation handbook*. Waziyatawin Angela Wilson, Michael Yellow Bird, and Angela Cavender Wilson, eds. New Mexico, School for Advanced Research Press, 2005, pp. 139-156.

Prah, Kwesi. "In tongues: African languages and the challenges of development." 2006. Accessed June 20, 2017. http://www.casas.co.za/.../204CV challenges.

wa Thiong'o, Ngugi. *Decolonizing the mind*. London, Heinemann, 1986.

Weiten, Wayne. *Psychology: Themes and Variations*, 8th ed. Wadsworth, Belmont, Cengage Learning, 2010.

Wiley, David. "'Tribe and Tribalism': Categories of Misunderstanding African Societies." 1981. Accessed August 13, 2017. http://www.africa.upenn.edu/k-12/tribe.

Endnotes

1 In 2015 university students across South Africa embarked on a wave of political protests that began with a one student-led protest (the student's name is Chumani Maxwele) at the University of Cape Town dubbed #RhodesMustFall. It was calling for the removal of Cecil John Rhodes' statue and all that he represents. This culminated into a bigger movement known as #FeesMustFall with clear demands for a free and decolonized education and the permanent employment of contract staff members who are predominantly black. What set these movements apart was the urgency of the demands and the articulation of what is meant by decolonized education. This articulation was a clear indication that students were thinking critically about what they learn.

Institutions of higher learning across South Africa and the national Department of Higher Education and training were thus forced to address the issue of pedagogy.

2   People of African descent across the African continent including South Africa.

3   Homelands, also known as Bantustans, were erected by the apartheid government as pseudo independent African states within South Africa. Their governments were constituted by indigenous people who were still controlled by the apartheid regime and they were set up according to language groups of the people of the land. The speakers of isiXhosa were allocated two Bantustans which were the Transkei and Ciskei, Setswana speakers were put in Bophuthatswana, Venda homeland was for tshiVenda speakers, Lebowa for speakers of Sepedi, KaNgwane for siSwati speakers, Gazankulu for Tsonga speakers, Qwaqwa for Sesotho speakers, KwaZulu for the speakers of isiZulu and KwaNdebele for the isiNdebele speakers. This was part of the apartheid regime's strategy to divide and conquer. The aim was to create divisions among indigenous people and language was instrumental. In a very negative way language was used to create superior and inferior groups of people. Schools in these homelands used indigenous languages as media of instruction. It was important for the apartheid regime to keep indigenous people in these homelands and control their movement in and out of the territory they had declared as belonging solely to Europeans. Indigenous people from the homelands needed to have passports to travel to any part of the country which fell under the Republic of South Africa.

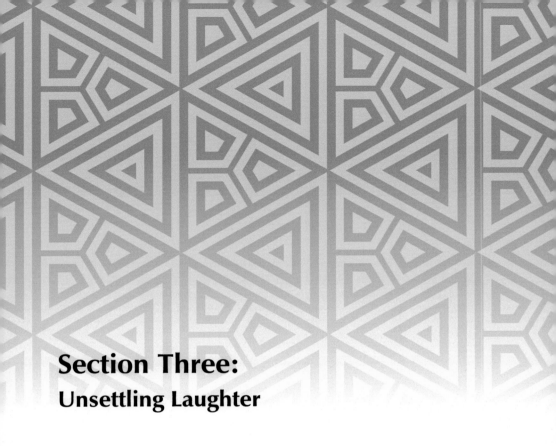

Section Three:

Unsettling Laughter

5

Gradations in a blur:
Some thoughts on what it means to be contemporary in South Africa

Ashraf Jamal

> The contemporary is the person who perceives the darkness of his time as something that concerns him, as something that never ceases to engage him.
>
> Giorgio Agamben

> We are now living through a period in which the center of gravity is transferring to new worlds.
>
> Hans Ulrich Obrist

I first used the phrase "gradations in a blur" in 1996 in my novel *Love themes for the wilderness*. Evoking calibrated clarity within an unclear schema, the phrase responded to South Africa's uncertain transitional years in which blindness and insight were perceived as irrevocably bound. This essay returns to this notion of a graded blur and, in the broader context of Africa, examines why the phrase may have a continued purchase. Now that it finally looks as though African art is assuming a prominent role and place in the world's art market, the question I ask myself is why this is so and what it means? There are no final answers provided here; rather, in keeping with the logic of a graded blur I make some propositions which it is hoped will assist us in thinking the contemporary in Africa today.

El Anatsui's meteoric rise to global fame, or El Selahi and Meschac Gaba's stellar presence at the Tate Modern are cases in point. In *Africa Outside The Ghetto* Liese van der Watt reminds us that "the redress started in the 90s when shows like *Seven Stories of Art in Africa* tried to put straight the mystifying damage that Magiciens de la Terre did to the field of contemporary African art by constructing an exoticised and decontextualized show in 1989" (2013, 61). This redress is on-going. As Chris Dercon former Director of the Tate Modern notes, the museum now seeks to create a "truly international collection, showing African artists as part of a global history of modern and contemporary art" (Ibid.). This move to finally include contemporary African art within what to date has been a Western-centric focus is a salutary one. That said, we should not forget that the very notions of globalisation and the contemporary are in-and-of-themselves problematic. This essay therefore also examines the conceptual problems built into these categorical imperatives which are so avidly in operation today.

There is no doubt that global interest in Africa and its arts is on the rise. The question is why, after over 500 years of exploitation and misrepresentation the dialogue has—seemingly—changed. No longer a privative other, Africa is today at the epicentre of a global shift in ethics and the creation of a new humanism. This grand claim—my own—is built on the core principle of sustainability—or sustainism—which, I argue, lies at the centre of the new perceptions of art and its value in a rapidly changing world. The global ecological and cultural focus on sustainability is a shift which marks an epistemic leap from modernism and postmodernism. Developed by Michiel Schwartz and Joost Elffers, sustainism is the key to their "cultural manifesto" for the 21st century. If modernism is a system which strived for coherence, integration, objectification, centralization, linearity, autonomy, then, for Schwartz and Elfers, sustainism seeks dispersal, immanence, decentralisation, flow, collectivity. The pervasiveness of this new consciousness today cannot be underestimated. My challenge is to link this new thinking and activism to a changing art world, and, in particular, to uncover its relevance in African art practice. My engagement in this regard is largely speculative. Nevertheless I do see some canny links between the logic of the contemporary and that of sustainism—both systems signal a break from modernism, and its conceptual fall-out, postmodernism. In other words we are, today, living in a very different era.

As Julieta Aranda, Brian Kuan Wood, and Anton Vidokle point out in their introduction to *What is Contemporary Art*, with this shift "the grand narratives and ideals of modernism [are] replaced by a default, soft consensus on the immanence of the present, the empiricism of *now*, of what we have directly in front of us, and what they have in front of them over there" (2010, 6-7). Clearly not a universal category, the contemporary is, rather, strikingly geographical and temporal. In "Now and Elsewhere" the Raqs Media Collective adds: "Different places share the same time because of the accident of longitude. Thus clocks in London and Lagos (with adjustments made for daylight savings) show the same time. And yet, the experience of 'now' in London and Lagos may not feel the same at all" (43). It is therefore the disjunctive untimeliness of the contemporary which matters. This realisation importantly qualifies the push for a generic globalised vision of culture. Later I will discuss the tensions between the local and the global, or as the Raqs Media Collective puts it, the "asynchronous [...] strange tug of more than one time and place" (2010, 45).

This global shift in values is tied to the deep and gnawing realisation that the principles of modernism—along with its conceptual and reactive crack-up postmodernism—mark an end-point in the West's Enlightenment project and that, today, in a decentralised global world of hyper-connectivity, a world increasingly at odds with controlling dehumanised systems, what is needed all the more is the human touch. The ecological revolution—sustainism—now runs concurrently with a cultural revolution—the contemporary—founded on compassion. How this shift impacts upon art practice is my key concern. Tino Sehgal, championed at No. 54 in ArtReview's Power 100, conducted by Mark Rappolt, best manifests through his art practice and ideas this growing need for understanding and compassion. His interactive, "relational," and deeply intimate public works are, he says, "nothing less than an anticipation of truly dialogical relations in contemporary culture" (2013, 132). Sehgal reiterates this theme in Hans Ulrich Obrist's "Manifestos for the future":

> I thought the twenty-first century would be, hopefully, more like a dialogue, more like a conversation, and maybe that in itself is a kind of manifestation or whatever. I am careful in even using that word. I just think the twentieth century was so sure of itself, and I hope that the twenty-first century will be less sure. And part of that is to listen to what other people say and to enter into a dialogue, to not stand up and immediately declare one's intent (2010, 65).

Once again it is a lack of clarity that matters; an openness and attentive and profound sense of context. Along with Jeremy Deller and Nicolas Bourriaud, the philosopher behind Relational Aesthetics, Tino Sehgal's interventions have come to define the slipperiness of the contemporary moment. As Hans Ulrich Obrist points out, we are dealing with "a plurality of temporalities across space, a plurality of experiences and pathways through modernity that continues to this day, and on a truly global scale [...] We are now living through a period in which the centre of gravity is transferring to new worlds"

(65). It is because of this decentralisation of a Western-centric artworld, and the subsequent relocation or broadening of the logic of centres, which explains the increased nodal pull of zones such as Dakar, LagosPhoto, or the Johannesburg Art Fair. In keeping with Tino Sehgal's view this shift has also meant the dispersal of taste, value and provenance; the concerted attempt by those, like Sehgal and Deller, who seek to free the art experience from the fetish of the object, resulting in artworks which are also increasingly amorphous, indeterminate—caught in a graded blur.

Via Giorgio Agamben, Obrist also turns to this perceptual blur of forms and intent. "The one who belongs to his or her own time [...] does not coincide perfectly with it," says Obrist. "To capture one's moment is to be able to perceive in the darkness of the present this light which tries to join us and cannot." Agamben follows: "The contemporary is the person who perceives the darkness of his time as something that concerns him, as something that never ceases to engage him." Hans Urich Obrist sums up Agamben's view: "To discern the potentialities that constantly escape the definition of the present is to understand this contemporary moment" (2010, 67). It is precisely within this perceptual schema, this horizon of unknowing, that I began this essay. It is not my intention to be wilfully obscure; rather, with Sehgal, Agamben and Obrist I seek to affirm the criticality of an indeterminate, ceaselessly shifting, mercurial cultural moment; a moment in which contemporary African art in all its diversity finds itself staging its own uncertain yet nevertheless invigorating narrative.

In South Africa, Willem Boshoff's landmark work *Blind Alphabet* from the mid-1990s precisely captures the slippage of meaning in the instant of its visceral impact. Boshoff carved a wooden sculpture every day for a year. The sculptures were inspired by Latin—a dead language. He then placed the sculptures in a funereal black box. The box was meshed, the objects vaguely discernible within. The artist then placed a metal sheet stencilled in braille on the top of the box—the text explaining the content of the box. Only those who could read braille could understand the contents. In a gallery context, in which touch is strictly prohibited, it was the blind who now become sighted. A brilliant installation—and a critical conceptual intervention in contemporary African art—Boshoff's *Blind Alphabet* evokes a new language for a new era. If for the sighted the work proved obstructive and obtuse, it also spurred a new perception, a new mode of orientation.

In the context of South African art, the *Blind Alphabet* remains a landmark work which defines a society in need of what Albie Sachs in "Preparing ourselves for freedom" termed new "apertures." Created in the era of democracy, the *Blind Alphabet* signals a new openness or spirit of play which defines South African art today. That said, it should also be noted that the best art holds onto the specifics of place and the locality of its imagining.

In other words, with all the talk of globalisation and uniformity of expression, it should be stated that the conceptual heft of Boshoff's *Blind Alphabet* is not only universal, it also, all importantly, elicits a certain particularity—for it quintessentially defines the shift in power in South Africa, the collapse of apartheid along with its morbid polarisations and the balkanisation of its people. A work which effectively blurs differences and morphs perception, the Blind Alphabet serves here as a key example of a contemporary sculptural artwork which captures the epistemic imprecision so central to us today. The presence of Boshoff's *Blind Alphabet* at Frieze 2013 affirms all the more its prescience and its currency.

Irrespective of the medium one practices, my view is that a graded blur is inescapable. In *Babble* Charles Saatchi addresses this matter. He begins by quoting Pablo Picasso—"painting is a blind man's profession. He paints not what he sees, but what he feels, what he tells himself about what he has seen"—then links this proposition to a medical anomaly, "selective bilateral damage," the ability, despite total blindness, "to detect emotion on a person's face." The patient, it seems, "responded appropriately—with emotions such as joy, fear, and anger—to a variety of social expressions" (2013, 265). Not only was the patient able to respond to emotions, it was discovered that he could also navigate and avert a series of obstacles placed in his path. The term given for this startling ability is—Blindsight. As Saatchi notes: "Because his strokes damaged only his visual cortex, his eyes remain functional and as a result can still gather information from his environment." For the patient "sight has changed [...] from a conscious to a largely subconscious experience. He no longer has a definite picture of his surroundings, but he has retained an innate awareness, demonstrating to the researchers what they described as 'the importance of these evolutionary ancient visual paths'" (266).

It is as a conceptual trope that I adopt the intriguing term "blindsight." For in the context of the contemporary art world what interests me is the disappearance of discernible grids. In South Africa the canon which was created to explain the role and agency of our artists during the resistance and post-resistance years is also no longer satisfactorily operable. Rather, it is the heightened fusion of the local and the global and the consequential blurring of that deemed discrete or singular which has emerged as the outcome of the new internationalism and transculturalism. For J.J. Charlesworth in his essay "Local vs Global" this development marks a new "Esperanto." "As the artworld becomes increasingly global, does it run the risk of destroying cultural difference in its efforts to promote art that is legible, easily understandable, instantly translatable and culturally exchangeable?" (2013, 154). Charlesworth's question is a critical one, for the pursuit of a unifying Esperanto can also produce the dulling effect of sameness; hence the need to blindside this tendency; or the need for a new kind of blindsight evident in the interventions of Tino Sehgal, Jeremy Deller, or Willem Boshoff.

"The artworld of 2013 is no longer simply international, but global," says Charlesworth. "There is a difference between the two where once there were national art cultures, something different has begun to emerge—a single 'artworld' that is no longer dominated by a few powerful national scenes." We live today in the age of "the 'networked artist'—the artist who finds opportunities in multiple localities across several continents, facilitated by the equally global curator" (Charlesworth 2013, 154). Within this "dispersed, nodal, twenty-first century paradigm," Charlesworth chooses to hold onto the criticality of the local. Art's task, he says, "is the task of all localities, together, against the power of the global." For as Charlesworth repeatedly points out, as cultural difference converts into a globally recognisable product, "the local then comes to mean merely one of many localities that constitute the global artworld. Ironically, the consciousness of difference homogenises it—an artworld Esperanto" (155). It is the homogenisation of cultural difference which we must be wary of. At the same time, we must also be wary of the reification of cultural difference, for if the former orientation disperses singularity or cultural distinctiveness, the latter tendency fetishizes it; hence the importance of a graded blur, or what the Raqs Media Collective calls an "asynchronous contemporaneity" (2010, 45).

To occupy a graded blur is to best mediate these competing interests. There is no doubt that this new twenty-first century artworld paradigm is alluring, for with an accelerated globalisation comes "the spread of common intellectual points of reference, as critical production is dispersed across centres, further consolidating artistic communities around common questions" (Charlesworth 2013, 155). The problem of course is that within such a paradigm local matters only become relevant once they have found their parallel elsewhere in the world. However, despite all the hype about sameness, differences prevail. Omar Al-Qattan addresses this matter in his essay "Culture and Power in a Globalised World." Al-Qattan's view is anything but favourable: he sees the globalised market as "nothing but a colonial market by proxy." It is precisely this globalised market—this Esperanto—which, he says, will nullify "cultural turmoil, conflict and contradiction." The danger is that the local is being "swallowed up by a world in which artistic expression is made banal by easy money and borrowed ideas and fashions, and marketing and public relations considerations rather than the struggles for freedom, equality, authenticity and originality that some artists, thankfully, continue to consider as central to their creative endeavours" (Al-Qattan 2013, 119).

Al-Qattan's critique is a sound one, though the author himself recognises that there remain—and will continue to remain—anomalies to this withering absorptive system:

> If authenticity is no longer even conceivable because so many world cultures have undergone cultural genocide […] we must ask ourselves what value a work of artistic expression can have if it does not at least express a point of view; if it relinquishes historical accuracy; if it loses sight of issues of genuine universal concern for humanity or remains stuck in narrow identity politics, conceptual game-playing or formalistic posturing, as so much globalised culture has been in recent years.

While Al-Qattan's prognosis is justly bleak and to the point, my own intervention asks that we hold fast to the loopholes in this vision: those who succeed in eliding what Al-Qattan in no uncertain terms calls a "cultural genocide." His concluding answer is that we must look to those "whose work genuinely resonates among the poor, dominated and marginalised grassroots; who can find alternatives to violent ideology and dominance through their inspirational work and who can offer a genuinely universal and liberating voice in a global cultural conversation held on an equal footing between all its participants" (119).

It is telling that as the artworld becomes increasingly depoliticised, or rather, as it increasingly adheres to neo-liberal free-market principles, that Al-Qattan should return us to the culture of resistance and post-resistance which defined South Africa's cultural struggle. What Al-Qattan is clearly reminding us of is a need for on-going activism through our arts. My view is that this is in fact the case, but that, today, it is no longer defined by overarching ideological principles; that, instead, the struggles have become increasingly minoritarian, or "grassroots"; localised, immanent, piecemeal. In the Cape Town area in South Africa, for example, the Greatmore Studio Collective is a case in point, as is the Burning Museum Collective and the Maboneng arts initiative in Guguletu. Operating outside the official gallery arena, these movements among many others signal the resurgence of makeshift "pop-up" cultural interventions. However, these myriad minor movements may also need a bigger bolder face to capture their counter-cultural visions, and here, perhaps, we could, after Al-Qattan, consider El Anatsui as a "genuinely universal and liberating voice in a global cultural conversation" (2013, 119).

In an amusing but revealing piece, "The International Curator Karaoke bus, or how to lose faith in your contemporary art education in four weeks," Mika Conradie comes to grips with what she considers the South African artworld's disjointed relation with global concerns. The home context Conradie declares to be "extra-provincial," a term at once devastating and precise. Conradie's gripe is not about being out of synch with a Western-centric art culture, but about a failure to be responsive to a more pliable intellectual and cultural context and more aware of "larger intellectual movements in contemporary Art." All importantly, for Conradie the key question which must be posed today is: "What Does It Mean To Be Contemporary (in Africa)?" (29). In the light of Conradie's view, Willem Boshoff's Blind Alphabet re-emerges as an aesthetic and cultural intervention all the more singular, for it broaches a possibility which has not been sustained. I am well aware that here I am contradicting myself. My point is that it is impossible to determine just how effective this counter-cultural, grassroots, minoritarian, or relational movement in fact is.

With all the talk of globalisation we find ourselves returning not to the "extra-provincial" matter of nationhood which has a tendency to essentialise cultural differences, but, rather, to the question of 'Africa', yet another nominal category, but one which will not be synthesised or integrated despite all attempts on the contrary to read and even experience the continent as a trope for either the romantic or barbarous other, as begging bowl, or as hospice for palliative care. In other words, Africa as a global cultural signifier has, historically, always been crippled by fantasy or prejudice, always othered-yet-exploited as an economic outpost and raw resource, or as a realm for fantasy or site for a brute unconscious. The art of the African continent has rarely been perceived as illustrative of human evolution, or as a marker for global culture; rather, once again, it has proved to be yet another raw material to be exploited and redeployed without any regard for its provenance. This is an all too familiar story which I am not interested in reprising. Rather, it serves as a preamble to Conradie's more searching question: What does it mean to be contemporary in Africa?

Returning to the notion of Blindsight, or the importance of what the discoverers of this condition called "evolutionary ancient visual paths" (Saatchi 2013, 266), we can begin to develop another paradigm which locates Africa at its core, while recognising all the while that Africa too is both nodal and dispersed; that as a conceptual zone it must be conceived intra-regionally and intra-continentally. For if Mika Conradie is as insistent as she is in shifting the focus away from the extra-provincial ghetto of a national imaginary it is because she realises the greater value of a PanAfrican and Afropolitan focus. Conradie, of course, is not alone in this push. 2013 saw the launch of the first West-based African Art Fair, aligned with Frieze in London. Titled *1:54*, the fair is the first international market for art out of Africa. By locating it within a major metropolis, and aligning it with an internationally celebrated contemporary art fair, Frieze, *1:54* marked a new era in the cultural manufacture and dissemination of African art worldwide.

1:54 is by no means an isolated phenomenon. 2013's *ArtReview* lists El Anatsui at no. 98 in its Power 100, a first for an African artist. The *Art Review*'s rationale behind this selection is worth quoting in full:

> Although the sixty-nine-year-old Ghanaian-born, Nigeria-based sculptor and teacher has been active since the 1970s, the last decade has seen El Anatsui's reputation rocket. His breathtaking, shimmering curtains made of thousands of throwaway metal objects—bottle caps. Aluminium wrapping, metal graters, printing plates—have wowed crowds across the world this summer, from the Brooklyn Museum of Art to the Royal Academy's Summer Exhibition and the Venice Biennale. El Anatsui's work, meanwhile, has been yielding record prices at auction and waiting lists at his galleries, as collectors and institutions find in his flowing, abstract 'fabrics' both aesthetic wonder and a stoic commentary on globalisation, consumerism and the cultural, social and economic histories of West Africa (Rappolt 2013, 168).

El Anatsui's relatively recent meteoric rise, after decades in the field, is a salutary sign for African art more generally. But if El Anatsui proves representative of an emergent and growing belief in African art as "the next big thing," it is because his art mirrors not only an obsession with rarefied and inflated commodities, but because his art is also at the forefront of a new world defined by sustainability. By recycling waste to create his "fabrics," El Anatsui's work has captured the imagination of a world caught between austerity and innovation—a world, in other words, urgently preoccupied with tempering excess while maintaining growth, and with holding onto creativity and the power of the imagination in an increasingly fragile climate.

In *Sustainism*, a non-paginated Cultural Manifesto for the Sustainist Era, Michiel Schwartz and Joost Elffers set out to define the contemporary ethos: "The confluence of globalization, the Web, Climate Change, Localism, Media Democracy, Open Source, Environmentalism, and more." In the sphere of art practice all these elements are operational, all key to the redefinition of what art does today. For Schwartz and Elffers "the sustainability revolution is in essence a revolution of culture." Following J.J. Charlesworth's caveat, they also point out that "sustainity is not intent on making everything global but recognises that all locals are globally connected." Schwartz and Elffers then follow up with the reversible formulation: The Culture of Sustainity will Transform Art. Art will Transform the Culture of Sustainity.

Some of the core dynamics and elements which define this new era include diversity, interdependence, flows, variegation, complex simplicity, and the recyclable, all of which are keys to the creation of El Anatsui's work. So while his works may be revered because they are "breathtaking" and "shimmering," thus inspiring awe, it is also all important to remember that in the instant they become deified, they also return us to the fundamentals for our survival. El Anatsui, the son of Ghana—dumpsite for the world's computers—emerges as the artworld's recycling conscience. In beautifying waste materials, in sanctifying trash, the artist is also offering solutions to what to do with products we fail to recycle. A bricoleur, collagist, creator of the assemblage, El Anatsui is also an ecological activist. By fusing sustainability and culture, the high modernist traditions of Europe with the ingenuity borne out of the African slum, the artist effectively connects the world.

This connection of Africa and the rest of the world is developing at a rapid pace. I have already mentioned *1:54*, to which I will return, but there are numerous instances of the growing prominence of African artists and art centres in the world's marketplace. A further case in point is *LagosPhoto*, or the Tate Modern's first African biennale. My own focal point—the better to address Mika Conradie's point concerning what it means to be contemporary in Africa—will be the intervention of Koyo Kouoh, the Artistic Director of *1:54*. Kouoh's vision is of art institutions and art museums as power stations and producers of new raw energy. Kouoh is also the Director of Raw Material, a company which focuses on "art and intellectualism as a raw material for human development" (2013, 18). In her view the globally feted El Anatsui has relevance not only because his work beguiles and dazzles, but because it redefines the raw materials for art making and the very principles for its existence. As the power of the Western-centric art world buckles, as new centres emerge elsewhere in the world—in the East most prominently; in Beijing, Shanghai, Guangzhou, Shenzhen, Hong Kong, Seoul, Tokyo, Mumbai, Delhi, Beirut, Tehran, and Cairo—we find, according to Koyo Kouoh, the emergence of:

> new economies, new dialectics, and most importantly: a highly intelligent audience. This trend is especially real in Africa, where during the last decade a variety of independent private art initiatives has emerged to fill the vacuum left by unfulfilled promises of cultural and artistic programmes led by the governments" (2013, 16).

Koyo Kouoh's question is as follows: "How is Africa after fifty years of independence, really determining its artistic landscape?" (2013, 17). While positive minded, Kouoh like Omar Al-Qattan calls for more "platforms of criticality and production" which "question hegemonic viewpoints, canons and narratives of art, and develop and manifest approaches of knowledge production outside state institutionalisation" and which "permits 'in-between' zones, spaces in flux that connect theoretical, visual, practical and local knowledge." Simon Njami similarly asks: "Can we grasp the needs of our times with contemporary tools? Can we move beyond the codification of a monolithic history of the world that is outrageously simplified? Can we change the analytical schemas whose purpose was to lock identities into geographic essentialisms?" (2013, 23). For Njami, Kuouh, Al-Qattan, and Conradie what is needed is a post-national, post-institutional vision—one in which a given institution becomes, after art historian and curator Alexander Dorner, "a power station, a producer of new energy," (Kuouh 2013, 7)—and in which, after Njami, "a new citizenship is being developed … that rejects all forms of elitism and destroys the barriers between those who know and those who do not know" (Njami 2013, 23).

In the light of these perceptions of African art practice what are we to make of El Anatsui's standing in *ArtReview*? Clearly the position is twofold: it absorbs the artist into the existing—Western—star system while, at the same time, acknowledging his local and global agency as an alchemist of waste products. My own investment in the works of El Anatsui is an ethical one: while justly awed, I am all the more inspired by his innovative recycling of consumer products. El Anatsui has reworked the cargo cult on a grand scale—the quasi-mystical re-appropriation or detournment of Western products. In effect the artist has taken a disposable waste product and converted it into a shimmering Idea, for it is not only the visceral or spiritual impact which his work imparts that matters; rather, and all importantly, it is the Idea which the works provoke which, in the 21st century counts the more, for it is the Idea—rather than infrastructure, machinery, or money—which is the key to economic and cultural vitality of a society, a business, a nation, a continent. In the contemporary artworld, El Anatsui's method and affect marks a breakthrough. As a modernist and a sustainist, or change agent, the artist straddles tradition and innovation. At the core of what the artist does is the call to *remake the ways we make things*.

There is no doubt that El Anatsui is at the pinnacle of his career. The question which remains, even in this globalised world, is whether he matters more to the Western imagination—as an aesthetic appeasement for its guilt regarding waste, as trope for an othered-now-revisited African unconscious, as mirror for a spirited and ethical Idea—than he does within Africa? In other words, how global and contemporary is the African imagination? As Koyo Kouoh and Simon Njami have pointed out, much needs to be done to create "a new [global] citizenship." And as Francois Verges reminds us: "We still have not finished with the decolonization movement that promised to reorganise the world more fairly and 'decolonize our minds'. Europe, the West, the Occident, these certain territories denoting economic, military and cultural power continue to dominate even though they are increasingly threatened by other centres of power" (2013, 37).

Here we find the paradox succinctly captured by Omar Al-Qattan. While matters seem to be changing, they also remain the same. As Liese van der Watt notes, "for as long as the playing fields are not level, African art will remain is separatist limbo, whether gallerists and artists like it or not. African art is simply not represented internationally and efforts from within to change this should be applauded" (van der Watt 2013, 61). Koyo Kouoh in an equally emphatic tone asks: "Where is our Tate, MoMA and so forth doing the work that they are supposed to do?" (Jamal & Kouoh 2013, 65). Clearly we are confronted with an on-going battle for visibility, provenance and value, rights which have repeatedly been stripped away or denied to Africa. That said, we should also optimistically remind ourselves that our Tate and our MoMA has finally been created. I am referring here to Zeitz MOCAA, the Museum of Contemporary Art Africa, which opened in Cape Town in September, 2017.

The brainchild of Jochen Zeitz, the ex CEO of PUMA, Zeitz MOCAA (the Museum of Contemporary Arts Africa) sees itself as the talismanic centre of contemporary African art housed on the continent. Ranking with museums in Sydney, San Francisco, and Bilbao, Zeitz MOCCA also promises to be our Tate Modern. Described as "By us, about us, for us," Zeitz MOCAA is set to "define the culture of our time" (Jamal 2013, 30). An ambitious PanAfrican project, Zeitz MOCAA seeks to define African contemporaneity for the world. Based in a renovated grain silo on Cape Town's Waterfront—which is also Africa's biggest shopping Mecca—the museum promises to not only deepen our experiences of the role of art in today's world, but to connect a divided continent. While it remains too soon to state what the impact of Zeitz MOCAA will truly be, I believe that the writing is on the wall, the initiative on point. As Jochen Zeitz notes:

> We want to use this institution to connect our artists with the rest of the world […] and vice versa. For so long, so many African cultural artefacts were taken from us. But now we are—very fortunately—in the position where we can import these back to where they belong. And this, in turn, allows us to export our cultures ourselves; to take them all over and make a much broader cultural community aware of exactly what we have here. (Clark-Brown 2014, 9)

Here Jochen Zeitz conveys the prevailing turnaround and the new position African art is assuming. Perhaps one could see El Anatsui as the epigone of this new moment in Africa's art history. Then again, perhaps one could see the artist as an anomaly and therefore by no means representative of change for the better.

Given the split vote regarding African art and its role in the world, I prefer to stick with Zeitz's optimism and, contra Liese van der Watt, see the provenance of African art as stemming from something more than a filtered and rarefied system of exceptionalism. I refuse to fix the continent's artists in some ghetto of the imagination. If decolonization of the imagination, according to Verges, is not completed, it is certainly under way. In "Digital Africa" J.M. Ledgard more optimistically reminds us that "Connectivity is given: it is coming and happening and spreading in Africa whether or not factories get built or young people find jobs. Culture is being formed online as well as on the street: for the foreseeable future, the African voice is going to get louder, while the voice of ageing Europe quietens" (Ledgard 2011, 62). Once again it is networking, flexibility, open source, and flow which prove the determining factors in changing the fate of Africa—that along with its vast captive youthful population. To understand how Africa can be changed we have to understand its youth. And, as Ledgard reminds us:

> Speaking is still preferred to writing and Africa happens to have timed its digital age to coincide with new voice-activated technologies. The generation gap between those who were trained to guide a fountain pen with their fingers, those whose kinetic memory is dominated by their thumbs, and those even younger who are used to the sweeping movements of the touchscreen, will give way to the return of voice—Africa's voice (2011, 68).

Ledgard's vision is a provocative one, and, for those concerned with what it means to be contemporary in Africa and the role of art-making therein, the vision suggests a very different digitised scenario. In this current-yet-futuristic context it would seem that despite its vision of sustainism, that the work of El-Anatsui seems rather retrograde. I am uncertain on this matter, preferring to hold onto both the analogue and digitised worlds. And perhaps the role of contemporary African art is to find new reasons for bridging what, after all, is nothing but a false divide. In an essay on renowned architect, Norman Foster, J.M. Ledgard affirms the prevailing view that it is cities that "supercharge ideas," and that in these cities it is the slums which supercharge ideas all the more. Ledgard further states that "most of the economic growth in the world in the coming years will be from the poorest bits of cities in the poorest countries" (2012, 64). It is evident that in Africa innovation will continue to about hunger, that inspiration and desperation will remain snagged together. Perhaps it is this rich complex which could help us to create art for this world? It is not a solution I am offering here, but a way of interpreting the world we live in; a world that is indisputably uncertain, in which the very grid that defines the value and meaning of art is vanishing before our very eyes.

As Jonathan T.D. Neil reminds us, "contemporary art today, on the whole, doesn't know how to authorise itself. It doesn't know what values it subscribes to or what good it is for. Absent of its own authority, art must look elsewhere to be taken seriously, and increasingly it appears it wants to be nothing more than familiar" (2013, 57). It is the last word in this statement which is the most difficult to countenance—art as one's familiar, art as familiar. Stemming from a culture of hyper-connectivity, facebook, and the grotesquerie of the "selfie," the notion of the familiar, ironically, also supposes a distanced-if-intimate relation to oneself and to others. Familiarity is not intimacy—it operates by proxy; vicariously; through trickery or a sleight-of-hand. To be "nothing more than familiar" is to be nothing more than something banal; something with the fleeting illusion of a presence. This is most certainly a spectral and digital notion—defined by a swipe or a press of a button. If this is the defining zeitgeist of contemporary Western art, then how are we to connect and interface with it? How, in other words, is African art going to make sense?

I say this in the full knowledge that one cannot synoptically define either Western or African art. However, what I am battling to communicate is the dilemma of location, presence, and reception. These are the questions central to Liese van der Watt's reflections on *1:54*, but, more generally this is a dilemma which remains central to the question of the contemporary in Africa: How "African" is African art? How transcultural? How diasporic? Are our South African artists as disposed to the blithe ease and banality of the familiar? Or are we seeking to create a different point of interface? If we have moved beyond the moments of resistance and post-resistance culture, does this mean that our artists similarly are now unable to mediate themselves? Or that they now lack a critical grid? In "White Knuckle" Anna Stieleu comes to grips with the gnawing vacuum which seems to define the present moment in South African art practice: "Resistance art, characterising much of the creative output of the Apartheid era, was more long drawn out scream than exhalation." She says:

> [I]t was raw, hurting, crying out in the dark. But now, as the born free generation—and I number myself among them—stretches it's lungs to wail, there is a pervasive sense of discontent. We lack the coherent call of the struggle. We are, in a very real sense, still hunting for something to shout about at equal volume […] and some contemporary practice seems to be tiring of holding its breath. Perhaps boredom is too strong a word.

Stielau then makes the all-important qualification: "This is not the monotony of ennui, amounting to little more than ideological emptiness, but a kind of white-knuckled, thwarted frustration; a brand of boredom that drums its heels irritably on the floor" (2013, 62).

Returning to J.J. Charlesworth's debate, "Global vs Local," we find that a culture of sameness can as easily become a culture of indifference; that all the more one must hold onto the imperatives of the local if we are to interface effectively in the world at large. Which is why, as the world begins to blur, I have asked that we learn all the more to calibrate. Perhaps, despite Ledgard's optimism, we should continue to remain out of step with the digital revolution - or at least out of step enough to reflect on the implications behind the technology we use. My children, doubtless, will guffaw in the face of this preposterous and belated proposition; all the more now that global giants such as Samsung are today at the forefront of Africa's digital revolution—rendering the familiar ubiquitous. As Samsung's advertorial pitch goes: "Nowadays we Instagram our lives. Social networks have become photo albums. Photography has become the universal language of communication." Or as Nana Ocran notes in her Samsung catalogue essay "Lagos Photo: The African city as an art gallery," "the digital revolution is transforming the way in which African stories are being told and consumed and in the process it is changing much of the politics behind the continents various (2013, 50). If Ledgard emphasises the power of the African voice, then the spin-doctors behind Samsung's African invasion fast-forward to the global taste for the visual, the true Esperanto of the 21st century. When speed meets economy of scale, when narrative meets optical precision, and the "image stabiliser" meets "photo suggest" —as in the case in Samsung's Galaxy S4 Zoom—it is the photographer who becomes the camera's familiar and not the other way around. This inversion, coupled with the disappearance of the auteur, affirms the more the separation of the artist from the creation.

In Western aesthetics this is already a common parlance and lore. The question is whether we are caught in the same slipstream? And, once in this slipstream, how does it affect the stories we tell, and the way we live our lives? Nana Ocran has already pointed out the massive impact the digital revolution has on our politics. My question is: Does this seismic digital shift mean that the disconnection between Africa and the rest of the world is—finally—breached? Or does is merely generate yet another voyeuristic portal for passive and disaffected consumers? With all the hype about connectivity—are we truly connecting; truly speaking each to each?

The art critic Matthew Collings runs counter to the prevailing and blithe view of easy connectivity. Contra the digital age, Collings looks forward to "a physical, unalienated relationship between the art object and the person who's making it. The artworld lost sight of this, and as a consequence a hunger will be answered, and making will return" (2013, 65). "A proud 'digital-idiot'," Koyo Kouoh concurs, noting that "Painting and drawing were declared dead for a long period for the benefit of installation, video and process-driven productions. Yet one cannot deny the power and the high level of critical content in the body of work of an artist like Johannes Phokela" (Jamal & Kouoh 2013, 66). This resurgence of the tactile is heartening, returning us once again to the visceral and eye-popping works of El Anatsui. It also returns us to the words by Pablo Picasso: "Painting is a blind man's profession. He paints not what he sees, but what he feels, what he tells himself about what he has seen" (Saatchi 2013, 265).

Curiously, at this point in my rumination Picasso's words connect as seamlessly to the world of painting as it does to the world of digital photography, for if we are to believe Samsung's fiction then Instagram persuasively serves as a blind man's vehicle; for in a culture defined by speed one no longer photographs what one sees but what one feels. A process of synaesthesia is at work, a confusion of receptors, in which we relate false interpretations of our actions; interpretations which become increasingly less important the further we move away from consciousness into some big global sleep. My point here is that perhaps we have happily transformed ourselves into somnambulists, and, so doing, have given up the preoccupation with a clear divide between the waking and dream worlds. As the bold backdrop of morality fades away, as our ethics becomes increasingly makeshift and contingent, our narratives lose their overarching frame and their rudder. After Jonathan T.D. Neil, we, like the art we make, or are drawn to, find that we are unable to authorise ourselves, that we don't know what values to subscribe to, and that we don't know what they are good for. And yet we go on and seem to make sense; we have a canny capacity to make sense of non-sense, to suture difference. We read promise in a vat of faeces, hope in a puddle of gasoline. Through the prosaic we find the sublime, and, having suffered a stroke, still we continue, blindly—still we teach ourselves to see.

Charles Saatchi's account, in *Babble*, of the man who lost his sight after suffering two consecutive strokes which destroyed the visual cortex of his brain, is a salutary one. Stroke one destroyed the one hemisphere of his brain, while stroke two destroyed the other, rendering the victim clinically blind. The remarkable outcome of this sad story is that the patient—because of the peculiarity of the "selective bilateral occipital damage"—nevertheless could "see." I am speaking in metaphoric terms here, for the aim of this essay is not to relay a medical condition but to alert the reader to what is called "blindsight." I began my essay with a variant of this formulation—the graded blur—and wish to close by returning to it because, in my view, blindsight captures new apertures which we must open if we are to take up Mika Conradie's question: What Does It Mean To Be Contemporary (in Africa)? In my view this involves a slippage between the analogue and the digital—the worlds of El Anatsui and the worlds of Instagram. It involves holding fast to what, after Schwartz and Elffers, I call "Sustainism"—a belief that "the future of our built environment and our life-world will be shaped by the ideas of sustainism." As Schwartz and Elffers affirm: The sustainability revolution is in essence a revolution of culture. If I have chosen to frame my reading of the work of El Anatsui within a sustainist precept it is because, today, it best splices culture and change, thus freeing the artist from the honorific vestments of high culture which must surely oppress him or her.

Contemporary art (out of Africa) should, therefore, embody a "blindsight" —it should neither reproduce the aesthetic and values of a preordained (national) repertoire, and neither should it cravenly try to manifest an imagined-other-global aesthetic. Eschewing dialectics, by-passing bipolarity, the art of the current age should not-quite-know itself yet possess a canny self-possession. An adjustable aperture: a work should become what others aspire it to be while, at the same time maintaining its own light—rather like the lamp-lit sea creatures of the deep. This evocation of a deeply recessed light returns us to the thoughts of Giorgio Agamben and Hans Ulrich Obrist, namely: "To discern the potentialities that constantly escape the definition of the present is to understand the contemporary moment" (2010, 67).

The November 2013 issue of *ArtReview* similarly explored the power of a recessed light, a blindsight, or what I term a graded blur. While the cover artwork for *ArtReview Asia* is crisply clear—we read the capitalised words POWER EATS THE SOUL without impediment—the *ArtReview* distributed in the rest of the world is blurred. The first cover provides a 20/20 vision while the latter provides vision which reads 20/400. A collaborative work by Rirkrit Tiravanija and Phillipe Parreno, the blurred cover artwork is a visual record of Tiravanija's uncorrected eyesight. A Metaphysical conceit— drawing attention to itself through affectation or an unlikely metaphor—the cover for *ArtReview* gets to the crux of art practice today: while forced to be subjective, we do not in fact inhabit the subjective positions we assume; while trying to be objective we overreach the mark. What counts is the indecisiveness, when one is forced to correct a vision—never quite certain if one is truly seeing the world clearly. That this collaborative work is that of two relational aestheticians—artists, like Deller and Seghal, who locate their works in deliberately indeterminate contexts—affirms all the more the uncertainty of the contemporary moment—a moment in which, in the loosely framed African context, I has attempted to foreground the power of art which refuses to be absorbed into a global sameness; which holds onto the urgencies and drives of a given locality; captures the power of the asynchronous; and, all importantly communicates its passions across the world. Perhaps this is Africa's global moment to galvanise its struggles, network its strengths, and share—its blind alphabet.

Bibliography

Al-Qattan, Omar. "What Defines Culture and Power in a Globalised World." *ArtReview*, November, 2013.

Aranda, Julieta, Brian Kuan Wood, Anton Vidokle. *What is Contemporary Art?* e-flux journal, Sternberg Press, 2010.

Charlesworth, J.J. "Global vs Local," *ArtReview*, November, 2013.

Clark-Brown, Gabriel. "Launch of Zietz MOCAA." *Art Times*, December 2013-January 2014.

Collings, Matthew. "Great Critics and Their Ideas." *ArtReview*, 26, November 2013.

Harney, Elizabeth. "El Anatsui: Irradiance, Wisdom, Weight." *Art South Africa*. Bell Roberts Publishers, December 2013.

Jamal, Ashraf. "Zeitz MOCCAA." *Art South Africa*. Bell Roberts Publishers, December 2013.

Jamal, Ashraf and Koyo Kouoh. "1:54: a conversation." *Art South Africa*, Bell Roberts Publishers, December 2013.

Kouoh, Koyo. *Condition Report: Symposium on Building Art Institutions in Africa*. Ostifedern, Hatje Cantz Verlag, 2013.

Ledgard, J.M. "The Space he's in." *Intelligent Life*, November/December 2012.

—"Digital Africa." *Intelligent Life*, Spring, 2011.

Neil, Jonathan T.D. "Is the artworld's celebriphilia merely the symptom of a deeper insecurity?" *ArtReview*, November 2013.

Njami, Simon. "Imagined Communities." *Condition Report: Symposium on Building Art Institutions in Africa*. Ostifedern, Hatje Cantz Verlag, 2013.

Obrist, Hans Ulrich. "Manifestos for the Future." *What is Contemporary Art?* E-flux journal, Sternberg Press, 2010.

Ocran, Nana. "Lagos Photo: The African city as an art gallery." S13, Samsung, 2013.

Rappolt, Mark. "Power 100." *ArtReview*. November 2013.

Raqs Media Collective. "Now and Elsewhere." *What is Contemporary Art?* E-flux journal, Sternberg Press, 2010.

Saatchi, Charles. "Painting is a blind man's profession." *Babble*. Booth-Clibborn Editions, 2013.

Schwartz, Michiel and Joost Elffers. *Sustainism is the New Modernism: A Cultural Manifesto for the Sustainist Era*. New York, d.a.p./Distributed Art Publishers, Inc., 2010.

Stielau, Anna. "White Knuckle." *Art South Africa*. Bell Roberts Publishers, December 2013.

van der Watt, Liese. "Africa outside the ghetto." *Art South Africa*, Bell Roberts Publishers, December 2013.

Verges, Francoise. "Mapping 'invisible lives'." *Condition Report: Symposium on Building Art Institutions in Africa*. Ostfildern, Hatje Cantz Verlag, 2013.

6

To Make Light of a Dark World:
Resilience and Resistance in South African Art

Bhavisha Panchia

ightness, humour, and laughter are terms seldom associated with South African art, particularly with regards to artwork produced dating from the 1960s onwards. The country's subjection to violence and dehumanisation under the apartheid government mobilised a particular approach to aesthetic production that favoured more serious, direct forms of representation. Such artistic responses contributed to a saturation of images depicting the spectacularly violent and traumatic. Subsumed in the struggle against apartheid, these artists' works were gathered under the genres of 'protest', 'resistance', and 'township' art.

During the late 1970s, the figure of the cultural worker emerged, and championed art as a political weapon in the struggle for freedom and basic human rights. Collectives such as the Gaborone-based Medu Art Ensemble, for example, played a key role in advocating for an aesthetic and cultural approach to political resistance, including the furthering of Africanist cultures. The Medu Art Ensemble was founded a year after the 1976 Soweto Student Uprising. Most of its members were South African exiles, who through visual art, poetry, music, and literature worked together in the struggle for basic human rights. Former Constitutional Judge Albie Sachs, and public intellectual Njabulo Ndebele would later challenge this instrumentalisation of arts and culture, arguing that such rhetoric flattened and limited creative production to more spectacularised representations of the human struggle facing black South Africans.

Pivotal events informing the political landscape and its accompanying aesthetic sensibility in the field of visual arts can be loosely mapped by the following events: the 1976 Soweto Student Uprising, followed by the murder of Stephen Bantu Biko in 1977; the State of Emergency declared in 1985, and the escalating insurgence, uprisings, and demonstrations that followed thereafter. All these events would come to define a psychological heaviness across South Africa. Atrocities of apartheid were documented and disseminated to raise awareness of rising human right violations, and as a way to challenge the government's doctrines. Photography in particular played a significant role in the recording and dissemination of these images to the rest of the world. Ernst Cole, Santu Mofokeng, Alf Khumalo, Peter Magubane, and Omar Badsha are a few seminal photographers who made visible the effects of apartheid's heinous policies both locally and internationally.[1] The circulation of these images within Western Europe and North America furthermore came to represent the social and political ethos of South Africa.

In the late 1980s Albie Sachs reflected on the prevailing state of arts and culture in South Africa. In his text, *Preparing Ourselves for Freedom*, Sachs (1991, 187) astutely remarks, "Our artists are not pushed to improve the quality of their work; it is enough that it be politically correct. The more fists and spears and guns, the better." Sachs went as far as to say: "The range of themes is narrowed down so much that all that is funny or curious or genuinely tragic in the world is extruded" (1991, 187). It is important to underscore Sachs' bemoaning the exclusion of that which is funny or curious by creative practitioners working during this time. The appreciation of lightness and beauty of the world was set aside and replaced with anguish and torment. This resistance period marked a time that pushed aside the joy of laughter in favour of the fight. Sachs furthermore speaks to the limitations of political art, arguing that there is no room for ambiguity and contradictions. He writes, "Ambiguity and contradiction are completely shut out, and the only conflict permitted is that between the old and the new, as if there were only bad in the past and only good in the future" (Sachs 1991, 187). Sachs saw the power of art in its "capacity to expose contradictions and reveal hidden tensions" (1991, 188).

Commenting specifically with regards to the visual arts during this period, artist, and cultural activist Steven Sack, touched upon these conceptual and aesthetic reductionisms. In the exhibition catalogue of *The Neglected Tradition: Towards a New History of South African Art (1930-1988),* Sack offers a distinction of art produced by black artists during the 1960s and 1970s.[2] He writes,

> The art of the sixties and seventies shows two distinct orientations. One was an attempt to reflect social reality, and the repression of the 1960s. This art was often introspective and "tortured"; at its best an indictment of the social conditions caused by apartheid, at its worst, a "self pitying" and sentimental art (Sack 1988, 17).

The second distinction, noted by Sack, is held to be art that is "a site of hope rather than despair" (1988, 17). Artists such as Fikile Magadlela, Thami Mnyele, and Peter Clarke who were inspired by music, literature, and poetry, according to Sack, "reacted against the prevailing township imagery of hopelessness." Sack's distinction of these two polarizing aesthetic sensibilities reveals two different aesthetic approaches and concerns to resisting dominating structures and ideologies, which continue through the 1980s and 1990s. Publications such as Sue Williamson's *Resistance Art in South Africa* (1989) and Gary Younge's *Art of the South African Townships* (1988) testify to these preoccupations.[3] Both these publications in their different ways brought together artists whose work demonstrated resistance against the apartheid regime, and emphasised the political and social context in which the work was produced.

Art of the South African Townships attempted to offer a selection of artwork from the racially segregated townships of South Africa. Many of the artist's works featured in the book, according to Younge, reflect on and respond to oppression in South Africa, and accordingly, their works are discussed in terms of their cultural significance and political attribution. Fixing these artists in the realm of political struggle left many black artists restrained within this burdensome framing. Younge's survey book would furthermore entrench the association of the 'township' as a subject with a syndrome of suffering. Aside from this reductionism and limited readings of these works, books like *Art of the South African Townships,* have furthermore misread artists' work to fit within the established framework of 'resistance' and subversion. One such case is Younge's rather stretched interpretation of deaf-born artist Tommy Motswai's pastel drawing titled *The Tea Party* (1987). This work was awarded a merit prize in the Volkskas Ateljee Award and depicts a simple tea party gathering between two middle-aged couples. The scene is that of a modest looking living room occupied by two couples as they jovially converse over tea and cake. The host reclines in his chair and entertains his guests while the hostess offers them milk for their tea.

Younge's description of *The Tea Party* on the other hand, will demonstrate the narrow and pre-determined lens through which he recounts Motswai's drawing. He writes,

> In *The Tea Party* his victims are a smiling middle-class couple who are being entertained in an excruciatingly average South African home. Whilst the image of the aproned maid bringing in the milk may be somewhat passé, white South African viewers should squirm with embarrassment at the accuracy of his jaundiced colour scheme and telling choice of paintings (1988, 50).

Younge's over-politicising of Motswai's artworks is problematic in the way it over-determines and inscribes Motswai's work as satirical and critical. His interpretation of the hostess as the domestic worker serving a white middle-aged family reveals his inaccurate visual analysis of Motswai's cartoon styled depiction of his subjects, which all appear to be of the same indeterminate race. This failure is furthermore indicative of his essentialising and reducing artworks to the trope of 'resistance' and 'protest' art, and partly explains his careless and negligent analysis and interpretation of *The Tea Party* as critical and satirical. Satire, one of the more politically charged forms of humour, ridicules and mocks its object of choice by exposing its weaknesses and faults, often with the intention to create an awareness of prevailing social ills. Satire is explicit in its operation and object of attack. Counter to Younge's assertions, Motswai's work does not employ satire as I have just described. Motswai instead offers a positive perspective on a society haunted by a traumatic history with an insupportable inhumanity.

Motswai depicts the humorous, the lighter, more positive side of everyday South African experiences, offering viewers optimistic representations of human relations in a society wrestling with a haunting history of inhumanity. His drawings were appreciated and recognised for his use of anecdotal representations of South Africans that were described by arts journalists (Levin 1995; Louw 1999) and writers (De Jager 1992; Arnold 1996) as humorous and satirical. Many South African art critics responded to his work as being naïve and lacking seriousness, perhaps a result of his brightly coloured cartoon-like style of drawing. His mission focuses on those human experiences that tend to be neglected: moments of leisure, laughing, smiling and rejoicing. Motswai portrays celebration not desperation. His work, one could argue, resists spectacular and violent representations, especially of life in township areas. While his work did receive significant praise by the South African and international art world during the mid 1990s, having received the Standard Bank Young Artist Award in 1992, his work also encountered severe criticism.

Art writer and critic Ivor Powell is one of the few writers during this time to critically engage with Motswai's style, content and subject matter. In the article titled 'Wallpaper for the new South Africa', Powell provides a dismissive evaluation of his work making up the 1992 exhibition at the Standard Bank Gallery. For Powell, his drawing style neither 'possesses the illusionistic possibilities of a more definitively naturalistic mode, nor the individually expressive possibilities of a more personalised manner'; rather he asserts, "Motswai strikes me as being little more than a designer of wallpaper for the new South Africa" (1992, 31). It is a kind of wallpaper "that will not clash with the mental furniture of your prejudices or with your historical unease." In short, Powell considers Motswai's drawings as "Paper for the psychic walls of the suburban whiteys, muzak for their souls" (1992, 31). Powell's criticism of Motswai's stylistic undertaking, together with his choice of subject matter is illuminating in that it reveals both the artistic climate and art market trends. Yet Powell's observation, nevertheless fails to consider Motswai's drawings as imaginative renditions that stretch beyond the veracity of the world at hand. Motswai's drawings are constructed visions; thus, reading them as a form of realism would be misguided. They are subjective representations, products of Motswai's invention, imagination, and selection. Narratives of dreams and aspirations are allowed to surface, laying bare a society emerging with hope and expectation. On the surface his renderings may seem naive and cheerfully optimistic, but they also provide a way for us to imagine a South Africa filled with possibility, not restricted to depictions, reflections and representations of pain, suffering, and oppressions.

Returning to Sach's criticism of art's reduction for political ends, we could read Motswai's oeuvre as resisting limited representations of the everyday, to instead offer more anecdotal renditions of life in South Africa undergoing transition. Writer and public commentator Njabulo Ndebele furthers Sachs assertion that dreams of love, hope, compassion, newness and justice were sacrificed to the negative spectacle in black South African literature and visual art production (2006, 42). In his essay, *Rediscovery of the Ordinary: Some New Writings in South Africa*, Ndebele reflects on spectacle and the failed attention to detail in black South African literature. Ndebele rebukes the over-deterministic nature in which the political came to foreground cultural production in South Africa. As Ndebele points out, such determinations of spectacle are mistaken or conflated with what is considered the everyday, or ordinariness of life. In this important essay he demonstrates how this preoccupation with 'spectacle' over the 'ordinary' mistakes the "concern with 'seeing' with the engagement of thinking" (Masilela 2009, 28).

Even though Ndebele focuses on black South African literature, he notes that the representation of the spectacular is also present in visual arts, such as painting and sculpture, both of which are creative sites wherein we are most likely to see "grotesque figures in all kinds of contortions indicative of agony" (2006, 38). His essay is important as it discusses those human practices and experiences that tend to be neglected and repressed under hostile regimes. He sought to capture the "multidimensionality of lived experience that is constantly in the process of historical becoming" (Masilela, 2009, 25). When Ndebele asks us to rediscover the ordinary, he invites us to pay attention to unattended human tendencies such as humour and lightness—even if Ndebele does not name it as such.[4]

Humour and Hurt

"Humour seeks to make light of a dark world" (2007, 13), wrote artist, theorist and critic Colin Richards (1954-2014). For Richards, humour was an instrumental mechanism used to cope, give hope, and live more fully. For the 52nd Venice Biennale in 2007, Richards wrote an exhibition proposal titled *Punch-Line: Hurt and Humour,* an edited extract of which was published in the art journal *Art South Africa.* Here Richards expands on the relationship between hurt and humour within a post-apartheid and postcolonial context, framing humour as a positive mechanism and form that can enable subjugated and subordinated subjects to approach their circumstance or conditions with hope, resilience and lightness. The dark world that Richards refers to is the remnants and current states of worlds, nations and people that have been exploited and suffered abuse, while the inflicted hurt, as he further elaborates, is most often understood "as a consequence of colonialism and its after-effects in Africa" (2007, 13). The forcible takeover of land and resources not only managed to steal the wealth and riches of (neo)colonised countries, but also simultaneously impacted the psychological well being of these subjects, as Frantz Fanon has argued in *Black Skin White Masks* (1967) and *The Wretched of the Earth* (1968). Fanon articulates not only conditions and experiences but also responses of human subjects struggling against being degraded, despised, exploited and in short, dehumanised by the violent systemic rule of the coloniser. As Fanon points out, this reduction resulted not only in physical hurt through slavery and war, but also through a psychological stripping of the self. The dark world Richards refers to, is not only an incomprehensible space where wars, xenophobic attacks, racism, hate, rape and murder, brew, and manifest, but also an incomprehensible psychological space.

Humour is used broadly in Richards' text, and understandably so. It is discursive in function and form, making it a difficult task to define, considering terms such as wit, joke, comedy and farce all share similar characteristics and are often used interchangeably. Moreover, humour is universal and particular; it is both social and anti-social. It can be found in all societies, yet is also culturally specific. The manifestation of humour relies on ambiguities, ambivalence, uncertainties, and shifts in perspective and representation. It is multi-faceted, contradictory and paradoxical, can make light of a situation, while also offering critical viewpoints and judgments. Social psychologist and scholar of humour, Herbert Lefcourt argues that the study of humour belongs to the "part of psychology that is concerned with investigating 'positive processes', particularly the study of the positive effect." Lefcourt's research shows how humour can help "individuals maintain positive effects during encounters with negative events" (Lefcourt as cited in Billig 2005,

20). He distinguishes "positive humour" as that which "encourages group solidarity" from "negative or aggressive humour that separates, divides and excludes" (22). Such humour functions 'sociopositively' because it brings groups together. In the book *Art and Laughter*, Sheri Klein also stresses the positives of the humour when she writes:

> An encounter with visual humour offers artistic, aesthetic, intellectual and psychological benefits. Humour from art, as experienced through smiling and laughing, can be a catalyst for personal and collective healing, wellbeing and improved psychological health. Laughter as a medicine for social ills and everyday problems is known to increase vital functions, relax nerves and aid in digestion. Looking at art that brings laughter can bring both pleasure and meaning, and allow us to extend our capacity to feel joy (2007, 5).

The social function that humour played in South Africa during this period should not be understated or overlooked. As a tool for grappling with adversity, humour, lightness, and play formed part of the everyday lived experiences of black South Africans, irrespective of the condition and circumstances endured under the apartheid government, or the new democratic dispensation.

This is demonstrated in Peter Clarke's (1929 - 2014), *The Only Way to Survive* (1983). This drawing portrays three young black men facing a wall sprawled with graffiti. In large letters we see word "CHE," a reference to Argentinean Marxist Revolutionary Ernesto Che Guevara. Towards the right, names of black squatter settlements, such as Lourdes Farm, Crossroads, Kraaifontein, Vrygrond and Snakepark are written, making reference to the 300,000 squatters in the Cape who were forcibly removed from their homes. Scribbled below is a passage from James 2:15-16, which reads, "Suppose a brother or sister is without clothes and daily food. If one of you says to them, 'Go in Peace; keep warm and well fed,' but does nothing about their physical needs, what good is it?" This graffitied wall assumes the role of a notice board for its community, keeping them informed, critical and hopeful. On the left side of the drawing, another message reads as follows:

> The only way to survive these days is to have a sense of humour
> So…we live
> We perform
> And we survive…

The Only Way to Survive is one of Clarke's many works that demonstrate the perseverance of black South Africans living under violent conditions. Humour scholar Michael Billig affirms this when he writes, "it is most certainly not the case that only societies living in happy circumstances experience humour. Joking can appear in the direst of social environments; in fact, it can provide a way of demonstrating that one has not succumbed to exigency" (2005, 185). Even during apartheid, those whose lives were seemingly left to the mercy of the state, experienced laughter, love, and pleasure. His statement is empowering and hopeful. His calling upon humour as a means to overcome and survive is a message to black South Africa to not to succumb to the negative conditions surrounding them.

Peter Clarke played a significant role in shaping the visual representation of communities that were subjected to the forces of the apartheid state. Clarke, one of South Africa's most formative artists, was dedicated to showing the struggles and successes of his community in the Cape. He carried out his artistic practice in Ocean View, Cape Town, after the Group Areas Act forcibly moved him from Simon's Town in 1973. His paintings and graphic prints portray the everyday life of Cape communities in ways that are resilient, dignified, and nuanced. The tender and lyrical treatment of his subject matter, countered the proliferation of agonised black bodies represented within the field of visual arts. He committed his work to depicting the everyday lived experiences of his community in the face of violence and oppression, and his oeuvre is testament to this survival and resilience, including his refusal to yield to social and political exigencies. Having worked as a full time artist since the late 1950s, Clarke produced a body of work that encapsulates South Africa across six decades, from works that depicted the trauma of forced removals from Simonstown, to more celebratory representations of South Africa in the 1990s. His oeuvre stands as a testament of the restorative process of expression through which new values and subjectivities can be imagined and produced.

The Only Way to Survive stands as a reminder to live and laugh, not despite of the circumstances at hand, but as a continuation of living; living which is not without moments of joy, pleasure, and laughter. It is important to reiterate that not only despair spread throughout South Africa during the late 1970s and 1980s: laughter and love also formed part of the black lived experience. The more recent publication of *The Lighter Side of Life on Robben Island: Banter, Pastimes and Boyish Tricks* (2012) written by Fred Khumalo, Paddy Harper, and Gugu Kunene, attempts to restore these narratives of lightness and pleasure that lie alongside the existing narratives of hardships endured by political prisoners on Robben Island. This collection of anecdotal stories shed insights into the lighter side of the prisoners' experiences almost twenty years after its closure. Comic relief as shared in this book, not only reveals its use for survival, but also as lived, human experiences that were shared among the prisoners. These anecdotes tell a story wrapped in music, fashion, gossip, and love, and offer a refreshing counterpoint to the trauma-based narratives that have been reproduced and circulated.

Resistance does not only take the form of shock and spectacularity. The visual rhetoric of resistance and resilience took divergent aesthetic forms within South Africa during apartheid. In this essay, I have attempted to demonstrate the capacity of humour to offer a light, not necessarily less serious, way of engaging our surroundings, but also as an important mechanism for the revitalisation, transformation, and celebration of life. Humour and laughter have been key forces to resisting the weight of physical and psychological violence afflicting black South Africans under apartheid. Subtle and nuanced representations of everyday experiences of black South Africans, as made visible by Clarke and Motswai show an alternative visuality to resisting dominant narratives of the forlorn and anguished black body. Sach's observation that "if you look at most of our art and literature you would think we were living in the grayest and most sombre of all worlds, completely shut in by apartheid" (1991, 188), is arguably challenged by Clarke and Motswai who work to establish and show imaginative spaces that lie beyond the material and psychological confines of apartheid. These representations reveal pleasure, dignity and compassion in ways that resist and act beyond the systemic confines of apartheid's socially engineered values. Moreover, positive mechanisms of humour as I have discussed, facilitate resilience and survival, and help bear better that, which for the moment, is unalterable.

Bibliography

Arnold, M., Tommy Motswai. *Contemporary Art of Africa*. A. Magnin and J. Soulillou, eds. London, Thames & Hudson, 1996.

Billig, Michael. *Laughter and Ridicule*. London, SAGE Publications, 2005.

Critchley, Simon. *On Humour*. London, Routledge, 2002.

De Jager, E.J. *Images of Man: Contemporary South African Black Art and Artists*. Fort Hare, Fort Hare University Press in association with the Fort Hare Foundation, 1992.

Erichsen, Ulrike. "Smiling in the face of adversity." *Cheeky Fictions. Laughter and the Postcolonial*. S. Reichl. & M. Stein, eds. New York, Internationale Forschungen zur Allgemeinen und Vergleichenden Literaturwissenschaft, 2005, pp. 27-42.

Fanon, Frantz. *Black Skin, White mask*. New York, Grove Press, 1967.

—*Wretched of the Earth*. New York, Grove Press, 1968.

Khumalo, Fred, Paddy Harper, and Gugu Kunene. *The Lighter Side of Life on Robben Island*, Makana Investment Corporation, 2012.

Klein, Sheri. *Art and Laughter*. London, I.B. Taurus, 2007.

Levin, D. "Deaf artist to exhibit his works in Canada." *Sunday Times Metro*. May 7, 1995, p. 3.

Louw, D. R. "Fanning the creative fire." *Mail and Guardian*. July 2-8, 1999, p. 4.

Masilela, Ntongela. "The Historical and Literary Moment of Njabulo S. Ndebele." *English in Africa*, 36.1, 2009, pp. 17-39.

Ndebele, Njabulo. *Rediscovery of the Ordinary: Essays on South African Literature and Culture*. Kwazulu-Natal, University Of Kwazulu Natal Press, 2006.

Peffer, John. *Art and the end of apartheid*. University of Minnesota Press, 2009.

Richards, Colin. "Humour and Hurt." Art South Africa, 5.4, 2007, p. 13.

—"Aftermath: Value and Violence in Contemporary South African Art." *Antinomies of Art and Culture*. T. Smith, O.Enwezor, N Condee, eds. Durham and London, Duke University Press, 2008, pp. 250-289.

Sachs, Albie. "Preparing Ourselves for Freedom: Culture and the ANC Constitutional Guidelines." *TDR (1988-)*, 35.1, 1991, pp. 187-193.

Sack, Steven, ed. *The Neglected Tradition: Towards a New History of South African Art (1930-1988)*. Johannesburg Art Gallery, 1988.

Williamson, Sue and Ashraf Jamal. *Art in South Africa: the Future Present*. Cape Town and Johannesburg, David Phillip, 1996.

Williamson, Sue. *Resistance Art in South Africa*. Cape Town and Johannesburg, David Phillip, 1989.

Wylie, Diana. *Art and Revolution: the life and death of Thami Mnyele*. Auckland Park, Jacana, 2008.

Younge, Gary. *Art of the South African Townships*. London, Thames and Hudson, 1988.

Endnotes

1   For more information on the role of photography during apartheid see O. Enwezor and R. Bester, eds., *Rise and Fall of Apartheid. Photography and the Bureaucracy of Everyday Life* (Munich, London, and New York: International Center of Photography, 2013).

2   Curated by Sack, *The Neglected Tradition* is a seminal exhibition of black artists that was held at the Johannesburg Art Gallery in 1989. The exhibition and its accompanying catalogue re-evaluated South African art and its histories by tracing the development and influence of black South African artists.

3   Other publications concerned with art and cultural prodsuction and its relationship to the apartheid system can be found in Williamson, S. & Jamal, A. (1996); Wylie, D. (2008); Peffer, J. (2009).

4   Colin Richards furthers Ndebele's critique of the spectacle to reflect on South African art practices in the essay, *Aftermath: Value and Violence in Contemporary South African Art*. Here Richards (2008, 232) observes a form of spectacularity in the displays of violence and agony in a number of contemporary artworks, including Alfred Thoba's *Riots* (1977), Billy Mandini's *Necklace of Death* (1986) and Jane Alexander's, *The Butcher Boys* (1985-6), all of which fell under the banner of 'resistance' art.

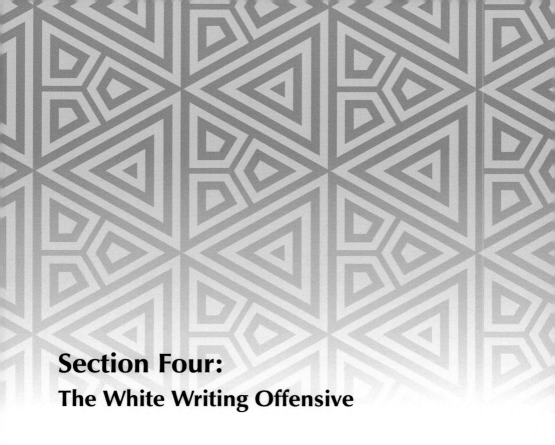

Section Four:
The White Writing Offensive

7

Entanglements:
Post Apartheid South Africa

Abebe Zegeye

Introduction: TRC and the Discourses of Entanglements

Lewis Nkosi (2008) makes an astute observation which is that in South Africa, a numerical minority controls the means of literary production. In this unequal matrix which is a continuation of the many discriminatory practices of apartheid of past entanglements, a numerical majority is held hostage intellectually and does not have venues for their literary works; their views are ventriloquised by white liberals who set the agenda on what constitutes the new creative practice in post-apartheid South Africa. Nkosi has articulated his concerns that in South Africa,

> There is a sense for example, in which a numerical majority in a multiethnic society like ours can be seen to be effectively a 'minority' in the field of cultural production, producing at best a 'minor' Literature, while a numerical minority, through access to cultural capital and through control of institutions of symbolical and commodity exchange, can be seen to be constituting the real 'majority' (2008, 10).

For Nkosi this situation which has been naturalised is cause for embarrassment. Both publishing and its literary gatekeepers are continuing the legacies of apartheid and promoting institutional conditions that silence and suppress critical examination of systematic oppression. In fact, long before its demise, apartheid in the literary establishment had authorised discourses which made it inconceivable to examine the complex social factors that shaped institutionalised anti-Black racism. The same literary gatekeepers worked tirelessly to endorse titular black leaders that were wedded to propping up its apparatus. Just as genocidaires of Rwanda, warlords of Bosnia, and the architects of the Jewish holocaust are still being hunted down out of their lairs and made to stand account at international legal tribunals, this gang, too, must be brought to book. Indeed, if their literary criticism has justified a "deferral of justice" in which the "state is trading, by negotiated political instruments and constitutional amendments, the due process of law to merely the publicity brought to bear on crimes arguably otherwise establishable as facts under extant bodies of evidence," (Eze 2004, 757) these critics are accomplices to the crime of academic non-disclosure.

Concluded in 1995 the Truth and Reconciliation Commission as an instrument of sovereign post-conflict nation building had a unique ability to protect and provide a hedge around the interests that apartheid represented. In this context, international critics following the lead from the South African white liberals, on one hand, and Tutu and Mandela, on the other, wrote of the benefits of the TRC as more significant than its negatives. For example, James L. Gibson declared that the TRC "did not undermine reconciliation within any of the groups in South Africa, and that for Whites, Coloured people, and those of Asian origin, truth may actually have caused reconciliation" (2006, 410). Previously, Tutu had boasted that the uniqueness of the South African TRC spectacle had been "its open and transparent nature" because "Similar commissions elsewhere in the world have met behind closed doors. Ours has operated in the full glare of publicity" (Tutu in Beitler, 2012, 9).

Not only did Tutu shape and influence the TRC, but the fact that his actions were answerable to GOD and to a coterie of white liberals constituted "a plea for the public and the state to substitute the order of the law for a higher, moral, order" (Eze 2004, 757). The requirement that antiapartheid liberation movements should stand trial for atrocities committed during the struggle was a paradox which Tutu and Mandela either deliberately chose to ignore for political expedience or which they did not understand. The TRC process and its discourses about transparency, truth, and reconciliation as a means for spiritual cum political redemption resulted in an elaborate and sophisticated project of spiritual and political pacification for black people (Lazreg 2007). In this context black peoples' "enforceable rights" to protection from atrocities which emerged from the law and the state as fundamentally characterised by violence were revealed to be a non-existent birth right (Humphrey 2013, 6). What they did understand is that their views pardoned apartheid on behalf of the antiapartheid movement—made up of many black people and a few whites who were opposed to it. Most significantly, the spectacle of excessive forgiveness on the part of the black architects of the TRC encouraged a pernicious discourse in which the perpetrators and agents of apartheid—largely white and some blacks could now claim an equal share of blame. This meant that the forces of liberation movements, who internationally had been recognised as legitimately fighting a system described as a crime against humanity could, at various times be described as terrorists. By careful choreographing of pain, mourning, and sorrowing at the TRC, South African histories were being re-written in ways that rendered it possible to plant doubt in the capacity of back people to be historically righteous. Following Njabulo Ndebele, the credo became that if apartheid was ugly, then every one of the black people was also ugly, and perhaps in the same ways. It follows the logic that human history, though complexly embedded in each other's experiences, should be to disengage and disentangle from the labyrinth so that social relations are re-seen more clearly. Against this liberatory perspective, Nuttall gives the impression that entanglement is the end of historical efforts to break up experiences into recognisable pieces, with the end desire to understand how these pieces of experiences have contributed to oppression. As argued by Mor and Terno, using the analogy of physics, it *is* possible to

consider a disentanglement process in which local properties of an entangled state are preserved, while the entanglement between the subsystems is erased. Sufficient conditions for a perfect disentanglement into product states and into separable states are derived, and connections to the conditions for perfect cloning and for perfect broadcasting are observed.

Markus Götz, another scholar borrowing from science, suggests that human relations are never entirely entangled to a point where it is totally impossible to disengage. For Götz (2017), there are several strategies of disentangling which involve deforming, stretching, squeezing and even shrinking the human relations under which humanity is entangled. West-Pavlov suggests a theory of cultural disentanglement that recognises and emphasises a shift from conceiving humanity only as fragile, to embracing unity. The critic's argument implies that very awareness that one is entangled is the beginning of the process of cultural and intellectual disentanglement which signals a movement from celebrating collapsing identities to highlight even 'coherence' that is informed by different human subjectivities. In other words a theoretical project of disentanglement has as its ultimate goal, the desire to know, to explain social phenomena and have control over it so as to harness it for social enlightenment and not obliteration. A project of disentanglement that I submit in this essay should not wish to be swallowed by the complexities of social phenomenon to a point where one's identities are utterly collapsed into other identities and rendered unrecognisable.

Let me propose another analogy in order to reveal how Nuttall's pernicious politics of entanglement amounts to camouflaging the previous dominant group into the previously dominated group in order to pass as victim. Thus, we read that the world is a global village with big and small, poor and rich countries entangled. But, during moments of economic crises such as economic depressions, recession, and busts, big and economically powerful countries can easily disentangle themselves from these crises and return to their former positions of being dominant. The economically weak countries take long, many fail to recover for good, and the worst irony is that the economic medicine to "disentangle" poor countries are prescribed and administered by powerful countries on weaker nations through structural adjustments economic programmes. This is what happened during the Obama era of the Wall Street crises. Thus, what weak countries should have learnt is that it is not possible to equate, or flatten, the experiences of countries as if their economies are evenly strong and comparable.

And yet, this is what Nuttall wants black Africans in post-1994 South Africans to believe, like fish, grabbing hook and sink, in her book, *Entanglement: Literary and cultural reflections on post-apartheid*. Antjie Krog has, ironically, but correctly, described this malevolent change of speaking position, as a change of tongue. Gramsci theorised the same phenomenon as a distinction between a war of position (ideology) and a war of maneuver (shifting and occupying and dominating new spaces in a different guise).

Entanglement: Pre-emptive strike, complicity, and disarming Black Politics in South Africa

Entanglement is an untidy and premature rehash of liberal pro-apartheid narratives that criminalised the entire anti-apartheid generation for the crimes committed by apartheid. Further entanglement robs future generations of their inheritance of a powerful struggle against anti-blackness. Beyond this aim, the book also celebrates the cult of victimhood by obscuring who was at the receiving end of historical injustices and pre-empting campaigns seeking legal accountability against state crimes that have been designated crimes against humanity. At a rhetorical level the convoluted verbiage used in *Entanglement* mirrors the idea itself:

> Entanglement is a condition of being twisted together or entwined, involved with, it speaks of an intimacy gained, even if it was resisted, or ignored or uninvited. It is a term which may gesture towards a relationship or set of social relationships that is complicated, ensnaring, in a tangle, but which also implies a human foldedness (2009, 1).

Götz rejects the idea of entanglement as a mere entertwining and posits that there are moments where their phenomenon is joined together where it is not easy to enter and exit at will. Entwining' in Nuttall's formulation suggests wrongly that humanity "remains trapped within a logic, albeit attenuated, of binaries and oppositions" (2017, 5). Even Mbembe is aware that entanglement is not rigid as it relates to human-human relationships, since the latter are "at times distinct, at times mutually entangled, at time superimposed" (Mbembe 13). Other critics who have commented on the rhetorical language and histories of "monstrous intimacy," like Christina Sharpe in the eponymous book where she coined this term (Duke University Press, 2010), and other unwanted contacts that were "resisted, ignored or uninvited," have largely focused on the power dynamics that reveal how legacies of systematic, institutional racialised, sexual violence and domination can be disentangled (Gqola 2016; Gqola 2010; Graham 2012; Sharpe 2010; Hartman 1997; Sexton 2008; Gordon 1997; Rassool and Hayes 2002; Kunnie 2000; Woodward 2002; McKittrick 2006; Christianse 2007; Harris and Baum 2009).

While this is largely a settled question in most quarters, it bears repeating that having self conscious erotic agency about ones survival as a person subjected to sexualised antiblackness, is not the same thing as being in a relationship. Romantic love as it were, has nothing to do with it. Today when such stories are turned into passion plays they repeat the cultural work that has been done in the past to shore up "racial regimes" that intensify the life of slavery under racial capitalism and that deliberately misname coercion and force as *seduction* (Robinson 2007; Hartman 1997). From this roundabout definition of entanglement come a series of summaries of ideological positions previously advanced by other critics on entanglement. Each of these summaries is punctuated by expunging race, class conflict, and racial capitalism. For example, race is grudgingly acknowledged as having shaped the communities of black and white people's modes of knowing, their situatedness in apartheid and post-apartheid South Africa such that, as Nuttall explains, "whites became dependent on backs and blacks on whites" (2009, 2). What is suppressed or left unsaid in this cavalier formulation of the political economy of the displacement of black Africans is the fact of a very lopsided dependency in favour of white people. Paul Gilroy (1994) among others captures this unequal relation in the Black Atlantic as being articulated on the ironical plane of dependency and resistance. The point I am making here is that, since colonial politics were "never simply about colonial subjugation and anti-colonial resistance" (2009, 2) as Nuttall suggests, it is then baffling to imagine that in the same utterance, readers are urged to conclude that poverty and economic underdevelopment is the fault of categories of racially inferiorised people.

From this denial of the historical consequences of colonial subjugation and the repudiation of the achievements of anti-colonial movements, Nuttall moves swiftly to Achille Mbembe's formulation of entanglement as a condition *sui generis* to a postcolony which "encloses multiple durees made up of discontinuities, reversals, inertias, and swings that overlay one another, interpenetrate one another" (Mbembe in Nuttall 2009, 4).

As I have argued above, entanglement is not a recent future of the post colony, nor of post apartheid. Entanglements of different kinds have been with Mankind from the cosmogonic man hammering stone on stone and these entanglements will continue. However, while recognising that entanglement is a permanent feature of human experience, the question is whether to consider such entanglements as beyond disentanglement. Nothing could be farther from the truth since historical and dialectical materialism are meaningful theoretical frames through which it had been possible to understand colonial subjugation and anticolonial movements prior to the 'post' in post-apartheid South Africa. Indeed, every society that has experienced colonial subjugation and anticolonial movements has been transformed through consistent but uneven struggles to disentangle, gain political clarity, make enforceable alliances when necessary and useful, and usher in new societies. *Entanglement* further celebrates complicity and collusion between black political leadership and white liberal thinkers in post-apartheid South Africa.

According to Nuttall, approvingly paraphrasing Sanders "The question of complicity as a context for assuming responsibility is integral to black intellectual life and to the tasks that have faced black intellectuals" (2009, 6). With this speculative statement, Nuttall validates the authority with which black intellectuals speak for the black masses even when there are divergences of visions between the two. Such an argument that casts black intellectuals as the interlocutors in a historical argument collapses the class boundaries between the masses and black intellectuals (Barchiesi 2011; Desai 2002; Kunnie 2000). Furthermore, a reasoning that places blacks in binaries also ignores the fact that even within the class of the masses of people, there are multiple subjectivities. This is also the same with the so-called intellectuals; they are never found manifesting themselves in one hue. And thus, the task of disentanglement politics is to seek to find out why, so as not to fall into the pit of glorifying entanglement. In other words, writing about black people as one homogeneous group is ahistorical. It is an assumption to fix entanglement as an unassailable or a contestable thought. Although South Africa has resolved some obstacles towards cultural tolerance, the unfinished business is contained in the class differentiations that continue to inhere in South African society. The Entanglement concept attempts to banish analysis of race, racism, and class while it is steeped in a language that reveals the continuing legacy of these very axes of power and domination. Nuttall explains that entanglement "enables us to work with the idea that the more racial boundaries are erected and legislated the more we have to look for the transgressions without which everyday life for oppressor and oppressed would have been impossible" (2009, 12).

One way of explaining this confusion in Nuttall's account of entanglements is that she is herself entangled in critical concepts whose semantic valence her work is not prepared to exhaust. Another way of explaining Nuttall's failure to think with the (black) people with whom she feels entangled is that the position that black intellectuals and the masses occupy in post-apartheid South Africa is one in which they are spoken to by the liberal discursive violence in concepts such as entanglements. Nuttall believes that entanglement is a game that whites and blacks participate in. Thus both are involved in entanglements at their own volition. Entanglement is too playful a theoretical term and does not bring out too many frames of entanglements to comprehend itself. It, therefore, needs solid historical and dialectical materialism to explain how, where, and why blacks in post-apartheid are entangled and to what. This important because there is no single force and single remedy to entanglement. Entanglement is not necessarily entrapment because to think so, as Nuttall does, is to succumb to permissim which leads to the legitimation of slavery. Susan Pollock, et al, argue that working with the theory of entanglement might expand our perspectives of the past by way of "following links and chains in a fashion that is rhizomatic rather than linear or dentric." However, the critics qualify their view on entanglement when they submit that on "epistemological grounds [...] a theory of entanglement that sees no possibility for disentanglement, other than the collapse of an existing system, turns into a self-fulfillling prophecy" (155). In other words, theories should consider different kinds of entanglements in different places orn even different directions not all of which involve a growth in the degree of entanglement. The same idea, put differently, it is not possible to take a neutral position when it comes to theorising entanglement. An awareness that one is entangled necessarily generates a will to disentanglement, as just as an abject life can spur a desire for a better life. Glorifying entanglement as Nuttall does, results in "being caught in other, even more entangled kinds of nets" (153). The point I stress here is that the world can be reconfigured and steered in different directions and it is from this human agency that it becomes possible to imagine disentanglement is a "process that proceeds in degrees that can be enhanced, or reduced, sped up or slowed down."

So far, I have attempted to demonstrate that there are multiple and conflicting subjectivities at work as Nuttal theorises entanglement. There is first the recognition that white people as a race are no longer in control, at least politically, and this instills fear in Nuttall as the critic does not know what this new reality will mean for the numerically white people. There is, second, a calculated desire to embrace a new ideology of racial integration without entirely renouncing the baggage of social iniquities such as lack of equity that any form of racial discrimination will bring.

The above theoretical lacuna in Nuttall's understanding of post apartheid South Africa also reveals the workings of the TRC template in which past oppressors demanded equal treatment from the new government most of whose ordinary black people's feelings the system of apartheid deliberately injured. The assumption that was popularised by the TRC was that blacks have an infinite capacity to forgive and forget. Even critics such as Derrida (2001) had concluded that South African blacks were moral entrepreneurs because, as he believed, the essence of their forgiving mentalities resided in forgiving the unforgivable. But Nuttall does not want to be forgiven, for that would establish that whites in the first place had transgressed on the rights of blacks. Instead this theory wants to forgive blacks for ever waging a war against apartheid, and she wants blacks to feel that their being forgiven has been accepted in the human foldedness which is a euphemism for collective guilt between whites and blacks. This way, the path of South African development after 1994 would proceed from or with carefully selected acts of amnesia and nondisclosures. However, in her book, Nuttall feels the compulsion to demonstrate acts of intimacy and entanglements and for this task she carefully identifies the space of the city—of Johannesburg's Hillbrow surburb for that choreography where human deprivation is elevated to an aesthetic category.

Secrets of Lies: The Black Middle Class and White Militants

Entanglement focuses on the black middle class by equating the material advantages between white and black middle classes and by imagining that the black middle class is larger than the white middle class.

The claim by Nuttal that the black middle class has superseded the white middle class in post-apartheid South Africa (Ibid., 731), is disingenuous on two registers. First, there are no statistics to back this speculative view. Second, in a population of over 50 million in which between 5 to 10 million are whites of different backgrounds, it is both saying something and not saying anything at all to focus on the emergence of a black middle class larger than that of whites. The numerical advantage of blacks should have guaranteed at least this decades ago. The second issue with this wrong-headed attention to the black middle class is that apartheid and its plans for black economic development get the credit for having created its existence. The argument pretends to discuss class and perhaps hints that there might be something important to examine about class but then refuses to consider what kind of material property that this new black middle class own. To own a mortgaged house in Sandton and a mortgaged car is not the traditional definition of how one is described as middle class. As Fanon (1963) reminds us the European middle class in the West and in Africa are distinguished by the extent to which they own the productive forces of the country and the creativity in technological inventions which are remunerated at a rate which produces wealth. Without this ownership what we witness in South Africa is actually a more pervasive and deepening racial wealth divide (Lui et al 2006) that pays little concern to the gravid mass of whites and blacks on the margin of the South African economy and diverts the attention of those masses who are also entangled with class wars with other blacks. While the history of the black middle class is deployed to celebrate apartheid and obscure class conflict white militants are introduced to suggest that they were tokenised members of the antiapartheid movement. No one can dispute the fact that the late Ruth First, and Joe Slovo amongst several other surviving whites who were targets for elimination by apartheid, took up arms against the system (Nuttall 2009, 63-5). "First and Slovo were political activists involved in the military dimensions of political struggle, and it is this oppositional work which situates the production of whiteness in their lives and writing" (2009, 65). Introduced both to reinforce the cult of white victimhood and to remind readers that white people must be accorded space as a political and demographic minority in post-apartheid South Africa, *Entanglement* is incorrigibly patronising explaining that "Slovo [...] was seen by black South Africans as a black man" (2009, 63). This argument *must* be crafted to parry unsaid verbal blows from an imagined critical black voice. But, there is no one who has argued that contributions of white people to the liberation movements in South Africa amount to nothing. Such a stance flies in the face of South African history. Nuttall defends Ruth First, Joe Slovo and other white people. Of course some whites have contributed immensely to the freedom of South Africa. Despite this truth, Nuttall's motivation for writing this book seems to lie elsewhere. It is the desire to re-install white nationalism at the core of post 1994 discourses of belonging by authorising a narrative that wants to raise the contribution of these few whites to the same if not higher moral ground than what black people who suffered apartheid policies and continue to suffer during the rule of the comrades have gone through.

Throughout this book Nuttall has been arguing in a way that attempts to minimise racial politics both during apartheid and in post-apartheid South Africa. And yet, in post-apartheid South Africa whites can become both black and white at the same time. Telling the life histories of white militant antiapartheid activists must be more than verbal sparring meant to displace black struggle. Many white South Africans sacrificed their lives for the common good. These white people who participated in the liberation struggle did so from well-considered perspectives knowing the potential disastrous consequences of doing so. They were not entangled in the sense of the meaning offered by Nuttall. Some whites commanded senior positions and planned for the demise of apartheid. They are/were heroes just as the mass of blacks that fought apartheid out of necessity are/were heroes. Nuttall advances a neoliberal argument calculated to elevate white revolutionaries to heroism which makes it easier to conclude that there should not be black access to the country's resources, wealth, welfare, social services, community programs, and other entitlements. This malicious reasoning repeats the violence of the TRC process.

In short, and to use Borzaga's phrase, Sarah Nuttall's notion of entanglement has become a "fashionable metaphor" (2014, 8) meant to deflect the possibilities of raising more critical questions about how to let democracy meet the truth of black and some white people, still leaving in abject poverty. Nuttall has not theorised the necessary and sufficient conditions for possible disentanglement, which is why her project hits a cul de sac in which individual permissism is universalised. Part of the problem with the way Nuttall thinks about entanglement is that this has not been done without assuming an explicitly political position on the subject matter. The critic has not created sufficient distance from the phenomenon of entanglement being analysed. As a result, she has narrowed the debates on the perspectives when she has attempted to make efforts to solve the problem that arises from entanglement.

Conclusion

The aim of this chapter was to reflect on Sarah Nuttall's notion of entanglement in her book of that title. Nuttall's preoccupation with flattening the experiences of whites and blacks in an attempt to present these lives as equally affected by the neuroses of post-apartheid society is meant to pre-empt harder questions about black and white life in South Africa and to obscure the assemblage of cultural factors responsible for shaping post-apartheid South Africa. Banishing race and class analytics in favour of an amorphous notion of entanglement refutes what many commentators now take for granted that in many ways the agenda of the liberation movement has been stalled and in some cases tabled indefinitely. *Entanglement* and its cavalier handling of the post apartheid period must not be understood in isolation. The TRC provided, and its past pronouncements still provide, misguided ideological templates which many authors rely on and which many funders and publishers assiduously pay for. The TRC implied that the history of South African began anew in 1995, that the past with its ugly policies was as much a result of apartheid as it was the fault of black liberationists, and that after 1995, black and white people are starting on the same footing. This hagiography popularised by Nuttall in her book is useful in that the book propounds the notion that everybody in South Africa is festooned to an ugly past in ways that are not only difficult to disentangle but equalises the experiences of blacks and whites. The fact that this view is not normally said in public has come out and is not only bold but a brazen attempt to uncritically embrace and use the notion of the rainbow nation in ways that purchase the idea of an unproblematic citizenship for whites in South Africa. However, and I agree with Gerard Ralphs, when the critic writes that it is "vital in ensuring that the paradigm of [South] Africa's victimhood is indeed dismantled and displaced, rather than its scaffolding upheld and its discursive structures replicated" (2007, 18). Dedicated social research that is attendant to history and structures of domination and the powerful analytics of race, class, and gender have amassed an important legacy scholarship for doing precisely this and none seem mystified by entanglement.

Bibliography

Barchiesi, Franco. "Precarious Liberation: Workers, the State, and Contested Social Citizenship in Postapartheid South Africa." Albany, State University of New York, 2011.

Beitler, James. "Making More of the Middle Ground: Desmond Tutu and the Ethos of the South African Truth and Reconcilation Commission." *Relevant Rhetoric*, 3.2, 2012, pp. 1-21.

Bennett, Leronne. *Forced Into Glory: Abraham Lincoln's White Dream.* Chicago, Johnson Publishing Company, 2000.

Borzaga, Michela. *Trauma as Entanglement.* 2014, pp. 1-10. Accessed April 21

Brundage, W Fitzhugh. "Opinions on Current Reading: A Contrarian View of Abraham Lincoln as the Great Emancipator." *The Journal of Blacks in Higher Education*, 27, 2000, pp. 129-131.

Christianse, Yvette. *Unconfessed.* New York, Other Press, 2007.

Desai, Ashwin and Richard Pitthouse. "'What Stank in the Past is the Present's Perfume': Dispossession, Resistance and Repression in Mandela Park." *South Atlantic Quarterly*, 103.4, 2004, pp. 841-875.

Desai, Ashwin. *We Are the Poors: Community Struggles in Post-Apartheid South Africa.* New York, Monthly Review Press, 2004.

Eze, Emmanuel. "Transition and the Reasons of Memory." *South Atlantic Quarterly*, 103.4, 2004, 755-768.

Fanon, Frantz. *The Wretched of the Earth*. London, Penguin Books, 1963.

Derrida, Jacques. "On Forgiveness." *On Cosmopolitanism and Forgiveness*. Mark Dooley and Michael Hughes, trans. Abingdon, Routledge, 2001, pp. 25-60.

Gibson, James L. "The Contribution of Truth to Reconciliation: Lessons from South Africa." *Journal of Conflict Resolution*, 50.3, June 2006, 409-432.

Gordon, Avery. *Ghostly Matters: Haunting and the Sociological Imagination*. University of Minnesota Press, 1997.

Götz, Markus. "Basic Strategies to Solve Disentanglement Puzzles." http://docplayer.net/47242281-Basic-strategies-to-solve-disentanglement-puzzles-by-markus-gotz-goetz-de.html

Graham, Lucy Valerie. *State of Peril: Race and Rape in South African Literature*. Oxford University Press, 2012.

Gramsci, Antonio. *Selections from Prison Notebooks*. New York, International Publishers, 1971.

Gqola, Pumla. *What is Slavery to Me? Postcolonial/Slave Memory in Post-Apartheid South Africa*. Johannesburg, Wits University Press, 2010.

—*Rape: A South African Nightmare*. Johannesburg, Jacana Media, 2016.

Harris, Duchess and Bruce Baum. "Jefferson's Legacies: Racial Intimacies and American Identity." *Racially Writing the Republic: Racists, Race Rebels, and Transformations of American Identity*. Duke University Press, 2009, pp. 44-63.

Hartman, Saidiya. *Scenes of Subjection: Terror, slavery, and self-making in nineteenth-century America*. Oxford University Press on Demand, 1997.

Humphrey, Michael. *Politics of Atrocity and Reconciliation: From Terror to Trauma*. New York, Routledge, 2013.

Krog, Antjie. *A Change in Tongue*. Johannesburg, Random House, 2003.

Kunnie, Julian. *Is Apartheid Really Dead? Pan Africanist Working Class Culture and Perspectives*. Boulder, CO, Westview Press, 2000.

Lazreg, Marnia. *Torture and the Twilight of Empire: From Algiers to Baghdad*. Princeton University Press, 2007.

Lui, Meizhu, Barbara Robles, Betsey Leonard-Wright, and Rose Brewer, eds. *The Color of Wealth: The Storybehind the U.S. Racial Wealth Divide*. New York, New Press, 2006.

Mbembe, Achille and Sarah Nuttall. "Writing the World from an African Metropolis." *Public Culture*, 16.3, 2004, pp. 347-372.

McKittrick, Katherine. *Demonic Ground: Black Women and Cartographies of Struggle*. University of Minnesota Press, 2006.

Mor, Tal and Daniel Terno. "Sufficient Conditions for a Disentanglement." *Physical Review A*, 6.6, 1999, pp. 4341-4343.

Ndebele, Njabulo. *Rediscovery of the Ordinary: Essays on South African Literature and Culture*. Scottsville, University of KwaZuluNatal, 2006.

Nkosi, Lewis. "The Ideology of Reconciliation: Its effects on South African Culture." *Baobab: South African Journal of New Writing*, Autumn, pp. 7-11.

Nuttall, Sarah, *Entanglement: Literary and Cultural Reflections on Post-Apartheid* (Johannesburg: Wits University Press, 2009).

—"City Forms and Writing the 'Now' in South Africa." *Journal of South African Studies*, 30.4, 2004, pp. 731-748.

Pollock, Susan, et al. "Entangled Discussions: Talking with Ian Hodder About His Book Entangled." *Forum Kritische Archäologie*, 3, 2014, pp. 151-160.

Ralphs, Gerard. "The Contribution of Achille Mbembe to the multidisciplinary study of Africa." *Postamble*, 3:2, 2007, pp. 18-29.

Rassool, Ciraj and Patricia Hayes. "Science and the Spectacle: Khanako's South Africa, 1936-1937." *Deep Histories: Gender and Colonialism in Southern Africa*. Wendy Woodward, Patricia Hayes, and Gary Minkley, eds. Amsterdam, Rodopi Press, 2002, pp. 117-161.

Robinson, Cedric J. *Forgeries of memory and meaning: Blacks and the regimes of race in American theater and film before World War II*. University of North Carolina Press, 2007.

Sexton, Jared. *Amalgamation Schemes: Antiblackness and the Critique of Multiracialism*. University of Minnesota Press, 2008.

Sharpe, Christina. *Monstrous Intimacies: Making Post-Slavery Subjects*. Duke University Press, 2010.

Woodward, Wendy. "Contradictory Tongues: Torture and the Testimony of Two Slave Women in the Eastern Cape Courts in 1833 and 1834." Cross/Cultures: Readings in the Post/Colonial Literatures in English Series, 57. *Deep Histories: Gender and Colonialism in Southern Africa*. Wendy Woodward, Patricia Hayes, and Gary Minkley, eds. Amsterdam, Rodopi, 1994/2002, pp. 55-84.

West-Pavlov, Russell. "Reading African Complexities Today: Generic Folding in Gaile Parkin's *Baking Cakes in Kigali*." *Research in African Literatures*, 46.1, 2015, pp. 142–159.

8

Colonialism and Capitalism in South Africa Today

PA Hudson

Introduction

The principal aim of this article is to refine the concept of colonialism and its articulation with capitalism in South Africa today, i.e. to advance a new conception of the status of colonialism under current conditions, as well as a new way of thinking about the relationship between colonialism and capitalism in South Africa today.

This is done via a concept of colonialism as unconscious, of the colonial unconscious, which develops Fanon's conception of the latter by drawing from Zizek.[1] Finally, I show how this colonial unconscious intervenes in economic practice—i.e. how colonialism and capitalism are integrated, but not structurally interdependent, as was previously the case, in South Africa today. Under current conditions there has occurred a shift in the mode of colonial enjoyment or *jouissance* in South Africa, such that today, capitalism occupies the very place of colonial enjoyment.[2] Whiteness is not merely (see infra), a symbolic construction but an identity in which white subjects emotionally invest and to which they are passionately attached. Colonial enjoyment thus refers to the affective charge which white subjects derive from their identification as 'white'. Under current, i.e. democratic, conditions this "existential electricity" (Daly 2014, 80) is repressed but is able to 'return' via the gap provided by capitalism in the fabric of non-racial democracy.

This unconscious is as objective as it is subjective (see infra) and operates inside the relations of production of capitalism. The capitalism-colonialism relation is no longer one of structural interdependence, but a new articulation, one of structural integration in which the colonial relation intervenes in the effectivity of the relations of production via the colonial unconscious: here the unconscious is a social practice, not shored-up and inaccessible.

And, yes, it looks a bit like the last redoubt of CST (Colonialism of a Special Type) theory, a desperate last ditch attempt to link race and class, long after the 'objective' conditions that Marxists and (some) liberals saw as the economic 'basis' for colonial domination have gone—and also, (but not so long), after what many see as the final death knell of CST, the 1994 Constitution.[3]

What is being proposed is thus a new articulation, not interdependence—as when capital accumulation depended on the articulation of modes of production and the colonial apparatus—but one in which an unconscious colonialism continues to thrive and thus splits South African society from within and by means of the powers of property constitutive of capitalism.

The Status of Colonialism

The status of colonialism has always been controversial and contested on the South African Left. The two conceptions of colonialism outlined below mark the basic co-ordinates of this dispute.

The Strong Conception

From this stand point (defended primarily, but not exclusively, by the Congress Tradition—today, the Alliance—and also Nolutshungu 1984) colonialism is a *sui generis* social relation of domination and exploitation with its own irreducible effectivity. This specific relation is dominant when it comes to the structuring of the South African social formation—dominant, i.e., over capitalism: it is not just co-constitutive with, but always more constitutive than, capitalism. The colonial relation saturates the subjectivity of all subjects, including members of the working class. "Lived experience" is here colonised, 'colonially constituted' lived experience. Colonialism has its own figures of the subject, of its lived experience, as well as its own *sui generis* mechanisms of appropriation and reproduction, its own logic and motor.

Hence the receptivity of colonised members of the working class to a specifically **national** democratic interpellation, which focusses on colonialism as it penetrates the capitalist relation and thus working class identity; herein lies the working class **content** of the NDR (National Democratic Revolution), which isn't thus socialist but anti-colonial. (The *sui generis* character of colonialism entails, in other words, that a category mistake is committed when it is asked of the NDR whether or not it is anti-capitalist) (see Hudson 2014).

This conception is 'strong' insofar, then, as it attributes a dominant role in the structuring of South African life to colonialism—this latter itself thus causes the fundamental divisions in South African society, including the distribution of assets and life-chances (while not eliminating other structural causes of inequality, e.g. capitalism) and reproduces itself.

As we'll see shortly, this strong conception can take two forms, one, where colonialism continues to exist as an active cause and reproduces itself, and one where, although it continues to exist it does so with a diminishing ontological valence over time. Here, colonialism exists, perhaps for a very long time, but as 'residual'; here we encounter (see infra) the 'structural inertia' thesis in terms of which, as cause, colonialism is temporally distant from its effects in the present; these latter thus exist as the aftershock of a cause which itself, as structure, has already been eliminated.

In the first form referred to above, let's calls it the 'strong' strong conception, the cause (colonialism) is not temporally distant from its effect but simultaneous with them, and continuously intervening in their production. Here, then, colonialism is not residual, not reduced to the effects of an 'inertial causality' but characterised by a 'simultaneous causality' in which cause and effect are not temporally separated.

The Weak Conception: colonialism as subject to the causality of capitalism

Here the point of departure is that colonialism only exists, i.e. is taken seriously, to the extent it contributes to the reproduction of South African capitalism. It has no logic nor motor of its own but only exists in so far as it enters the radar screen of a Marxism only able to identify objects in as much as they are functional for the reproduction of South African capitalism. As such, colonialism is thus—once South African capitalism moves to a new alignment of the relations and forces of production—marked from the start as destined to become 'residual', 'a left over'.

This division between conceptions 1 and 2—colonialism 1 and colonialism 2—has split the Left—with CST aligned with 1 and what is commonly called South African neo Marxism (inter alia, Wolpe, Kaplan) aligned with 2.

However, the same split can be discerned within the CST position itself which is often, and correctly, criticised for oscillating between 1 and 2. This doesn't erase the distinction between it, CST, and its 'neo Marxist' counterpart, because CST does oscillate, whereas, for all its Althursserian inflections, all its talk of relative autonomy, reciprocal causality and specific effectivity, its neo Marxist counterpart doesn't, i.e., C2 is 'in' C1 but not vice versa.

The question I'm posing is how is colonialism understood today in CST theory, or, how is today's colonialism understood in CST theory; in other words, how is colonialism understood under post-Apartheid non-racial and democratic conditions? Has its status and mode of causality changed, and, if it has, in which ways?

Revisiting CST-Where is Colonialism Today?

Turning to the NDR text, i.e. the (2007) Polokwane Statement on "Constructing a National Democratic Society," we are presented with the following indications, none of which are, however, satisfactory from the point of view of the question we have posed concerning the exact status of colonialism in South Africa today. These attempts to describe the current relationship between colonialism and democracy in South Africa, pull in two opposing directions—one emphasising the break with colonialism, and the other, the latter's resilience. But we are not offered any conceptualisation able to hold these together; the invocation of the form / content distinction being merely a repetition of the problem in the guise of a solution (see ANC 2011, 234).

> "Steadily the dark night of white minority political domination is receding into a distant memory" (224)

> "With the definitions of the past starting to fade" (244)

> "Overall, since 1994, the balance of forces has shifted in favour of the forces of change" (239).

> "We should not be blinded by form, the fact that blacks are, for the first time, occupying the highest political offices in the land – as distinct from content, the reality that colonial relations in some centres of power, especially the economy, remain largely unchanged" (234).

> "The progress made since the attainment of democracy is such that we are still some way from the ideal society of national democracy" (240).

> "the 1994 Democratic breakthrough" (247)

All the ambiguities in the CST theory of colonialism today are concentrated in the signifier "breakthrough'. This term covers several possible states of the relationship between democracy and colonialism, which need to be distinguished but aren't in CST discourse, and all of which have also to square with the unshakable thesis (which permeates the text) that South Africa is still a colonial society, that the NDR is not over yet and that specifically national democratic forms of anti-colonial struggle are still called for.

When it is said that there has occurred a 'breakthrough' does this mean colonialism was 'broken', or 'broken through' as in 'decisively damaged'? And, if so, just how does colonialism live on inside the democratic state? We want to be told just how colonialism and democracy have 'interacted' since 1994 and how they 'interact' today. How, in other words, does democracy simultaneously bar and repress colonialism and accommodate—if not legitimate—it? Are whites still able to access the libidinal and ontological enjoyment of being 'white' and if so how (see later)? Is it perhaps that colonialism exists in the gaps or interstices of the Constitution and thus (somehow) 'slips through' the strictures of democracy? But how is this possible?

'Breakthrough' certainly suggests an antagonism between democracy and colonialism and some form and degree of displacement of colonialism from its previous status as the dominant structuring principle of South African society, but precisely just what has changed in the role and mode of operation of colonialism in South Africa since 1994? If the 'strong conception' of colonialism has to be modified how is this to be done?

When we examine what kinds of colonialism might be compatible with an anti-colonial breakthrough having taken place in South Africa we need to recall that conceptions (1) the strong colonialism also has (like 2) room for a conception of 'residual'—there is a residual form of strong colonialism just as there is a residual form of colonialism as capitalist effect: and, as CST is silent on the question of the precise status of colonialism in South Africa post 1994, a conceptual space is created for the possibility that today CST theory conceives (more or less unconsciously) colonialism as precisely residual.

Let's unpack this shift from 'strong' to 'residual' colonialism in CST discourse. There could be said to have been a breakthrough against colonialism without the latter having disappeared if colonialism is now understood to function according to the category of inertial causality—i.e. the interpretation of colonialism in South Africa today in terms of the theory of 'structural inertia': here the 'rewards' accruing to an occupant of some place in the structure get transmitted down across generations even though the place and the structure have been eliminated: here the structure is inert, 'dead', but its effects live on—causality here is at a temporal distance, as opposed to the simultaneous causality of a cause still active in the production of its effects.

Here 'colonialism' is a residue of colonialism, today's colonialism is the effect of the strong active colonialism that once existed being subjected to the democratic act which turns colonial causality into inertial and today's colonialism into a 'residue', in the process of dying out—even if this happens very slowly and takes a long time; over time it is vanishing because its causal motor is no longer current and it does not therefore intervene in the here and now in the reproduction of colonialism. This afterlife of colonialism is thus the colonialism of today, post the democratic 'breakthrough'.

The political implications of such a shift in the semantics of colonialism hardly need to be pointed out—if colonialism is running out of steam and no longer able to reproduce itself, this surely changes its status as object of the National Democratic Revolution (NDR).

What I have tried to show above is how CST theory 'deals with' democracy, how it deals with the question of the relationship between democracy and colonialism—and what I've suggested is that the term 'breakthrough' leaves a door wide open for the theory of colonialism today as an effect distant from its original cause and, no matter how resilient it might seem, on the way out. In other words, it exists but only under the impetus of what it once was, i.e. strong colonialism, whose heavy inertia ensures it an afterlife as residual, as no longer reproducing itself under its own steam but as a 'left-over'—which might last a long time but which is, no matter how imperceptibly, fading.

In what follows we attempt to outline a conception of how colonialism in South Africa might still be said to be of the strong (i.e. 'strong' strong) type, while, at the same time, giving 'full weight' to 'the event' of 1994.

Beyond Structural Inertia

What distinguishes the CST analysis of SA today, i.e. twenty years after the transition to democracy, is its insistence that the colonial differential still exists in the heart of the SA economy, and still, thus, continues to divide assets and life chances. This sets it apart from several other understandings of inequality in SA today. First of all, there is the robust liberal individualist account which maintains that whites have, since 1994, earned their (relative) prosperity and have not relied on their (colonial) whiteness as was previously possible. Here there is no causal connection between 'whiteness' and prosperity, just a 'dead', inactive correlation. Whites may have found themselves sitting in the front row in 1994, and sitting there as 'whites', but, from that point on, it has been through their own effort and discipline alone that they have maintained this position. Importantly, on this perspective, these white agents have disconnected themselves from (colonial) 'whiteness' and are in no way influenced by racial identification. In their economic practice and interaction with others they identify themselves in generic humanist, not colonial/racial terms. They are, in short, 'non-racial' economic subjects. The left-wing version of this perspective ascribes concentrations of wealth and opportunity to class relations of production instead of individual merit, but also denies the specifically colonial relation it any causal efficacy.

More interesting is the structural inertia theory which maintains that the historic allocation of groups to positions of privilege produces an 'inertial effect', which advantages and disadvantages groups across generations. Here it is as if we're living the aftermath of colonialist—it still exists but only as the on-going consequence of what once existed—colonialism was so entrenched that it makes possible the cross-generational transmission of the colonial differential even though, since 1994, it hasn't 'really existed'— at least not as it did exist prior to 1994. Here 'white privilege' is being reproduced but the causal role of 'whiteness' needs clarification—is this cross generational transmission of the colonial differential just the after-effect of colonialism? Is it therefore vanishing, on the way out—does this effect get weaker the further away in time it is from the 'colonial event' that caused it? Be this as it may, structural inertia theory thus posits that whites still benefit from colonialism, but are not (today) reproducing it as Whites.

What is the status of colonialism in SA today? This is an important question in the wake of 1994 and the liberal democratic constitutional dispensation that has replaced Apartheid. Alliance theory insists CST still exists in South Africa because inter alia, de fact control of economic assets is still white and life chances in SA still split along racial lines (see Polokwane 2007).

But CST fudges the precise status of whiteness, of colonialism in SA today. It insists SA is still a colonial society (of a special-internal-sort) but isn't able to accommodate the post 1994 status of colonialism in a society in which colonialism is no longer the discourse/practice that **explicitly** structures the South African social—in other words, it doesn't confront the question of just what is meant by the **implicit** existence of colonialism in SA today.

The CST thesis, viz colonialism still exists because assets are still disproportionally in white hands, itself contains an equivocation or ambiguity. It doesn't explain just how colonial 'whiteness' is causally **operative in the present** and thus leaves open the possibility of a 'structural inertia' interpretation of the colonial differential in which colonial 'whiteness' is still operative but only in the mode of a residue, as an 'aftermath' increasingly incapable of reproducing itself, as 'vanishing'.

The 'structural inertia-residue' model wants to have it both ways—to recognise the ongoing effectivity of the colonial differential, on the one hand—and deny the latter still exists by describing its existence as 'residual', on the other hand.

CST theory must take on board the task of showing just how colonialism intervenes today in capitalism—how it continues to exist and reproduce itself—how it exists as **more than** residue, aftermath: in other words, instead of 1) "whites benefit from the colonial differential but don't reproduce it themselves as (colonial) whites"; CST should defend the proposition 2) that "whites benefit from the colonial differential and themselves intervene qua Whites to reproduce it," and it must also thus confront head-on the question of how 'whiteness' has helped such white subjects who, *ex hypothesi*, deny all identification with 'Whiteness', benefit economically.

Two historical transformations have to be dealt with by any claim that colonialism still exists—and it is principally the CST model of the tripartite alliance which claims this viz the shift from a regime of accumulation based on the articulation of modes of production to one based on the real subsumption of labour and relative surplus value production (see Wolpe 1988). Under the conditions of the former, colonial/racial forms of domination were a condition of existence of capitalism, whereas, under the latter, no such structural interdependence between capitalism and colonialism exists. What, then is the status and causal role of colonialism under the conditions of the latter? The temptation here is to think of colonialism as nothing more than a residue with a vanishing causality sustained only by 'structural inertia'. The second transformation refers to the advent of democracy which prohibits racists practices and imposes generic egalitarianism. What possible mode of existence can the colonial differential assume under such strictures?[4]

Thus if the theory of CST is to remain relevant in the analysis of South African society and the NDR project to be at all coherent, its very concept of colonialism needs to be rethought.

CST theory insists (see Polokwane) that colonialism still exists and structures the distribution of assets and life-chances, but it doesn't explain how this is possible after 1994 nor how colonialism **actually intervenes** in South African capitalism. Wolpe (1988) has already drawn the conclusion— from the fact that accumulation in South Africa ceases to depend on the articulation of modes of production—that capitalism and colonialism are **contingently**, not of necessity, articulated in SA, but leaves matters there, opening the way (as explained supra) to a reductionist conception of colonialism which denies both its *sui generis* character and its capacity to reproduce itself. The trouble with CST theory too, is that it can be read as suggesting that colonialism today is nothing more than a residue of colonialism *stricto sensu*, one that is trans-generational but bereft of the conditions of its reproduction in the present, and already on the way to dying out. What needs to be addressed is how, in view of the effect of 1994, which prohibits all and any racial discrimination, colonialism can continue to exist—and what is it in relation to South African capitalism given that the latter no longer depends on colonial domination (see Wolpe, 1988)?[5]

The Colonial Unconscious

Fanon's epistemological revolution consists in grasping that colonialism is not merely a matter of social, political and economic inequality, but involves ontological inequality and asymmetry. "Inequality? No, non-existence." (Fanon, 1998, 139). The colonised is relegated to a zone of "non-being" (Fanon, 1968, 131), whereas the coloniser enjoys an ontological plenitude conferred by the signifier of 'Whiteness'. 'Whiteness' is the master signifier under colonialism, but whites and blacks are asymmetrically interpellated by it: whites as enjoying (the illusion of) full self-possession and autonomy, and blacks as occupying an ontological void, caught between two impossibles— 'Whiteness' (from which they are barred) which defines the possibility of being, and 'Blackness' which is non-existence.

When it comes to the coloniser, Fanon insists that his inscription in colonialism can be more or less 'unreflected' (1968, 136). The degree to which his colonial identity is present to his consciousness varies according to conditions—and here Fanon invokes the role of democracy (106, 126). It can, in other words, be unconscious, i.e. "resist being raised to the conscious level" (136). Then it is a "collective unconscious" which is, however, cultural and comprises "habit" and not "instinct."

The transcendental turn of psychoanalysis involves invoking the hypothesis of the unconscious in order to account for the possibility of "the gaps in the phenomena of our consciousness" (Freud 1940, cited in Tauber 2010, 119). Zizek deploys this transcendental argument for the unconscious as comprising "gaps in consciousness" in an account of anti-Semitism. Here the concept of the unconscious does not refer to anything 'hidden away' but rather to those instances where the 'norm' (of fairness and equality) disintegrates, and where meaning and practice are interrupted via the irruption of the "disavowed beliefs and suppositions we are not even aware of adhering to ourselves" (2014, 94-95). These are not concealed but embedded in the observable social practice of the anti-semite even if he denies it.

Colonialism becomes unconscious when it is displaced and repressed by a different system of social relations and subjectivity. *Ex hypothesi* what occurred in South Africa in 1994 is the constitution of whites and blacks as non-racial citizens, no longer colonial subjects.[6]

Homo economicus and the colonial unconscious

Let's take three spaces where the colonial unconscious intrudes in South Africa today. Let's begin with everyday life—when whites behave in racist ways, in the workplace, in the street, in the syntax and inflexion of their speech, without being aware of doing so. This is a very widely identified phenomenon. Here the appropriate question, which leads to the unconscious, is "why are they doing this—because they're doing it, whether they know it or not?"

Jokes are an interesting phenomena in this perspective—those racist jokes that just slip out—a "word play" that isn't planned but happens anyway. Here the question is "why did you say that? —"you must unconsciously have all along held the belief that blacks are like that, i.e. the way they come out in your joke."

Politics too, from pamphlets to voting patterns, is readable as being structured or steered by unconscious beliefs. Here however, under the stipulation of our earlier hypothesis, the coefficient of (democratic) repression is high and the presence of the colonial unconscious far from obvious or transparent. Returning to our earlier theme, let us now consider economic practice in this light.

When it comes to economic practice, clearly something has gone wrong—what is being produced and reproduced is the very racial differential constitutive of colonialism. *Ex hypothesi* there is no conscious and deliberate racial discrimination in the economic sphere: economic decisions are made on the basis of non-racial individual economic merit, and yet white relative prosperity is maintained and reproduced. Unless we posit that employers are themselves striving for non-racial outcomes, we are not tackling the implication of the 1996 Constitution and are wishing away the very problem of the status of colonialism in South Africa today.

What then justifies invoking the concept of a collective colonial unconscious in order to be able to account for the economic practice of non-racial economic subjects? Precisely the 'racial colonial' outcome of this non-racial economic practice, viz the reproduction of white prosperity. Here is the warrant for saying that something is going on here that needs to be accounted for and which cannot be accounted for unless we posit that, in some way, colonialism is still at work.

What has happened is that capitalist property powers enable whites to continue to act, albeit unconsciously, as colonial subjects who systematically discriminate in favour of whites and against blacks. Capitalist property powers license these decisions in relation to employment, remuneration and procurement which, it is claimed, are based on pure economic rationality, but which attest, above all, to 'Whites doing business with Whites'. It is this 'gap in consciousness' that warrants the introduction of the concept of the colonial unconscious, the causality of which is embedded in and inferred from social practice, from the objective collapse of the avowed non-racial norm.

Capitalism allows the white capitalist 'non-racial' subject to continue to keep a proper distance—an ontological distance—between himself and the colonised black subject. It allows him to be 'white' and to continue to enjoy his whiteness in his economic relations with blacks because of his individual sovereignty, so deeply installed and fiercely defended in capitalism: he can be White in his practice on account of the negative (non-interference) freedom to do what he likes with his capital, his property, within the law, i.e. he can be white without this being present to him, without him being conscious of this. This unconscious closure is how capitalism operates today, and this explains the reproduction of relative white prosperity.

What matters here is what these powers of property allow to 'slip through', viz a racial patterning—they allow the unconscious to determine the boundary of inclusion/exclusion without this appearing racist: closer inspection however, shows a racial patterning best explained via the concept of the colonial unconscious. What we are dealing with here isn't reducible to any 'unintended consequence' model either, insofar as we are not dealing with a series of self-contained and transparent actions which then go onto to produce something unintended—rather, here, these actions **themselves** are not what the agent thinks they are.

Here an unconscious racial norm operates, i.e. it must be assumed to operate if we are to account for the actual practice of white employers. Whatever they say, their practice says otherwise. They don't know they are doing it but they must be doing it. What they do slips under the radar screen of the Constitution because not done in the name of white hegemony, the Constitution only recognising avowed racism—but done nonetheless.

We are not talking about surreptitious racism or a racism more or less thinly veiled by code words, rather, it is a matter of unconscious racist practice in which the agent really is unaware of, and exceeded by, his own behaviour. Only if we are able to conceptualise colonialism as existing in this unconscious mode will we be in a position to defend the thesis that it still exists, in the strong sense, i.e. as more than a residue because still reproducing itself. If the colonial differential is to be grasped as sui generis, as irreducible, then it is more than residual and any emancipatory political project will have to incorporate this recognition of the complexity of the structure of domination in South Africa.

Capitalism facilitates the operation and reproduction of colonialism in South Africa today via the sovereign space of property ownership; this doesn't mean it is an expression, or effect, of capitalism—it is an irreducible sui generis and self-reproducing social relation of domination which is more than merely residual and dying out of its own accord.

In any case, there is no such thing as a stand-alone, pristine and self-sufficient law of capitalist accumulation; this latter is always and necessarily over-determined and is thus 'open-textured'.[7] The norm of capitalist practice does not speak for itself and is constitutively dependent on interpretation. The 'colour blind' South African capitalist is the bearer of a place in the relations of production, but this is never a sufficient explanation of his practice: he is, even if he denies it – interpreting the meaning of this place i.e. what being a capitalist carries with it in South Africa today. The rules are open-textured and the practices of capital always multiple.[8]

Our capitalist is still following the rules of colonial capitalism not any putative capitalism *per se*; even though we posit that he (sincerely) **is** 'colour blind', he follows the rules of colonial capitalism. He is conscious only of himself qua 'non-racial' and yet his practice is colonial/racially structured: even when he **is** colour blind, he, at the same time, is not, and the proof is that he could be 'doing business' with blacks, but he isn't. To deny this is to maintain that only our currently racially skewed capitalism is possible in South Africa today; in other words, nothing has changed; capitalism still depends on colonialism in South Africa, as it always has. But this fails to take into account the transformation of both the relations and forces of production referred to earlier.

To reiterate, we are not dealing with the claim that our homo-economicus is not racist although he only trades with whites because 'currently' only they, whites, 'add value'—this is just racist simpliciter and in that case the problem we are trying to explain falls away. *Ex hypothesi* the racist who maintains only whites can 'currently' add economic value, is, thus excluded.

The two ends of the chains, are then, 1) he really is (conscious of being) non-racial, and 2) in his practice he is racial, i.e. he maintains the colonial differential: and the hypothesis of the colonial unconscious is then invoked to square 1) and 2).

The claim that only whites 'add value' isn't non-racial: and we are positing that our subject is non-racial—that he really doesn't know—even 'deep down' (contra the Sartrean conception of the unconscious) —what he actually knows: his colonialism is an 'unknown known' (Zizek 2004, 94, 95).

Conclusion

Isn't this—it might be objected, the hypothesis of the colonial unconscious—just a heuristic device marking a limit position (i.e. the **'non-racial'-racial** subject) but not one of much reach? No, because if whites are taken as doing more than merely paying lip service to the Constitution, and yet, at the same time, as being racist, then this is the subjective economy which has to be supposed to be at work—this is what warrants invoking the concept of the colonial unconscious. If whites merely pretend to be non-racial, and *sotto voce*, justify 'doing business with whites' because only whites 'currently' 'add value' then there is nothing further to explain—their racism is not one of which they are unaware but one they consciously practice. So, the argument is that today in South Africa although colonial subjectivity is not (not necessarily) present on the theatre of consciousness, it has to be invoked in order to account for the reproduction of specifically white prosperity.

Our capitalist is following the rules of colonial capitalism. He thinks they are capitalist rules simpliciter because his colonial identity is unconscious. It is absent from his consciousness, but present in his practice. He is unconscious of the identification with 'whiteness' which is steering his practice. He doesn't see himself as colonial although in his practice he is.

What has 'misfired', 'gone wrong' here? He aims at non-racialism, but he doesn't practice it. In fact, what he's doing is systematically advantaging one race over another i.e. reproducing the colonial differential. He aims at 'non racialism' yet he gets the reproduction of the racial distribution of life chances. All you need then, to produce the latter, is initial capitalist class structural advantage and the colonial unconscious, which, as it were, 'tells him' how to interpret the rules of capitalism. The colonial unconscious intervenes to steer his 'interpretation' of the rules of capitalism so that racism gets objectively embodied in his practice —the very racism he disavows. He is trying to be non-racial and wants non-racial outcomes but he misfires— he ends up 'being colonial' without realising it. He says he is being non-racial because he sees, he says, only money—but, actually (assuming the possibility of a non-racial capitalism), if he saw only money he'd behave differently, without being conscious of it he sees colour not only money.

Post 1994, and the white colonial subject is now separated from the access to Whiteness that he previously enjoyed. Now the assertion of Whiteness is barred; however, at the same time, as has been discussed above, capitalism functions, under such conditions, as a stand in for such 'full' enjoyment, for the lost plenitude of apartheid, in that it makes it possible for the colonial subject to continue existing and to intervene in its own reproduction (and thus in the reproduction of the colonial /racial distribution of assets and life chances itself).

Bibliography

Althusser, Louis. *Philosophy of the encounter: later writings, 1978-87* London, Verso, 2006.

Turok, Ben. "From Building a National Democratic Society: A strategy and Tactics of the ANC." Extracts from 2007 African National Congress Conference Documents. *Readings in the ANC Tradition*. Ben Turok, ed. Johannesburg, Jacana, 2007, pp. 224 – 262.

Bloor, David. *Wittgenstein, A Social Theory of Knowledge*. MacMillan, Columbia, 1983.

Cronin, Jeremy. "Nationalisation of the Mines... let's try that again." *Umsebenzi*, 8.21, 2009.

Daly, Glyn. "Enjoyment / Jouissance." *The Zizek Dictionary*. Rex Butler, ed. New York, Routledge, 2014.

Deleuze, Gilles. "A quoi reconnait-on le structuralism?" *La philosophie au xx siècle*. François Chatelet. Paris, Hachette, 1973.

Fanon, Frantz. *Black Skin White Masks*. London, Paladin, 1968.

Hudson, Peter. "The Freedom Charter and the Theory of National Democratic Revolution." *Transformation*, 1, 1986.

— "The State and the Colonial Unconscious." *Social Dynamics*, 39.2, 2013.

— "Liberalism, Colonialism and National Democracy." *Theoria*, September 2014.

— "The Reproduction of Racial Inequality in South Africa: The Colonial Unconscious and Democracy." *Racism after Apartheid: Challenges for Marxism and Anti-Racism*. Vishwas Satgar, ed. Johannesburg, Wits University Press, 2019.

Lacan, Jacques. *My Teaching*. New York, Verso, 2008.

McGowan, Todd. *Enjoying What We Don't Have: The Political Project of Psychoanalysis*. Lincoln, University of Nebraska Press, 2013.

Nolutshungu, Sam. *Changing South Africa*. New York, Holmes & Meier Pub, 1984.

Stavrakakis, Yannis. *The Lacanian Left: Psychoanalysis Theory Politics*. Edinburgh University Press, 2006.

Tauber, Alfred. *Freud the Reluctant Philosopher*. Princeton, Princeton University Press, 2010.

Witgenstein, Ludwig. *Philosophical Investigations*. Oxford, Basil Blackwell, 1958.

Wolpe, Harold. *Race, Class and the Apartheid State*. Paris, UNESCO, 1988.

Zizek, Slavoj. *Organs Without Bodies*. London, Routledge, 2008.

—*Enjoy your symptom! Jacques Lacan in Hollywood and out.* New York, Routledge, 2012.

Endnotes

1   See Lacan on the prejudice that "a belief just is something I know I have" and that the concept of the unconscious is thus a contradiction in terms (2008). Instead of succumbing to such peremptory dismissal, the argument for the unconscious and its explanatory value needs to be assessed.

2   On enjoyment / jouissance see McGowan (2013), Zizek (2008), Stavrakakis (2006), Daly (2014).

3   CST is the acronym for "Colonialism of a Special Type" which is how the South African Communist Party has characterised South African society in its 1963 Programme *The Road to South African Freedom*. It refers to "a new type of colonialism [...] in which the oppressing white nation occupy the same territory as the oppressed people themselves and live side by side with them" (Turok, 69). CST became and still is the pivot of the alliance between the SACP (South African Communist Party) and the ANC (See *Building a National Democratic Society* in Turok 2011, 229). *Strategy and Tactics of the ANC – Polokwane 2007* (Turok, 229). NDR refers to the National Democratic Revolution which inaugurates a state of National Democracy in which all vestiges of colonialism, including those of economic class, are eliminated. See Hudson (1986; 2014).

4   Note that for both the EFF and NUMSA, colonialism is still a fundamental feature of South African society. But, in their discourse too, colonialism—the invocation by the EFF of Fanon notwithstanding—remains under-theorised.

5   Note too that while the Constitution makes provision for "just discrimination" to redress historic injustice, it doesn't mandate any such measures: they remain in the subjunctive, while the powers of property are always in the imperative. Affirmative action and BEE are, then, precisely responses to the on-going traction of the colonial differential but rest, as argued above, on an inadequate conception of colonialism, one unable to accommodate the "democratic effect" of 1994.

6   For a discussion of the colonial unconscious and the colonial fantasy which compares them with the capitalist unconscious and the capitalist fantasy and underlines the role of commodity fetishism and liberal democracy in the repression—and reproduction—of colonial subjectivity, see Hudson (2018).

7   "Accumulate, accumulate [...] that is Moses and the Prophets"—whilst this is the law of capital, note what sort of a law it is for Marx who is at pains to stress its over-determination by the historical conditions of its existence: it is not a self-enclosed and self-sustaining law, but one open, porous, to its contingent conditions of existence. Here is the colonial unconscious that over-determines, penetrates the identity of capitalist practice. See Althusser (2006).

8   On rules and interpretation see Bloor (1983) and Wittgenstein (1958)

9

Going Native or Double Dipping:
White Writing in Postcolonial Zimbabwe and Post-Apartheid South Africa

Robert Muponde

Introduction

This essay, contemplated in 2014 in the weeks leading to the 34th anniversary of Zimbabwe's Independence from Rhodesians and the 20th anniversary of South Africa's Freedom from Apartheid, is written to consider two different postcolonial contexts in which going native is undertaken by white writers in order to register how new and old racial and ethnic identities are being (re-)produced and questioned. I suggest that while the stimulus for going native is primarily the tide of conflict that is in favour of blacks, the ambivalences, opportunities and violence of postcolonial modernity require a series of experiments and immersions.

In colonial narratives of exploration, conquest, captivity and conversion, going native is associated with defection from the master race and its mores. In the imperialist eyes of the master race, going native is a form of treason. It represents the dangers of seduction and assimilation by the despicable other. In such a discourse and practice of going native, there is no room for positive transculturation and genuine assimilation. This is because, basically, colonialism evokes a situation and practice in which whites always saw themselves as the centre of things and meaning, and therefore "[m]any forms of mutuality were never a real part of the sense that white people had of the culture in which they lived. This fractured people's basic scheme of representation, only allowing each side to think about the other in those distanced terms and not to see mutualities of power and dependence" (Gosden and Knowles 2001, 12).

Going native in such circumstances of polarity and distance illuminates the ways of seeing, producing and repressing the cultural other. Precisely because it depends on reinforcing essentialism in both directions (in the one going native and the native culture being sought), it ironically "reinforces the racial hierarchies it claims to destabilize" by making the perspective of one who has gone native central, and the stories and actions of the native population he encounters incidental, as their primary importance resides in their relation to a guest who has become their hero and savior (Huhndorf 2001, 3). It seems a contradiction in terms for one who has gone native to be native. This is because there is always an underlying political project in going native, and imperialist cultures strictly enforced the binary between the enlightened self and the primitive other, and calculated tolerable risks of 'going native' in the process of empire building. In other words, according to Clark, the empire's strict interpretations of appropriate assimilation controlled meanings of the experiences of going native, which could only aid the purposes of empire if going native was a form of strategic assimilation where the ultimate and clear goal was that of "acclimating the native population toward European practices rather than the other way around when attempting to engender positive relationships between the two" (Clark 2011, 3). The regeneration of the white race, not of the host native cultures, is therefore central to going native; and for one who has gone native, there is always the possibility of reversion to earlier forms of security in imperial culture (Huhndorf 2001). It raises questions of double dipping.

In a postcolonial situation there are changes in the forms and directions of going native that may reinforce or upend colonial gains and hierarchies; and these are located in the peculiarity of experiences in each context. The post-imperial forms of going native are at the centre of my essay, as they hint at the identity crises occasioned by loss of mastery and influence.

There are some similarities between Eppel and Krog. Their works are published in the same year and respond to similar pressures on white cultures to transform in the face of changed political circumstances. In both countries political antagonists use race as a strategy of obtaining power. The formal end of violent white supremacy conceals underlying inequalities.[1] Both writers can be described as disloyal to their civilization (Ware 2013). John Eppel explores this revision of whiteness and raises discussions around possibilities of going black, or being with blacks, which in South Africa are depicted in Krog's *Begging to be Black*.[2] Krog's novel is a search for a theoretical vernacular to articulate the ethical and philosophical conundrums of contemplating blackness, or producing blackness as required, in post-apartheid post-racial discourses.

The White English Teacher as Houseboy and Curio

Absent: The English Teacher chronicles the predicament of an erudite white English teacher called George Jorge George. What precipitates his going native is his drunkenness and associated misdemeanors which cause him to lose his job. He ends up being a houseboy to Beauticious Nyamayakanuna, a black woman whose parents were once house servants to white people in colonial and postcolonial Zimbabwe. His predicament as houseboy intensifies the experience of being stranded on a racial, cultural, and political crossroads. The theatrics associated with the desire to 'authentically belong'—being trapped in the powerful clichés that describe and enliven the world of 'the white man'—and wanting to shuffle off 'the white man's burden' and take on models of a new post-mastery role, compound the tragicomedy that is synopsized in the curious name George Jorge George.

In Zimbabwe, 'the white man' is his farm. As farmer, he is invariably cast as a Rhodesian, the brute and the stealer of black land. So, for George Jorge George, not having a farm to lose in Zimbabwe means he can lose the Rhodesian tag and call himself a poet (10). This way he tries to distance himself from the repetition of history which has entrapped postcolonial politics and culture. He asks: "Why do people like Beauticious strive to out-Rhodie the Rhodies?" (*Absent*, 116).

George seems to be more perceptive and responsive when he has hit the rock-bottom of his suffering. His literary and English mind is his greatest asset, and the reason he survived the attrition he was subjected to during the period of social and political crisis. Nonetheless, and precisely because of the fabled riches of his literary mind, he is turned into something as vulnerable as the farm by the black police chief who needs help with his English distance-education assignments and Beauticious who converts him into a servant of many parts. He is robbed of the goods of his intellect in the same way the white farmers were deprived of land *en masse*. This way, like a creature after the Biblical flood, George Jorge George can have a fresh start, literally naked.

For example, after he had been arrested for being naked in a public park,

> In order to punish George for going to prison in her time, Beauticious arranged to hire him out for a wedding the following weekend. Normally he got a five per cent cut and he was allowed to keep any tips, but this time he would get no cut and he would have to surrender his tips. Fair is fair. I mean! Some months before, Beauticious had hired, for George to wear, an Elizabethan outfit, doublet and hose, from the theatre club (2009, 109).

His mannerisms and dressing, which are antiquated, lead to his miseries. His 'many parts' in this freak show are: a chattel, a chauffeur, a fool, a eunuch (Wilhelmine, his elusive girlfriend, says he is 'castrated', 97), an antiquity for display, a rarity as a black woman's own white monkey and white houseboy. In this role of monkey and houseboy he comes across as a "barbarian with reason" (Voigt 2009, 12) and an anomalous creature standing between barbarity and civilization (Clark 2011, 1). It is this versatility in loss and nakedness that makes George a true changeling and a collector's item in the postcolonial freakshow.

As a curio, he reminds me of the story of the career of a Yakshi, an ancient art object in India which Tapati Guha-Thakurta researched (2002). Like the Yakshi, in some respects, George is remade in the black market rhetoric of rarity and antiquity, and fetishized as an art object, while being increasingly fragile and endangered (see Guha-Thakurta, 106). He becomes a curio precisely because he bails himself out of the hegemonic white narrative. He manages to do so because in the first place he was on the margins of whiteness, and therefore could afford to be reckless and lose out on the dwindling white dividend. So, ironically, he survives being turned into a curio and Rhodesiana exactly because he exits two regimes of signification: the white narrative of whiteness and the black narrative of whiteness. He belongs to neither.

Going Native: 'Isn't it you look like a kaffir?'

There are about five ways in which George Jorge George might be considered to have gone native in ways that upend expectations of the colonial narrative, and augment and nuance the postcolonial narrative. Loss, captivity and conversion, adaptation and adoption, and primitivization are central tropes in his narrative of going native.

First, and the most obvious, is the way he is converted into a houseboy by a black woman called Beauticious Nyamayakanuna. If I suggest that it could be viewed as an important decolonial moment, it is because it reverses the colonial encounter and its attendant relations between black and white. In this instance, it allows George to experience what black people experienced under colonialism, and to become a better human being. He decolonizes himself. He actually becomes more caring to less privileged members of the society, including bailing out a black prisoner and saving a lost and malnourished black orphan girl he called Polly Petal and returning her later to her people as he finds his way to his own cemetery and final death. Of course in this reversal of the colonial encounter and change of roles is registered the tautology of colonial power in the relationship between George and Beauticious. He may not be well-equipped to champion the "re-embodiment and relocation of thought in order to unmask the limited situation of modern knowledges and their link to coloniality" in the spirit of decoloniality (Cheah 2006, 1), but his satirical methods make it possible for George to appreciate the entangled nature of the freedom he seeks. He becomes native because he has suffered deprivation and loss and has been *thingified* by social and political processes to the extent that his existence is as precarious as that of the majority of the struggling black people, with whom his fate is now aligned.

Second: the cypher of this loss, and going native, is first noticed by himself when he describes himself as not white but 'beetroot' coloured (1), the equivalent of white "ethnic scarring" and corrosion (Williams 1998, 253-255). Later on when he is arrested by the police chief for having been robbed of his clothes in a public park and is accused of "public indecency","" he is barefooted, and a black woman officer asks: 'Isn't it you look like a kaffir?' (89-90). A beetroot-coloured face will not make a kaffir, but someone on the margins of black and white, not coloured. It is neither a sign of a healthy native, nor of a healthy white man. The pejorative and reductive term 'kaffir' is not acceptable to both black and white people. It is proscribed and classified as the K-word. So, George has become worse than the black African who was forged by the colonial moment, because kaffir neither evokes autochthony nor a viable political threat, and is several removes from the quintessential 'white man'. In the postcolonial politics of resource nationalism, which is aimed at redressing economic and political imbalances caused by 'the white man', a native would be the one who would reap massive dividends.

While George's story of triple disempowerment by class, race and age may make him "readily decodable as socially black" (Williams 1998, 261), what Praise Zenenga (2013, 177) observes about the ways in which whiteness is performed by black people in Zimbabwe today as a "metaphor for black achievement, success and excellence" would eject him from the honorary status. His narrative is not one powered by the cathexes of racial and historical victimization but that of liminality and obsolescence.

Third: He goes native in the same way he imagines botanical imperialism and adaptation. He mentions how fruits and crops which were derived from places outside Africa, have become staple foods of cultures that actually inveigh against colonialism and its legacies. Maize, for example, he avers:

> has accrued a powerful symbolism, like bread in the Bible. It is a synecdoche for sustenance, both physical and spiritual. It is synonymous with our land, our sovereignty. It's the colour green on our flag. But it's a product of biological imperialism. So is the sweet potato. The colonisers introduced it. It has also, therefore, accrued a powerful latent symbolism. It is a synecdoche for oppression, exploitation (35).

The domestication and adaptation which has gone on for decades has taken the historical route/root of the crop out and made it part and parcel of the inalienable right to life of the colonized people. Whiteness, properly domesticated, democratised and nativised, could, like maize, potatoes and mangoes (products of botanical imperialism), be freed of the meanings of its original pathways and residences and naturalized. There is something botanical about George's roots, and like the enormous turnip in the children's story that he reads to Polly Petal, he feels deeply grounded and that, if properly propagated and tended, he could nourish the community. He seeks a route out of a whiteness beyond the borders of the colonial legacy, although curiously enough, he does not talk about being nourished by the same black community. The case of the Matopos below illustrates this glaring absence of mutuality.

Fourth: In seeking pathways out of Rhodesian whiteness, that sterile and violent legacy, he does not erase the complex politics of belonging and location traced back to the treks of the pioneer column led by Cecil John Rhodes who colonized Zimbabwe. His ancestors are part of the pioneer column, so he traces his aunt's roots and does what is called negative commemoration when one celebrates what is generally considered by another group an ugly history. George goes native by going to die in the Matopos Hills where his aunt is buried and rejects the impulse to 'diasporise' to Europe or South Africa as most white people did when Zimbabwe became independent in 1980, and also when it was in a political crisis post-2000 (90). He considers the heritage site at the Matopos as his to share in life and death.

The Matopos Hills is a place of historical contrarieties. This is where the founder of Rhodesia, Cecil John Rhodes, as well as the founder of the Boy Scouts, Baden-Powell, are buried. The hills entomb the bones of the colonial pioneers, and save as the shrines of the black Mwari (God). Mzilikazi, the leader of the Ndebele people, a warrior who fled from South Africa and founded Bulawayo, the second city of Zimbabwe, is also buried there. The Hills served as a hideout for nationalist guerrillas who ousted Rhodesian Prime Minister Ian Douglas Smith in 1980, and disgruntled armed black 'dissidents' prowled the area in their war against Robert Mugabe's regime between 1980 and 1987 (See Ranger 1999 for a history of the Matopos Hills). George recalls how about 150 of his armed pioneer ancestors had sought shelter there when under attack from the black insurgents who were resisting colonial occupation in 1896. A benevolent black chthonic "voice from a cave in the Matopos gave orders to the [black] warriors that the road to the south should be left open so that the settlers could run back to wherever they had come from. [...]. If it weren't for Mlilo [the voice], thought George with more sentiment than irony, I wouldn't be where I am today. The bastard!" (*Absent*, 108-109). The point of his flippant remark being that he would not have been born and would have been spared the ignominy of being a houseboy to a black couple. The Hills are a site of many origins and beginnings, and George's checkered history qualifies him as a pioneer of sorts. He belongs there. If he were to die and speak to Mlilo, the black God, he could speak about how the Rhodesians repaid his uncommon humanity, and how he George, their scion, made amends.

Nevertheless, in spite of the symbolic promise of his burial place, John Eppel's protagonist fails to articulate any conscious inspiration from, and nostalgia for, black African political figures and ancestral history. Unlike Krog in *Begging to be Black*, he does not take responsibility for his ancestors' land-grabbing, nor does he overtly condemn them. The only time he draws inspiration from the African canon is when he quotes Ngugi's *A Grain of Wheat*, a tragic story of what he calls the dialectic of loyalty and betrayal. But he subverts the force of this story by nativising 'illiteracy' and essentializing "the oral tradition, or orature, which enriched African culture before the white man brought the written word" (*Absent*, 99). So (with Rosaldo 1989 in mind), what is there to be nostalgic about black history, imagination and politics for a white writer who belongs to a race that trampled on black lives and civilizations for centuries?

Fifth: There are two scenes that recall aboriginal primitivism after George had willingly allowed the "collector of Rhodesiana" to strip him of his period safari suit in order for him to raise money to get the little girl some clothes (79).

The first is when Eppel remarks: "Luckily George wore underpants on Sundays, so he wouldn't have to go stark naked" (80). He recalls to us the selfless sacrifices that are necessary to protect the vulnerable. In the process, he has to strip himself of his colonial accoutrements, in public, in order to declare his oneness with the little black girl, as well as with nature. He also refuses to turn the little girl Polly Petal into a trophy. An act of charity, and sacrifice, not for country and king, but for self, helps him stave off charges of white philanthropic paternalism. He helps the little girl as a little man, with nothing to give or save except scraps of warmth left in his diseased body. By being a teacher of paradoxes, he readies the mind of Polly Petal, the little orphan girl, for a life of reflection, and helps her escape a postcolonial narrative of captivity in black corruption and consumption, in the same way he escaped his narrative captivity in unreconstructed Rhodesian discourse (Pilossof 2012).

> The second scene: when he is naked, he stumbles upon some mushrooms, and exclaims: 'Tonight, little girl, we feast!' (81).

> They gathered their mushrooms and made their way home, George taking care to avoid the lichen-splattered boulder where he located the image of a kneeling woman whom he loved to distraction. (*Absent*, 81).

The image of the kneeling woman brings to mind Wilhelmine, his unattainable white girlfriend, "going down on her knees," just a short page before, possibly to give her new black dreadlocked lover a blowjob right in George's view after she had just humiliated him in the park by having him undressed (80). The figure of Wilhelmine would symbolize vulgarity, treachery and instability, hardly the subject of a Petrarchan sonnet (*Absent*, 40). She turns out to be a phantasm of an ancient European convention, the marrow of George's aesthetic sensibility whose materiality is tested severely in the messiness of postcolonial experience. Finally confronted by evidence of the decadence and irrelevancy of received European conceits, he seeks the certainty of an ancient black pastoral in which simplicity translates to authenticity. In place of the whorish kneeling woman of his Petrarchan sonnets, he inserts himself in a primitivised space where, together with the figure of little Polly Petal, George is the hunter-gatherer father in the bushveld (142-145). His mock epic journey to the Matopos Hills to die where his white ancestors are buried places his remains among the rocks teeming with San art. He dies native in rock outcrops that potentially symbolize syncretic indigeneities. He collects himself in order for his remains to accrue complexity and "sets of significances" as they accumulate a history (*cp* Gosden and Knowles 2001, 3-4). Yet the continuous state of becoming that Gosden and Knowles believe characterizes the life of collected objects and histories is somehow arrested.

John Eppel's protagonist travels physically by journeying to the bushveld and the shrine where his ancestors are buried, and where he goes to die, and textually through a close critical reading of Shakespearean and African tragedies that reflect the disorder, oppression, corruption and chaos associated with postcolonial Africa. George tries to literalize these canonical tragedies in ways that confuse fact with fiction, and he dies *factionally,* so to speak. George's wanderings only point to something symbolic, something yet to be formed as white identities in Zimbabwe remain stranded in cultural quicksand after the political storm that hit the pillars of their economic and class certainties between 2000 and 2008.

Begging to be Black: re-versioning and re-purposing history

In Antjie Krog's narrative, going native or black is one way of re-versioning history and identity, and a quest for a theoretical vernacular and moral compass out of the quagmire of postcolonial whiteness. Her narrative underlines the harrowing soul-searching undertaken by one white writer in her efforts to grapple with the treacherous and murderous history of her race, and the conquest-ridden, haunted memories of blackness. She explores this hauntedness through three interrelated mechanisms: The Truth and Reconciliation Commission (TRC), the story of Moshoeshoe king of the Basotho, and the trip to Berlin, a city associated with Hitler's atrocities and the holocaust.

Berlin Trip and Writing Retreat: search for "multiple intactnesses"

Krog's writing retreat in Berlin is a spiritual, physical, and philosophical quest for perspective in her efforts to map a new South Africa based on a constructive and creative engagement with pain and loss, brutality and genocide, and how to build after the holocaust. Krog's Afrikaner race/ tribe was responsible for the atrocities of apartheid, and Krog acknowledges how implicated she is in the guilt of her race, although she did not participate in the war parties. The acknowledgement is a beginning in new and necessary steps towards a cultural and political renaissance undergirded by the uncommon black humanism exhibited at the TRC, and embodied in the person and politics of Nelson Mandela. It is important therefore for Krog to travel to Berlin to experience how another perpetrator race is carrying on and resolving its burden of guilt "with such consistent, sober and extended gravity" (199).

But the trip to Berlin is problematic, especially if its purpose is to understand post-holocaust sensitivities, care and order as they might never be experienced in South Africa. She goes to Berlin in order to understand South Africa and her relation to blackness (the fodder of white racism, violence and exploitation before the end of apartheid, and even after the advent of democracy in 1994). It is in Berlin that she encounters a white philosopher with whom she shares her notion of begging to be black, as black has become the new locus of an inimitable humanism and viable politics post-apartheid. The problem will be that Krog is a member of the perpetrator race that was responsible for the miseries of the black race in South Africa. She cannot be the one to use her perspective to re-organize blackness in ways that suit her own race's need to be accommodated in a new post-mastery politics of belonging. Nor should she be the one to re-version king Moshoeshoe's history for South African politics. There are chances that she could be accused of trying to manufacture difference and coherence in order to salvage and then assimilate into South African political ethics an ethnic history of the Basotho as an ordering principle.

In South Africa, Krog's race has lost direct control of the state. Its stake in the economy is being steadily eroded. The Freedom Front Plus, the political party that represents its interests, has been reduced to a mere pressure group, and its support base has dwindled to less than one percent of the national vote. Its language is now just one of the many languages one can use, it is no longer *the* language of government, business and education. Its culture is equally atrophying in many respects. In Berlin, the perpetrator race, though apologetic about its horrendous past, is firmly in control of the state, its economy, language and culture. There are therefore reasons for Krog to be excited about the order, attention to detail and care that she experiences in Berlin, which is not controlled by the victims of the holocaust.

Krog misses to the irony that on the one hand she is seeking to accept and transcend her race's guilt while on the other hand she is extolling the virtues and fortitude of a fellow perpetrator race which has learnt how to take care of its victims and its dreadful past. Berlin is a place in which her race consciousness can re-experience its erstwhile power to recollect and to reconstruct. Here, to recall Rosaldo, "a mood of nostalgia makes racial domination appear innocent and pure" (1989, 69). Berlin affords her immersion in 'guilt-redeemed' post-imperial discursive practices which, as Mehmet Ararguc observes, "In addition to practices to alleviate or absolve repressed guilt about the past, they often relate to discourses of power and regret that the past is no more. This type of nostalgia is another neo-imperialist form of exploitation by (ab)using or generating fluid, dynamic, and ever-evolving identities" (2012, 1).

It seems to me that her interest in how the Berliners enjoy a coherent culture which includes cultural productions by former victims of the holocaust is not a revolutionary discovery at all, as the same phenomenon is present in the United States of America where dominant classes, cultural and media discourses incorporate the cultural productions of African Americans (former slaves for centuries), and Native Americans (who survived genocide in the Wild West), and Jews (who suffered pogroms and discrimination for centuries at the hands of other white people). While in Berlin, Krog has every reason to be worried about the violence and disorder in South Africa, a state controlled by victims of her race's apartheid policies, a black race she and her white ilk still have to fathom after three hundred years of subjugating and objectifying their culture and life.

The idea of 'begging to be black' cuts in three ways. First, and to quote Hagen Engler, a South African white writer, it could be that,

> This is Africa, after all. So after a couple of decades of living in Africa [Engler should add: *ruling* Africa], one starts to feel a little embarrassed to not be black. The embarrassment is preceded by a series of insights, realisations and epiphanies about the status quo.

These make you wonder how you've managed to live a life of such utter, unleavened non-blackness for as long as you have (2013, 3).

Second, and related to the sense of shame, it could mean wanting to experience what black people actually went through and still go through in order to establish an empathetic identification with former victims. This identification, according to Engler, could essentialize black experience and "fetishize that blackness" which is viewed as a human essence that colonizing races have lost, and something that can only be found "unvarnished, unprotected, integrated," among certain classes and communities of black people, themselves, ironically long disintegrated by colonial experience. Third, it could mean wanting to share in the spoils of a race now much favoured by history. All the three views and the concomitant anxieties are discernible in Krog's *Begging to be Black*. They are projected in light of varying intensity and brightness, but whichever view is more clearly articulated and preferred, they all speak to the conundrum of post-apartheid blackness, and the difficulty of plotting it on a pocket-size map.

Matters of class, power and privilege define priorities in terms of who really gets bothered about wanting to be black, and who has time to ponder the possibility of being black. In South Africa, where the former ruling white race has lost political and cultural power, and is the one most likely to lose more if the Zimbabwean-style resource nationalism threatening South Africa today through the articulations of the Economic Freedom Fighters (EFF) cannot be skillfully staved off or deferred, it makes sense for Krog to proactively "bend over blackwards" (*Begging*, 173) and imagine a blackness that can accommodate what she calls "interrelatedness" and "interconnected humaneness" (227). Krog bends "blackwards" into African history and brings king Moshoeshoe's story centre-stage to underline the fact that this concept of interrelatedness which accommodated and humanized cannibals and missionaries, murderers and polygamists, war and peace, forgiveness and redress (a concept which is now associated with the exceptionalism of Nelson Mandela's political wisdom), is a complex politics and practice long understood by the Basotho, more than a hundred years before Mandela was imprisoned. It cannot therefore just vanish with Mandela's death as it forms the marrow of African humanism and community. Mandela's exceptionalism needs therefore to be historicized and restored to a long history of related practices in Africa (see *Begging*, 227-228), to avoid being jettisoned as a quack politics of the miraculous and the wondrous, an onerous burden on a society hard-pressed to produce another miracle worker.

To underline class preferences, Krog begs to be black in the regal fashion of Moshoeshoe and Mandela, but certainly not the underclasses associated with township 'necklace murders' and violent service delivery protests which cause her moral quandaries in her narrative. The authentic, viable blackness therefore lies in its embodiment in political and philosophical lineages and imaginaries that recall Mandela and Moshoeshoe. In the process of contemplating blackness, and begging to be black, Krog authenticates herself as someone who has credentials that identified with black struggles. It substantiates for herself an otherwise tenuous identity as white. So, as Eversley reminds us elsewhere, and as we see in Krog's politics, the demand for the real black might have originated with white people who wanted to define for black people what constituted a true useable blackness (2004). So, on behalf of the black people from whom she draws the blackness that she requires for her political project, she establishes the type of authenticity which "offers a double-edged opportunity for social recognition and cultural capital" (Eversley 2004, x). Moshoeshoe could then be dispersed as Africa's own contribution to modern African political philosophy, while Mandela, who extends him, would have a broader global iconic imprint.

Having defined for us what constitutes a propagate-able black authenticity, Krog probes for herself what it takes to belong to that black race as a white person. She wonders: is it "possible for a white person like myself, born in Africa, raised in a culture with strong Western roots, drenched in a political dispensation that said black people were different and therefore inferior, [...] to move towards a 'blackness' as black South Africans themselves understand it?" (*Begging*, 94). Her movement towards blackness, on a raft of post-mastery whiteness, results in her being a victim of reverse integration. In the end she opts to delight in contemplating the "terror and loneliness of that inability" to imagine black rather than to become black (*Begging*, 267). The promise of the sphinx in Berlin, "this figure from Africa" (274), a symbolic migrant and time traveller, a victim of a collecting colonialism which no longer speaks Africa in Africa, "[not] split, not guarding dichotomies, but presenting beingness as multiple intactnesses" (*Begging*, 275), speaks to her inability to imagine and become black outside of theoretical abstractions, the gimmicks of narratology and poetic licence.

Moshoeshoe, Casalis and Krog: nostalgia for 'interrelatedness'

For Krog, nostalgia is an essential part of collecting, recollecting and re-purposing African narratives and histories as well as 'mapping loss' in post-apartheid post-TRC literary imaginations. Shane Graham argues that mapping loss involves the central motifs of "digging and excavation," as spectral realities of a violent and murderous history (2009, 20). Krog was a reporter on the TRC proceedings, and was much influenced by the buried narratives that were confessed at the hearings. It is however not enough to "dig" and expose, with the hope that "if we only dig it out it will be revealed to us in all its totalizing explanatory power" (Graham, 20). In a carefully worded observation, which tallies with the impulse of Krog's imaginative project, Graham summarizes the direction and purpose of post-apartheid narrative excavations: "Recent South African literature teaches us, instead, that the tapestry of history must be read as a palimpsest, by paying careful attention to that which has been erased as well as that which is inscribed." In these erased and recovered narratives are "forgotten modes of social existence that might enable the birth of true radical democracy—which demands autonomy and self-determination on the part of all South African people. This includes enabling people to seize control over both the construction of social memory about the past, and the production of space" (20-21).

Obviously, Graham's 'true radical democracy' refers to the post-apartheid cultures of representation in the fields of the symbolic, and, like *Begging to be Black*, does not directly relate to the need for an equally pressing 'true radical democracy' of the economy as defined by left-leaning trade unions and political parties in South Africa. This patent mismatch between the symbolic and the material is a source of friction and crisis in post-apartheid South Africa. It privileges tokenism without addressing the inequities in the materiality of the symbol, very much like a placebo. However, redress and renovations in the field of cultural representations have a bearing on concepts and practices of freedom and self-determination in all spheres of life. In other words, Krog is availing herself of the radical democratic opportunity to tell the stories she wants to tell without being restricted in terms of whose story she should tell, who should tell it, and why and how she should tell it. She struggles to cut through the layered encrustations of biased white narratives about a black king, which she endeavors to re-member, re-compose, and re-purpose through a variety of techniques and forms. Her project of going black is therefore an attempt to attend to what Graham (quoting Frederic Jameson) argues is the postmodern "crisis of historicity," a "new depthlessness [and] a consequent weakening of historicity" in post-apartheid South Africa (Graham 2009, 2).

Viewed in this light, going black has a utopian and palliative function. It contributes to a "thinning of [white] skin" (Krog, 268) and its centrality in narrative, theory and philosophy, and an enriching of perspective on the part of white writers. Inability to relate creatively to African sources of inspiration destroyed the Rhodesian narrative and its economy, and leads John Eppel's protagonist to etiolate.

What seems to defeat Krog's project of going black are two interrelated issues

First, she is writing about begging to be black in a context of haunted historiographies. In writing as a white writer in Africa, and about Africa, she is aware of evoking the latent antecedent symbolism of the 'heart of darkness'. As a white female writer, the 'heart of darkness' could be construed as representing for her the pull of primordial desires, release from order, and the quest for self-immolation. Krog comes close to insinuating this kind of reading when she claims: "Blackness released me from my white capsule. It has liberated me from the rule of all laws; it has taught me how to become other than myself" (268-269). That otherness which she strives to become and to dissolve seems to be stalled before her contemplation of the blackness of Steve Biko which is closed to whiteness and minoritizes[3] whiteness (2004, 29-35) and the conflicted blackness of Franz Fanon (what she calls "Fanon-identified harms" of blackness, 94), which simultaneously reviles and apes whiteness: seeking freedom and autonomy through killing the white man while restoring forms of white power and culture in the postcolony. Her writing is inserted in these haunted discourses which define enduring ideologies of race. As with her trip to Berlin, which unfortunately can be read as an animation of spiritual and philosophical reveries of the 'intactness' of race and power, her nostalgia and agonized quest for 'interrelatedness' of human experience could be read as an instance of Rosaldo's cynicism about mourning what her colonizing race has killed or altered (1989).

Krog is quite conscious of how her project of going black is hobbled by her tenuous position as settler and native, the paradoxical status having been achieved through colonial conquest. Consequently, the text demonstrates "in its own self-conscious narrative, both the difficulties of representing or defining cultural others, and the inevitable historical and textual complicities underlying the location and legitimation of otherness" (Kanneh 1998, 2). Krog admits: "I cannot ever really enter the psyche of somebody else, somebody black" (267) precisely because "in a country where we have come from different civilizations, then lived apart in unequal and distorted relationships that formed generations of us, our imagination is simply not capable of imagining a reality as—or with—the other" (268). In being conscious of her oxymoronic status of (colonial) settler and (colonial) native, she also points to her sense of the hurdles such an anomalous position places in her efforts to imagine and articulate blackness. Her interest in and identification with black struggles is haunted by the dubious politics and origins of settler-native, and the protracted difficulties experienced in transcending this existential doubleness and residual strangeness. Engler notes a "strange type of dichotomy" in the white liberal tradition in South Africa, where "in our minds we are Joe Slovo, but in reality we are Cecil John Rhodes" (2013, 91).[4] The politics of double dipping are implicated in such conflicted, dichotomous perspectives.

Second, Krog is thinking 'blackwards' in a context of radical post-race discourses

It seems to me a belated politics of restituting blackness which comes across as salvage anthropology in which the white gaze on black history assumes a restorative function in a context where blackness is presumed by a specious post-race discourse to have lost coherence. In the war of interpretation and appropriation depicted by Krog, the French missionary Eugene Casalis authenticated, authorized, and gave coherence to Moshoeshoe's voice in order to present him to his church and queen as a big and rare catch in the conversion of black natives to Christianity and colonial modernity. In wanting "to speak black," and to represent "the life of a remarkable king," Krog's project of explaining Moshoeshoe and South Africa continues, rather than opposes, the work of the missionary Casalis (268-269; 227). She writes: "Without Casalis, Moshoeshoe's written voice lost its authority. The consequences were dire" (*Begging,* 219). Krog authenticates and authorizes the version of Moshoeshoe that she re-purposes for a new South African democracy. She reinstalls blackness at the heart of new South Africa at a time when blackness is presumed to have lost coherence by some liberal intellectuals and politicians who are championing post-race politics to overcome what they see as essentialism and untenability of native-settler, black-white dialectics in contemporary South Africa.

The irony is that the post-race discourse, which seeks to dethrone blackness as a coherent identity and politics, is coming across as a resurgence and replication of the double-standards of the white Western world in its dealings with blacks over the centuries. Toni Morrison, exasperated by the shifting of goal posts in the Western academy, observes that when for centuries black Americans insisted that race was not a useful distinguishing factor in human relationships, race was insisted upon. Ironically,

> When blacks discovered they had shaped or become a culturally formed race, and that it had a specific and revered difference, suddenly they were told there is no such thing as "race", biological or cultural, that matters and that genuinely intellectual exchange cannot accommodate it. [...] It always seemed to me that people who invented the hierarchy of "race" when it was convenient for them ought not to be the ones to explain it away, now that it does not suit their purposes for it to exist (1988, 126).

The intriguing story of the white-dominated Democratic Alliance renting prominent black faces in order to win votes, while espousing a mishmash of post-race and non-racial discourses, points to the meaning of Toni Morrison's rebuke. In comparison, Krog's dramatic abandonment of her going black project—"I simply don't know enough about blackness" and "I now think that to imagine black at this stage is to insult black" (268)—when she experiences what Blanco and Peeren called "loss of assuredness about what the historical narrative can translate about and from the past" in a haunted history (2013, 482), recalls a Leon Schuster practical joke from which the victim seeks relief and in its absence, experiences a perpetual nightmare. She balks at going black because she installed essentialism at what she construed as "the unassuming heart of blackness" (253) at a time when black politics and identities—exemplified by the story of Bonnini the Lesotho woman in chapter eighteen—instantiate what bell hooks theorized as "multiple black identities, [and] varied black experience" which challenge the one-dimensional representations of blackness by white supremacist ideologies (hooks 1990, 28). What the story of Bonnini hints at, and something that baffles Krog, is that there is no contradiction in maintaining the multiple sources of identity of a single race at the same time one is advocating redress (symbolic or economic) based on a singular race experience.

Going native by bending 'blackwards' to collect black life stories and histories in a situation where blacks like Bonnini have since found their own sources of narrative and power can only be "a reaction to the fear of a dystopic future" of the white race, and one way in which post-imperialist nostalgia can be considered to "serve an individual cathartic purpose" while feigning to search for community (Ararguc 2012, 2). As I have already alluded to by recalling Leon Schuster, there is a deadly joke behind Krog's project of "begging to be black." There is also an unreformed cynicism and haughtiness which the self-interrogation and extensive consultation and ripping of secondary sources hide or reveal. For example, responding to Bonnini's analysis of Krog's "single-rootedness" and her "inability to imagine [herself] consisting of others [as] a crude form of life," she figuratively thrusts the middle finger at her: "But it is that individuality that makes me survive anywhere, I wanted to say. In actual fact, I don't need to become more black, because for black to survive, it will have to become white" (217-218). Going native armed with a theoretical and anthropological vernacular of 'roots', 'community', and 'cohesive wholes' could only result in shattering despair. Bonnini, a true native who is ever in a state of complex becoming, turns away from Krog and marches "back across the bridge" which Krog had built between and beyond the races by reconstructing her guilt-ridden past and resurrecting Moshoeshoe (218).

Conclusion

The writing that Krog does demonstrates some hope that white South Africans have a better chance of deflecting the fate of Zimbabwean whites whose whiteness is destined to be wiped out together with the economic and symbolic infrastructure that supported it. The Zimbabwean whites, ironically, find themselves in danger of being frozen in time by an influential new coterie of white scholars of Rhodesian discourse such as Hughes (2010) and Pilossoff (2012). There is no real attempt to locate a space for articulating a different experience of postcolonial Zimbabwean whiteness, and its efforts to relate creatively to its past in new and untried ways, as the basis for a possible cultural renaissance. In the Zimbabwean case, the subsequent physical and symbolic destruction of the white farm in post-2000 inaugurates moments of a social crisis that is conducive for going native for the intended or unintended purposes of exiting the white frontier.

In Eppel's case, his protagonist escapes closure of the white narrative by performing symbolic acts of care and charity, insinuating that loss of whiteness in Zimbabwe is loss of a model of morality. George embraces and fetishizes marginality in order to recover lost white hegemony. However, the syncretic indigeneities that his death suggest are not worked out with the same rigour and imagination that Krog invests in the crafting of a white-serving working symbol of the 'interconnectedness' and 'intactness' of the human experience. Therefore, George's social life is as stranded in the cultural quicksand of Zimbabwe as his remains are trapped in the volatile histories of the shrines.

In Krog's narrative, going black is symbolically a revision and revitalization of whiteness, if not a reversion to earlier forms of security in whiteness which in South Africa can still be viewed as a form of property. Where in Zimbabwe the course of conflict has tragically beached the white narrative, in Krog's work we can see that the series of narrative experiments with transculturation, assimilation and collecting help stay or delay a similar fate on South African whiteness. Although Krog recoils at the idea of going black, 266 pages into her narrative and nine pages before the end of the narrative, and reverts to her earlier forms of unknowing and insecurity, she makes imagining black a work in progress which she suspends on the plane of poetic rhetoric and obfuscates in narratological ploys. She essentialises both whiteness and blackness in order to collect and speak black, but retreats strategically right at the moment when "the failure of Africa [...] becomes a problem" (266) that resists being converted into simplistic blackface[5] white historiography.

Double-dipping as a potential social prophylactic in the moments of crisis, is seen in the ways Krog stands to benefit in the moment of her pause, as an authority on post-apartheid whiteness and black-becoming; and the ways in which Eppel's protagonist accrues symbolic value as a *griot* of the decline of whiteness, a creature of the margins doubling as moral and intellectual authority through whom we make sense of postcolonial Zimbabwe.

Bibliography

Ararguc, Fikret Mehmet. "Imperialist Nostalgia in Master's *To the Coral Strand.*" *CLCWeb: Comparative Literature and Culture*, 14.1, 2012, pp. 1-8.

Biko, Steve. *I Write What I Like*. Johannesburg, Picador Africa, 2004.

Blanco, Maria del Pilar and Peeren, Esther. eds. *The Spectralities Reader: Ghosts and Haunting in Contemporary Cultural Theory*. London, Bloomsbury Academic, 2013.

Cheah, Pheng. "The limits of thinking in decolonial strategies." Townsend Center for the Humanities, 2006. http://townsendcenter.berkeley.edu/publications/limits-thinking-decolonial-strategies.

Clark, Amanda. "Review of Voigt, Lisa, *Writing Captivity in the Early Modern Atlantic: Circulations of Knowledge and Authority in the Iberian and English Imperial Worlds.*" H-LatAm, H-Net Reviews. May 2011. Http://www.h-net.org/reviews/showrev.php?id=32970.

Engler, Hagen. *Marrying Black Girls for Guys who aren't Black*. Johannesburg, MFBooks, 2013.

Eppel, John. *Absent: the English Teacher*. Harare, Weaver Press, 2009.

Eversley, Shelly. *The Real Negro: The Question of Authenticity in Twentieth-century African American Literature*. London, Routledge, 2004.

Gordis, Lisa M. "The Conversion Narrative in Early America." *A Companion to the Literatures of Colonial America*. Susan Castillo and Ivy Schweitzer, eds. Oxford, Blackwell Publishing, 2005, pp. 369-386.

Gosden, Chris and Knowles, Chantal. *Collecting Colonialism: Material Culture and Colonial Change*. Oxford, Berg Publishers, 2001.

Graham, Shane. *South African Literature after the Truth Commission: Mapping Loss*. New York, Palgrave Macmillan, 2001.

Guha-Thakurta, Tapati. "The Endangered Yakshi: Careers of an Ancient Art Object in Modern India. *History and the Present*. Partha Chatterjee and Anjan Ghosh, eds. Delhi, Permanent Black, 2002, 71-107.

hooks, bell. *Yearning: race, gender, and cultural politics*. Boston, South End Press, 1990.

Hughes, David McDermott. *Whiteness in Zimbabwe: Race, Landscape, and the Problem of Belonging*. New York, Palgrave Macmillan, 2010.

Huhndorf, Shari M. *Going Native: Indians in the American Cultural Imagination*. Ithaca, Cornell University Press, 2001.

Kanneh, Kadiatu. *African Identities: Race, Nation and Culture in Ethnography, Pan-Africanism and Black Literatures*. London, Routledge, 1998.

Krog, Antjie. *Begging to be Black*. Cape Town, Random House Struik, 2009.

Morrison, Toni. "Unspeakable Things Unspoken: The Afro-American Presence in American Literature." The Tanner Lectures on Human Values delivered at The University of Michigan, October 7, 1988, pp. 123-163.

Pilossof, Rory. *The Unbearable Whiteness of Being: Farmers' Voices from Zimbabwe*. Harare, Weaver Press, 2012.

Ranger, Terence. *Voices from the Rocks: Nature, Culture, and History in the Matopos Hills of Zimbabwe*. Bloomington, Indiana University Press, 1999.

Roediger, David, R. *The Wages of Whiteness: Race and the Making of the American Working Class (Revised)*. London, Verso, 2007.

Rosaldo, Renalto. "Imperialist Nostalgia." *Culture and Truth: The Remaking of Social Analysis*. Boston, Beacon Press, 1989, pp. 68-87.

Voigt, Lisa. *Writing Captivity in the Early Modern Atlantic: Circulations of Knowledge and Authority in the Iberian and English Imperial Worlds*. Chapel Hill, University of North Carolina Press, 2009.

Ware, Vron. "'A thinning of skin': Writing on and against whiteness." *Life Writing*, 10.3, 2013, pp. 245-260.

Williams, Patricia, J. "The Ethnic Scarring of American Whiteness." *The House that Race Built*. Edited and Introduced by Lubiano Wahneema. New York, Vintage Books, 1998, pp. 253-263.

Zenenga, Praise. "From the Fringe to Centre Stage: Performing Whiteness and the Changing Notions of Blackness in Zimbabwean Theatre and Everyday Life." *Imagining Citizenship in Zimbabwe*. David Kaulemu, ed. Harare, The Konrad-Adenauer-Stiftung, 2013, pp. 165-183.

Endnotes

1   The crises of whiteness in postcolonial Zimbabwe and post-apartheid South Africa can be described in many different ways, depending on the issues, individuals/groups, and contexts being explained and analysed. My analysis is based strictly on the literary reflections of two writers, not the literary views of all white writers, and does not attempt to extend itself into delving into the different racial orders in each country and their different roles in the global economy. This task would require a different project and methodology.

2   Interesting variants on this cultural, social, and political introspection instigated by postcolonial blackness explore sexual and social transactions be-

tween invariably guilt-ridden, and often derelict white males and black girls (some foreigners from other African countries) in post-apartheid South Africa. I do not have space to discuss these examples as I am more interested in the politics and contradictions of going native in works that respond more explicitly to public politics.

3   In *I Write What I Like*, Biko has an article titled "Black Souls in White Skins?," which echoes Fanon's *Black Skins, White Masks*. He argues strongly against unequal integration and white liberals, and stresses that, "For one cannot escape the fact that the culture shared by the majority group in any given society must ultimately determine the broad direction taken by the joint culture of that society. This need not cramp the style of those who feel differently but on the whole, a country in Africa, in which the majority of the people are African must inevitably exhibit African values and be truly African in style" (26). Antjie Krog is very much aware of this debate and context, and in *Begging to be Black*, she asserts: "But, actually, black people are in the majority and it is I who should be moving towards a 'state of non-personal power' within blackness" (94).

4   Joe Slovo is considered a white hero who fought against apartheid alongside the oppressed black people of South Africa. Cecil John Rhodes is the infamous colonizer who dreamt of handing over to the British Queen the rest of Africa from Cape to Cairo! He also had a country, Rhodesia, named after him. Rhodesia is the colonial name of modern Zimbabwe.

5   It is useful to make careful comparisons with David Roediger's study of blackface minstrelsy, where whites usurped black expressive arts and inventiveness at the same time doing violence to actual blacks.

Section Four:
Post-Script

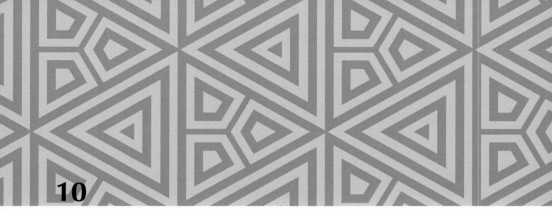

10

#WeAreNomzamo—Diasporic Intergenerational Testimonies Speaking Out Today Against the Erasure of Winnie Madikizela Mandela

Natalia Molebatsi & Jeanne Scheper

When the Anti-Apartheid freedom fighter, Winnie Nomzamo Zanyiwe Madikizela Mandela died at the age of 81, on 2 April 2018, a revolution was born. A fire was ignited, perhaps one that was always already there smoldering in smoke. This was a revolution that had been brewing out of necessity, not out of luxury—the necessity of being heard as women.

Even after a negotiated democracy in 1994, she knew that not all was well, and she continued to resist with her voice: a woman's voice, a Black woman's voice. Unlike many other leaders, she always embraced the most marginalized, continued to live in Soweto till her death, and was always particularly embraced by young people. So, when she died in April 2018, that day there was a spark that ignited especially younger women activists and feminists that refused to acquiesce to the constant refrain of demonization and erasure of our Black women icons—who are signifiers for all Black women. Recognizing these cruel erasures are systemic and epidemic, women refused to let these narratives that would demonize in order to diminish and efface stand unchallenged. In symbolic unison, women wore black and doeks, declaring #AllBlackWithADoek, and proclaiming Amandla! [Power!] to visually and symbolically unify and declare themselves the feminist afterlives of Mandela's work.

Winnie Mandela's life represents the utmost fight against the abuse of Black people. This is what matters, these young reignited activists have decreed. Her life, too, was and is a symbol of how racism and patriarchy always work against Black women, even the Black women who fight for the eradication of the same inequalities. Winnie Mandela's life gave birth to #WeAreNomzamo #SheDidNotDie #SheMultiplied among other declarations that echo through, but also go far beyond, social media and twitter hashtags. On 1 August 2018, the full scale and scope of the reverberations of her passing was expressed in the TotalShutDown. The TotalShutDown was an intersectional women's march against gender-based violence and an epidemic of rape that takes place today. As this movement made its way across the streets of Southern Africa, one of its catalysts and inspirations and truths was the life, the politics (both personal and universal), and the recognition of the significance and magnitude of the impact of the death/life of Winnie Mandela. TotalShutDown was the expression of this multifaceted loss in all its complexity and its power to ignite the future. This march was intended to multiply the personal and political work that this struggle icon embodied. This march was born out of the necessity to speak, walk, and live against the erasure and violence undergone by Black women in South Africa and globally.

Out of the death of Winnie Mandela come literary works such as Sisonke Msimang's *The Resurrection of Winnie Mandela*, which look at the icon's life before and beyond her struggle against apartheid—as well as beyond her representation as Nelson Mandela's wife. This book demonstrates how Winnie was a freedom fighter, an intellectual long before Nelson Mandela walked into her life. The book is narrated as a conversation between the writer and the late Madikizela Mandela.

This work and South African works like it are kin to the works produced here by students at the University of California, Irvine, students in Prof. Tiffany Willoughby-Herard's *African Feminisms* course, a seminar organized around contemporary political movements and campaigns against gender based violence in South Africa.[1] We see how what is being born out of the icon's death is an expanding intersectional, intergenerational, diasporic conversation, ignited for freedom. Out of research and reflection—tools that were historically blocked by apartheid's machinery—young Black feminists use their connection to the life of Madikizela Mandela, to her spoken and written words, to her acts both quotidian and monumental, as a touchstone and an elixir of courage. These young feminist freedom fighters will continue to carve a narrative and to clear a path with the fire of their own words that recognizes that truths and realities of all Black women, realities that require resilience, fierce truth-speaking, and a refusal to be locked away or silenced.

Endnote

1   The course Description reads: "Introduce students to concepts of gender and feminist activist movements generated and led by and about women and gender outlaws from the African continent and the context in which rebellion, social protest and transformation occurs. We will explore a range of texts: poetry collections, fiction, prison memoirs, social commentaries, films, and cultural and social histories. We will engage heavily (almost exclusively) on South African materials by poet Koleka Putuma; filmmakers Bev Ditsie and Rehad Desai; photographer Zanele Muholi; feminist cultural studies scholars Pumla Gqola & Devarakshanam (Betty) Govinden; and freedom fighter Winnie Madikizela-Mandela. Prominent exceptions include Ghanaian classic, *Our Sister Killjoy* by Ama Ata Aidoo; Senegalese filmmaker Ousmane Sembène's tour de force *Black Girl*; and British Zimbabwean director and screenwriter, Ingrid Sinclair's prized *Flame*."

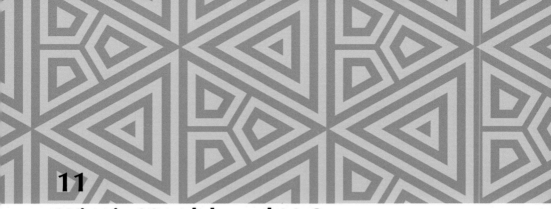

11

Winnie Mandela and Me?

Alyana Reid

Like Winnie
I wish I could believe in something so much
That my voice pours out of me into the ground.
I'd push my feet below the dirt
Even through the twigs, rocks, and glass
Plant myself so deep it's impossible to dig me out

But my voice is a whisper
Lost without direction
Standing still silently watching the world burn
Hiding alone cause we learned how to cry silently.

For Winnie
Behind walls she grew louder and louder
Stronger with power despite the prison cell

Her roots reached out to all who needed her
She sang words to ignite the world
She was fearless when they tried to cut her down
But her voice was too strong

To be lost without words has been my prison of thought
My voice hidden away has made me miss too much
But Winnie for me is all that I crave to be.

She's the words
The strength

The power
The selflessness
She moved through the waves that push me back

She is all that I lack.

12

491 Days:
A Visual Reflection

Aditi Mayer

Artist Statement:

In this visual series, photographer Aditi Mayer reflects on the memoir of Winnie Mandela's 491 days as a prisoner, exploring themes of bodily deterioration, solidarity confinement, and familial ties. The series includes excerpts from Winnie's journals and letters, documenting the highs and lows of her experience—from ruminating suicide, to the love for her family that frames her decisions.

The leading visual elements of the collection images include callousness of the human body, and motifs of erasure and solitude—both mental and physical, and generational legacy. The concluding photos pay homage to Winnie's legacy, who had aged through the brutal torture of the apartheid regime, yet left a history of resistance to be reflected in the future generation of activists.

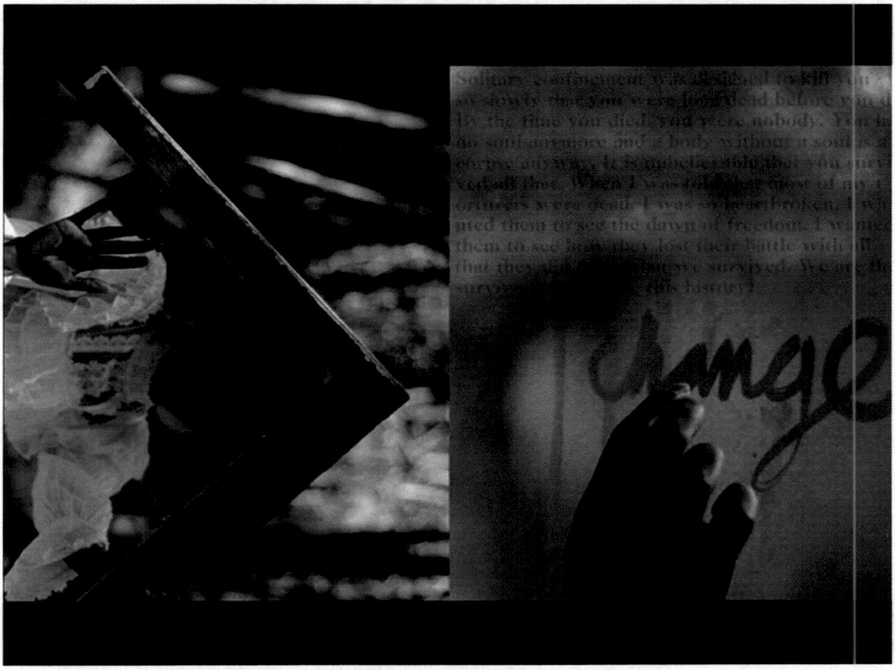
change

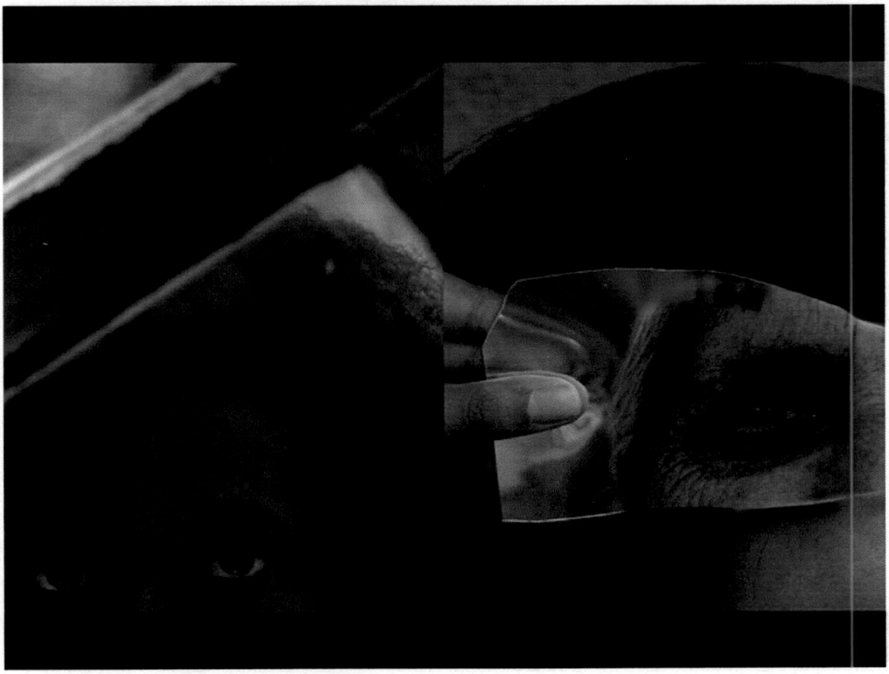

13

Frequently Asked Questions

Lara Nguyen

Dear Winnie,

I write this to you as I would write to my ancestors who have paved the long road towards liberation before me.
I write this to you as your husband did, with utmost admiration and respect for his hero, South Africa's hero, and mine.
I write this as co-conspirator in your everlasting plight for justice.

But admittedly, I do not understand:
My pessimism and detachment from reality derive nascent questions so intrusive, yet so superficial, I know, but a mind cannot fathom
How did you endure? (solitary confinement, legal torture, prison conditions)
Persist (for kinfolk, uncertain tomorrows, attempted suicide)
And live to recount the trauma of your 491 days as prisoner to your state? (without reparations)
Perhaps, there are no words in your colonizers' tongue that enunciate what fellow men are capable of
executing
Or perhaps there are yet words for black women who become militant revolutionaries, activists, and mothers
Out of survival for whole generations

You have humanized so much of what it means to be a foot soldier in the frontlines
of a struggle I am not quite sure we ever reign as victors
We are sliding, Winnie

Degenerating beneath the era of apartheid, into an age of Aryan reclamation and blissful ignorance
we supplement this reconfiguration of reality with buzzwords such as diversity or inclusion without questioning hypocritical pedagogy,
and wonder why emboldened supremacists can sometimes be your skin
shooting 16 gunshots in 14.2 seconds at Laquan McDonald
in a mosque,
emboldened by a manifesto, citing our president

For ephemeral hope, I look into your sharp mind
to play Monopoly better than our oppressor
When white men define "police brutality", my heart will mimic the steady knocks on your door when Zindzi and Zeni were orphaned at 2:30am
When McGraw Hill dilutes mass incarceration, the editors leave 'political asphyxiation of black consciousness' in the footnotes or

> Apartheid- systematic erasure/ murder
> Solitary confinement- death not liable
> Poverty- capitalistic rationing
> Neoliberalism- 21st century slavery
> Winnie Mandela- warrior of the underground, not just a wife

When I see Mandela quotes etched on the side of some suburban middle school, I'll champion Madikizela instead

But Winnie, I have a question or two
They say, 'the chains of your body are often the wings to the spirit'
to which I inquire, under whose sky? Robert Kelly's? Are our oppressors now, once our accomplices before?
It seems as though with every generation we metamorphosize back into old addictions
like biting fingernails or abusive relationships,
we say "this time is different"

> To subside the black lives matter protests
> To desensitize bombings against black and brown bodies
> To appease black moderates and appropriate Obama

Your soul must be tired, but your legacy tirelessly lives on...

Please respond at your earliest convenience.

Faithfully yours,
Lara

14

—The Afro-Boricua Blog—March 15, 2019
What Zanyiwe Madikizela Taught Me in 240 Pages[1]

Ariana Bolton

Recently in my African feminisms class I was assigned to read *491 Days: Prisoner Number 1323/69* by Winnie Madikizela-Mandela. Her book consists of pages from the journal she kept while in prison and the various letters written about her imprisonment, trial and personal life. In these pages we see the horrors of apartheid and the Nationalists government in South Africa in the late 60s and early 70s. We also see her resilience and commitment to her people.

Winnie is writing from prison where she and 21 others are being detained under the Terrorism Act of 1967 for their involvement with the freedom struggle and the African National Congress. Under this act, the state can keep her in prison for 8 years without charging her with a crime. For 491 days Winnie is kept in solitary confinement and is watched over by white female matrons who are brutal. She reports that her cell is 15 x 5 and that she is given two mats and some old blankets to sleep with. There is a light in her cell that is on for 24 hours a day. It keeps her from being able to discern what time of day it is. She has one bucket where she is expected to wash herself and her dishes and also use as a restroom.

The conditions in the prison are abysmal and made to dehumanize her and the other detainees. They don't always give them three meals a day and the meals they do get are often rotten and filled with maggots. They often are left in their cells for days at a time, not allowing them the exercise outside that the prisoners are entitled to. Winnie's cell is right by the torture room and she can hear screaming at all hours, which was a tactic to worsen her conditions in solitary confinement.

She details very extensively the dehumanizing tactics that the prison officials use. She talks about how their number one mission was to make them believe that they were no one, unimportant and forgotten about by everyone. This wasn't just the goal for the prisoners but for all Black people in South Africa. One thing that I found to be the most inhumane was the withholding of the medication she needed for her heart condition. As a result, she starts having "attacks" which consist of muscle spasms, blackouts, labored breathing and an irregular heartbeat. They also strip search her and force her to go without bathing since the shower they built was outside and unusable during winter. All these things were tactics to keep her weak, depressed, and hopeless.

But despite the fact that Winnie is subjected to these horrendous prison conditions she never gives up and this is what I love so much about her. She has a deep love for her people that sustains her when she feels like it might all be too much. Even when she thought of suicide, she was thinking about the benefit that it would have for her people. At every turn she is as witty and defiant as if she wasn't facing an oppressive regime that was determined to kill her. In May 1970 Winnie was taken to the Compol Building for an interrogation by Major Swanepoel and Major Ferreira. They had kept her awake for five days and six nights in an effort to get her delirious enough to answer their questions. But despite their best efforts Winnie was as sharp as ever.

When they ask her why she isn't happy or why she has lost weight she replies with, "I am not in the habit of answering the obvious" (37). She refuses to answer questions that they know the answer to. The prison conditions that they have put her through are the reasons for her depression, declining health and weight loss. They have deprived her of meals in sanitary conditions, of sleep, of her medication and of human contact and they have the audacity to ask her what's wrong. She is showing us how the state uses gas lighting techniques to try and make her doubt herself and her cause.

Later in the interrogation, Major Ferreira brings her a copy of the Terrorism Act of 1967 to remind her that they can interrogate her for as long as they like. However, the only copy they had was in Afrikaans. Major Ferreira asks her if she can read Afrikaans and Winnie recounts saying, "I speak the language of my first oppressor and that the raw and underdeveloped so-called language of my second oppressor was not compulsory in the Cape where I was educated" (38). She makes both Majors furious with her lack of fear. In one sentence Winnie disrespects everything the Afrikaners have tried to do. She calls their language "raw" and "undeveloped" reducing their language to something that is barbaric, an attempt at language. They think they hold all the power over Winnie but she reminds them at every turn that they do not. In the same interrogation she reminds them that she has the world on her side and they are an "isolated minority" (37).

This is the Winnie that electrified me and made me want to read more. This is a woman who is constantly being underestimated by the Nationalists. They assume that she's just Nelson Mandela's wife, someone so unimportant that her name not even be used when referring to her. But she is so much more. She is Zanyiwe Madikizela and she reminded the world of that with her activism and dedication. Being just Mandela's wife was never how she identified herself. In the epilogue she writes, "I will not even bask in his politics, I am going to form my own identity because I never did bask in his ideas. I had my own mind" (237). This is what I love about her. She isn't satisfied with being remembered as his wife, she was an integral part of the freedom struggle and a prominent leader of the ANC and she's not about to let you forget it.

She was involved in the military wing of the ANC and was also a leader of the underground struggle. Her involvement with the ANC was never about carrying out her husband's orders, she made decisions and plans on her own and was respected in her own right. She organized meetings and when she was on house arrest she often snuck out in disguise to recruit people to the ANC. Winnie's political activity didn't start when she married her husband. She had always had a strong sense of self and knew that she wanted better for herself and her people. She was a rebel and an activist and she constantly reminded her oppressors just how powerful, strong and determined she was.

Winnie taught me a lot about myself and the woman that I wish to be. Her devotion to her cause is what I loved the most. The Nationalists put her through extreme conditions that most people would never be able to cope with. She did struggle but she never let her oppressors know. Her ability to stay defiant even when faced with the torture room was supported by her knowledge that what she was fighting for was moral and just. Her fight was for the liberation of her people from this oppressive regime that wants all Black people to feel like nobodies with no value. She was fighting for her land back, for the life that her grandmother had lived when she was the first of the chief's wives to be a shopkeeper. She wanted her homeland to belong back to her people.

Winnie gives me the determination to continue forward. If she can be kept awake for five days and six nights and still manage to completely read her interrogators to filth, then I can challenge white supremacy in my everyday life. Her writings about fighting for her identity especially resonated with me. Winnie was writing in the 60's and 70's when women were expected to make being a wife and mother their main identity. This is still true for women today. While we enjoy fewer restrictions on how we should live our lives, there is still this expectation for us to put others before ourselves. She makes me less afraid to be strong in my convictions and reminds me that a woman's place is in the revolution, not just to serve as agents for other people, but as leaders.

In the epilogue, Winnie writes that she published her journal and letters so that future generations would know what it was like and so they can, "see to it that the country never ever degenerates to levels such as those" (239). That is the most important lesson in all of this. The reason she detailed every horrible thing that happened, every letter that was written and every conversation that was had, was so that we could understand how bad it can get. It was all to show us what the state was willing to do to maintain itself and what the state is slowly slipping back into. Her book is a call to action to wake up and look at the conditions around you. Winnie created a living archive while she was in prison. She knew that her story and the story of those around her would be important in mobilizing future generations.

For us in the United States, her message is crucial. With the rise of social media and technology, it is important for us to use all the platforms we have to say, "HERE. LOOK. Look at what white supremacy and anti-blackness are doing to them, to me, to us. Look at the tactics they use against us. Look at how they dehumanize us." Its important that we create living archives that capture our everyday reality. Whether it's a paper diary or an online one, we need to be creating the type of records that Winnie kept. It is often hard for us to view the brutality done to others in the past and connect it with our reality today, but it is crucial that we do so.

We are not free from the violence and oppression that Winnie faced. We are separating and detaining families that try to cross the border, we are incarcerating more people than any other country in the world, we have murderous police patrolling our communities, and extreme levels of hate crimes, rapes, and murders. We also have our own version of the Terrorism Act called the Patriot Act of 2001, which we must fight as fiercely as Winnie did. We owe it to her and future generations to document, fight and eradicate oppression and dehumanization where ever we find it.—A.B

EndNote

1   ARTIST STATEMENT: I decided that creating the Afro-Boricua blog would be the best way to present Winnie Mandela's life and activism. Blog posts are, typically, short and easy reads that can spark curiosity and conversation. They are also great for people who might feel alienated by academic writing and make topics like South African history more approachable. I spend a lot of time on social media, usually looking at things that aren't related to academics, so I thought it would make academics approachable for people who don't think of themselves as scholars. Often on social media platforms like Tumblr, there are people who write short, beautiful pieces of writing that can stimulate conversation on a topic. This was my hope for my blog

post on Winnie Mandela. After reading her book, I wanted others to understand the impact her words had on me. I wanted to give people who are just scrolling though social media a brief understanding of her book in hopes that they would read the book for themselves and allow Winnie to fill them with strength and perseverance.

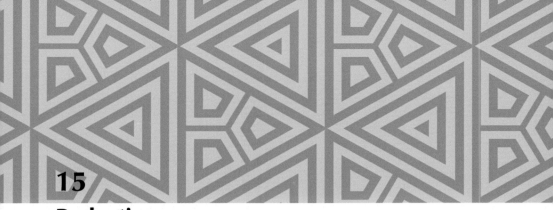

15

Redactions:
A Retelling of Winnie Madikzela-Mandela's Story

Callan Grace Garber

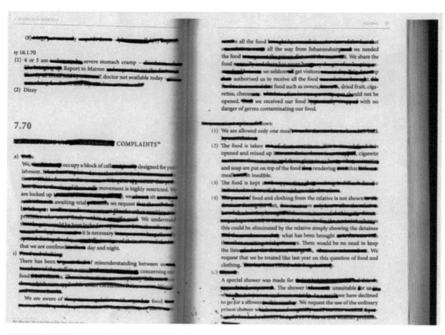

(8)

ty 16.1.70
(1) 4 or 5 am ▮▮▮ severe stomach cramp – ▮▮▮ Report to Matron ▮▮▮ doctor not available today ▮▮▮

(2) Dizzy

7.70

▮▮▮ COMPLAINTS"

a) ▮▮▮
We, ▮▮▮ occupy a block of cell ▮▮▮ designed for ▮▮▮ ishment. ▮▮▮ movement is highly restricted. ▮▮▮ are locked up ▮▮▮ awaiting-trial ▮▮▮ we request ▮▮▮ We understand ▮▮▮ it is necessary ▮▮▮ that we are confined ▮▮▮ day and night.

)
There has been ▮▮▮ f misunderstanding between us ▮▮▮ concerning ▮▮▮ food ▮▮▮
We are aware of ▮▮▮ food. ▮▮▮

▮▮▮ e all the food ▮▮▮ at ▮▮▮ all the way from Johannesburg ▮▮▮ we needed the food ▮▮▮. We share the food ▮▮▮ we seldom ▮▮▮ get visitors ▮▮▮ authorised us to receive all the food ▮▮▮ food such as sweets, ▮▮▮ dried fruit, cigarettes, cheese ▮▮▮ ould not be opened. ▮▮▮ we received our food ▮▮▮ with no danger of germs contaminating our food.

▮▮▮
(1) We are allowed only one meal ▮▮▮
(2) The food is taken ▮▮▮ opened and mixed up ▮▮▮ cigarette and soap are put on top of the food ▮▮▮ rendering ▮▮▮ this ▮▮▮ meal ▮▮▮ h inedible.
(3) The food is kept ▮▮▮
(4) ▮▮▮ f food and clothing from the relative is not shown ▮▮▮ this could be eliminated by the relative simply showing the detainee ▮▮▮ what has been brought ▮▮▮ s. There would be no need to keep the lists ▮▮▮. We request that we be treated like last year on this question of food and clothing. ▮▮▮
(c) ▮▮▮
A special shower was made for ▮▮▮. The shower ▮▮▮ unsuitable for us ▮▮▮ we have declined to go for a shower ▮▮▮. We request the use of the ordinary prison shower ▮▮▮

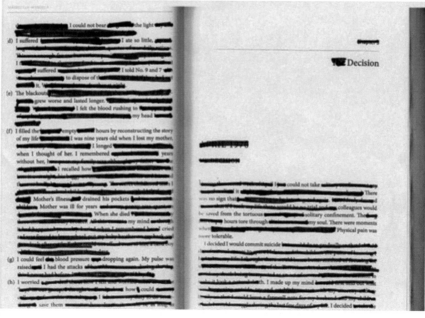

▮▮▮ I could not bear ▮▮▮ the light ▮▮▮
d) I suffered ▮▮▮ I ate so little, ▮▮▮
I ▮▮▮ suffered ▮▮▮ I told No. 9 and 7 ▮▮▮ to dispose of t ▮▮▮ it. ▮▮▮
(e) The blackout ▮▮▮ grew worse and lasted longer. ▮▮▮ I felt the blood rushing to ▮▮▮ my head ▮▮▮
(f) I filled the ▮▮▮ empty ▮▮▮ hours by reconstructing the story of my life ▮▮▮ I was nine years old when I lost my mother. ▮▮▮ I longed ▮▮▮ when I thought of her. I remembered ▮▮▮ years without her, h ▮▮▮ I recalled how ▮▮▮ Mother's illness ▮▮▮ drained his pockets ▮▮▮ Mother was ill for years ▮▮▮ When she died ▮▮▮ my mind ▮▮▮ cried ▮▮▮
(g) I could feel ▮▮▮ blood pressure ▮▮▮ dropping again. My pulse was raised ▮▮▮ I had the attacks ▮▮▮
(h) I worried ▮▮▮ how ▮▮▮ could ▮▮▮ save them ▮▮▮

Decision

▮▮▮ 1970

▮▮▮ could not take ▮▮▮ There ▮▮▮ as no sign that ▮▮▮ colleagues would be saved from the tortuous ▮▮▮ solitary confinement. The ▮▮▮ hours tore through ▮▮▮ my soul. There were moments when ▮▮▮ Physical pain was more tolerable.
I decided I would commit suicide ▮▮▮ h. I made up my mind ▮▮▮ I decided ▮▮▮

16

Winnie Mandela's Blueprint

Alexa Dorsett-Levingston

When telling the story of Winnie Mandela, I think it is important for people who have never heard of her to know that she was a strong woman, a mentally disciplined woman, a resilient woman, a determined woman, an intelligent woman and so on. Amongst other commendable characteristics, she gave the future generations an idea of what it means to fight, in an emotional, mental and physical aspect. Her journals that document her journey while in prison, capture the pain she endured while she was extremely sick and subjected to solitary confinement for over a year. More importantly, as she was isolated from her family with no knowledge of where her children were and subjected to inhumane living conditions; she never lost sight of the fight.

This is the chorus of her story followed by a spoken word.

> *Trying to break my spirit down, until there's nothing left in me*
> *You don't acknowledge that I have emotions*
> *You Don't allow me to feel anything.*
> *this is the fight of my life, for your life.*
> *Freedom is the destiny*
> *Can't lose sight all the power is in me…*
> *…*
> *How long could you last?*
> *Being forced to listen to cries and screams,*
> *Forced to suffer because your life is not even considered a life at all*
> *How long could you last in a chamber meant to break your soul?*
> *No writing allowed.*
> *No interactions allowed.*
> *No freedom allowed.*

How dare you ask for such a thing!
No fighting for your life.
You are placed here to die.
How long could you last not knowing where your family sleeps at night?
How long could you manage to stay sane, not knowing where your children are?
Give up.
Lose hope.
In this place, there is only room for brokenness…
You are not supposed to leave here the same.
You are to be broken.
Broken will be your new name.
How long could you last malnourished?
How long?
Maybe a day? Maybe a week? How about one month?
1 year.
Winnie Madikizela-Mandela survived 1 year.

It is important to Remember Mrs. Mandela's story because it shows what it means to fight for something. We should remember that people that speak against dominant structures in society become targets of the state. In the same way the Marikana Miners in the documentary film *Miners Shot Down,* challenged the way society was structured; we can observe how there is a very close relationship between the struggles of the miners and Mrs. Mandela. After watching the devasting and grossly inhumane shooting of the innocent Miners, I was deeply saddened at the blatant disrespect for human life. In the same way Winne Mandela's journals give an insight to the unethical arrest and treatment while incarcerated; there is a commonality in how power lies in our voices. It is evident however, that some people are not meant to speak and be heard, and when they attempt to open their mouths, they are reminded of how insignificant their lives are viewed as and their body's disposition in society. The tactics used to legitimize this begins with criminalizing the groups. When people are labeled criminals it automatically strips them of respect and justifies harsh and even irrational punishments. In both the film and book, we can see how both the miners and Mrs. Mandela were construed as a threat and danger that required control.

Another tactic used to try and destabilize these activists was through breaking them down mentally. In Mandela's case, solitary confinement slowly gnawed at her mind. Isolation is a devil, and it can make someone lose site of the big picture. My mother who worked in the Los Angeles Sherriff Department would tell me stories of how inmates would be taken to solitary confinement as punishment, especially for inmates who were mentally not well. One story in particular was about an inmate who was stripped from human contact, outside air, windows, and basically anything that gave a glimpse into reality; and he began to lose his sanity. Without the human decency of even having blankets, this inmate was being destabilized in every aspect. He later tried to claw his own eye out of his head. I remember hearing this story and wondering why anyone would do such harms to themselves. I believe the idea of solitary confinement is to break any hope left lingering. It is meant to make death seem more enjoyable than continuing to fight for life or freedom. I now understand the severity of what that inmate and countless others had to endure. Mandela's Journals express this process of incarceration taunting her to give up as she even plotted her own suicide strategically so that not only the other inmates brought in with her might be free in response to her death, but she could too.

The most challenging idea to swallow is that the people murdered and incarcerated in south Africa were not violent, yet such extreme forces of weaponry were used to mute them. And even in instances where the miners surrendered, with arms up, they were murdered for sport. The corrupt police force saw their deaths as a game. Listening to their tone, near the end of the massacre, I felt enraged at the lack of emotion and regard for humanity. It sends a message that certain bodies are not even bodies at all. One of the leaders of the miners says, "The blood of a rock driller is not different than that of a manager." Why does it take innocent bodies being shot at 14 times, dragged over one another, stomped on, and wounded to make people pay attention? Violence is too normalized, and we can observe how torture and pain plays an integral role in whose life matters and whose does not.

The fight for freedom and the fight for better compensation seems to be problematic because for the people suffering from it, it symbolizes the power to live. Apartheid in South Africa and the NUM maintained power structures that made it impossible for certain people to be seen, and it mocked their demands to be recognized as people with voices and a will to live. Even today, no police officer was charged with murder, which is a problem that also goes beyond South Africa. However, that only makes people yell louder and use their voices and dignity to form larger groups to speak up and continue the fight for freedom and life.

Standing over my dead body, the weight of your foot pounds on my half-beaten heart.
My life stolen
My body murdered... by the senseless movement of your trigger-happy fingers
Shot down because the power of my voice scared you.
My audacity to demand that you to recognize my life, shook you

Feel our presence
Hear our cries and listen
Let the voices left behind on this mountain, sink into the depths of your
rotten souls…

(reflective writing for the miners who fought)

The unwavering determination of Mrs. Mandela, to change apartheid in South Africa is what led her to be arrested under the Suppression of Communism Act. Her choice was beyond her life as this change would affect her children and the generations to follow. We should remember that she risked her life out of selflessness. To the People who have never heard of Winnie Madikizela-Mandela, she was targeted because she challenged the way society was structured. The fear that dominant structures invoked in people, sent a message that their voices were to be silenced. From being arrested in front of her children, separated from her husband, suffering from a heart condition without proper treatment, to being forced to live in unsanitary and inhumane conditions. The message being sent to her was that she was invisible, her pain was disregarded, and her dreams of freedom for herself and her children were impossible to achieve. The torture that she experienced was heartbreaking and unfathomable to wrap my head around. Those who were courageous enough to speak out against apartheid and injustices of the state, put their lives on the line with death or prison being a reality to face. However, she chose to take the risk and laid out a blueprint for future generations to follow.

17

The Audacity to Exist

Kamerahn Francisco-Latiti

I have sieged the reigns of the war
Without permission, I have dared to live
Without empathy, I have thrusted my body forward
Into the pit of inevitable agony

Chains, they suffocate the confines of my skin
No greater than the way illness finds comfort in my body

Still, I stare further into the horizon
Dreaming of the high-end grass fields
Where children play endlessly,
Running into an eternity of sophisticated chivalry

I reach the rendezvous point where love awaits my arrival,
And, subsequently I extend my hand to greet its presence
Pride, quite the entrance you have made
Will you stay a while longer?
Time is ticking, said time is not linear
So will you continue to exists in different realms
So that I may collide with tragedy
At times when you are needed the most?

[*A Personal Narrative*] I have taken a maternal leave from being an occupant
in my own children's lives
So that I may fulfill the duty of carrying the heart of a nation
In my fragile, yet sturdy womb

But is this the life that I asked for?

Perhaps the idea of consent is put into question
For one does not choose to be a revolutionary;
I live on the premise of higher fulfillment
And duty to those who need me
Even if it means being taken away
From those who love me

But is this the life that I asked for?

The question is counterproductive to the cause
So don't look for me when the time comes
When I must face the detriments
Of having **the audacity to exist**

If we wait forever to find distorted meaning behind our motives
We may forget to ACT when time calls for action
So of course,
This was never the life that I asked for
But it was the life that I found worth living
Through you, through I, through them, through we, through us.

18

Those Walls

Sydney Diane Lara

> In this cell so many of my people have spent tortuous moments. The
> walls are an encyclopaedia on the different types of persons held in the
> cell at one time or another […] It's so easy to tell what state of mind
> each prisoner was in, this mute expression—writing on the wall is the
> only emotional catharsis for a prisoner in solitary confinement. Why,
> you may even guess the prisoner's personality from this writing.
>
> Winnie Madikizela-Mandela[1]

The walls have a heartbeat
it's the echo of your steps
as you pace around the cell

The walls have ears
they listen to your stories
your tales of your families
having listened to countless others
a better listener than any person

The walls have arms
they pull you out of that drowning silence
and wipe away the tears
your hands are too tired to get
The walls have a voice
when all *They* allow you is
Nothing

you learn to hear it
to hear the stories it carries
they hold survival within
When *Their* treatment of you
your family
your people
gets too much
it reminds you
why you're fighting

The walls don't have eyes
the piercing gaze, the scrutiny, the surveillance
that washes over you
doesn't belong to the walls
It belongs to *Them*

Endnote

1   *491 Days 491 Days: Prisoner Number 1323/69.*

19

She Prevailed in the Face of Weaponized Isolation and Loneliness

R.M. Corbin

Winnie Madikizela-Mandela's *491 Days: Prisoner Number 1323/69* is a profoundly lonely book. But, not in the traditionally romantic or abstract sense: it's about a particular brand of institutionalized loneliness—the ways that solitude and the psychological discord that follows it have been weaponized by colonial systems in South Africa in an attempt to break the will and resolve of activists and radical thinkers like Mandela. More than this, the book speaks to the immense and formidable strength of will that Mandela possessed in the face of such sadistic methods of deconstruction. Given the formal nature of the book, a collection of diary entries and letters, the narrative speaks to a persistent dialogue despite long-term isolation and abuse: the strength inherent to and stemming from a constant reaching-out. Ultimately, what the reader receives is a message on the importance of persistent and constructive interpersonal connection to individual and collective restorative activism, an image of a system that is aware of that and attempts to stamp it out at any given opportunity, and the means through which one can persist or skirt these attempts in order to maintain and perpetuate activism despite isolation.

The theme of radical connectivity is present in the very skeleton of the book—Mandela's narrative is built from diary entries and letters, both of which are practical deployments of written dialogue. If the story had been presented omnisciently, as a presence that was not Mandela or the people connected to her (Nelson, her children, her family, fellow activists), it would have undermined the importance of the group around Winnie, both themselves as people and the social and political connections she had with them, to her survival while imprisoned. Though diary-keeping may not seem to be a dialogic practice, it can be seen as such in the larger understanding of interior language as well as, more importantly, Mandela's particular circumstances. Firstly, the nature and style of Mandela's diaries are not mere lamentation for her circumstances, but a concise and precise log of her time behind bars. They are purposeful. They're a kind of dialogue meant to not only keep Mandela intellectually and libidinally occupied, but to ensure that the entirety of her experience is logged for legal, personal, and larger educational potential. Through dialogue, Mandela both practically maintains and functionally perpetuates the importance of community to radical and restorative action. This practicality can be seen in her first actions upon being put into solitary confinement:

> The first thing you do when you get into a cell is to do a calendar, the very first day because you lose track of days when you are in solitary confinement because the light was on 24 hours and it was the brightest light - they never switched it off. You didn't know when it was sunset or daybreak, they never switched off the lights (9).

Mandela speaks of her experience not only as what she did, but what should be done if the reader ever finds themselves in a similar situation: she is fostering dialogue for both herself and for those who may find themselves in a similar situation—community within and without. The overarching nature of the entry shows an awareness on Mandela's part of not just connection across space, but across time. Her foresight reveals her understanding that her case will not be the last, and that pedagogy and shared experience are integral to the progress of social justice.

Isolation in Mandela's case was, ultimately, a means of quashing radical action among anti-apartheid forces by forcibly removing activists from their communities—the communities that they fought for and with, physically separating them from both the means and the end of their struggle. Mandela speaks to the psychologically damaging nature of solitary confinement:

> Being held incommunicado was the most cruel thing the Nationalists ever did. I'd communicate with the ants; anything that has life. If I had lice I would have even, I would have even nursed them. That's what this solitary confinement [does]; there is no worse punishment than that [...] with solitary confinement you are not allowed to read, you are not allowed to do anything, you have just yourself (57).

What Mandela truly longs for is some kind of communication: whether it be through a book, or even with insects. To be left alone, both in body and mind, is to be profoundly disempowered; which, given the pivotal notion of power, collective power, to radical movements, can be beyond damaging. But, through diaries and letters, the perpetuation of dialogue in the most practical and necessary forms, Mandela is able to retain communication, and thus retain her psychological fortitude and the community necessary to maintain and foster the future radical action that she will, undoubtedly, inspire.

It's important to recall the point of apartheid—the word literally means "separateness" in Afrikaans—being a system that attempts to manufacture false ontological rifts between people and peoples along race and gender lines in order to maintain minority rule in a hegemonic system. If one is able able to coerce or force the subjugated masses into splitting themselves apart, the population will lack the collective identity necessary to reinstate majority rule. It can come as no surprise, then, that solitary confinement became a regular tool of physical and psychological torture deployed against anti-apartheid activists like Winnie Mandela—it is the practical and poetic manifestation of the ideologies that drove and continue to drive apartheid and all other hegemonic states. But, on the other side, given her remarkable intellectual and psychological fortitude, it can also come as no surprise that Mandela knew this and had the clarity and foresight to understand that the demarcations created by apartheid and systems like it don't stop at physical or ideological space: they work across time, as well. Much like false racial categories and slavery separated African people from their histories, and thus the grander context through which one and many are able to establish a firm collective identity, solitary confinement separates an individual from time: a time that is necessary to own in order to possess political power. As quoted earlier, Mandela highlighted the timelessness that was necessary to solitary confinement, due to "the light [that] was on 24 hours" (9). This, like the rest of apartheid's subjugative systems, is not accidental. Just as it is integral to separate communities from their time, their historical context as well as control over their present use of time through exploitative work practices and curfews, apartheid systems must separate individuals from their time: both as a means of inducing disorientation and dissociation, but also to separate them from the power that possessed time can bring—control over narrative and action.

Speaking to control over narrative, it must also be noted that many of the letters sent between Winnie and Nelson Mandela did not make it to their addressee or had to be run through the Censor's office of Robben Island, whose entire position was to ensure that prisoners could not fully communicate with the outside world. Nelson Mandela spoke to this in a particular letter he wrote to the Commanding Officer of Robben Island on February 23, 1970 after not receiving letters that family had sent him:

> You will understand how important it is for a prisoner to be in regular contact with his friends and family. However most of the letters I have written in the last eight months did not reach their destination. Even the special and urgent letter that Colonel Van Aarde gave me personal

support for and which I gave to the censors on 19 November 1969 had
not reached its destination by 31 January (180).

Nelson's concerns not only speak to the enforced isolation of imprisoned
activists in South Africa, but the need for the systems that imprisoned
them to control the content of communication between prisoners and their
connections in the outside world. The very presence of a Censor's office
and the need for Nelson or Winnie Mandela to write their letters through
administrative or bureaucratic midpoints reveals the importance of a
possessed narrative to systems of colonial power—reality is formed from
collective discourse and collective experience—if you isolate individuals
or groups, control the quantity and quality of communication they can
carry with those outside, then you can attempt to dictate and control those
prisoner's perception of reality, manifesting the confusion necessary to
mask the sins of the state. Multiple letters in the book are addressed either to
Robben Island's Commanding Officer as an intermediary or mentioning the
black hole of the Censor's office that ensured letters never made it to their
destination (102, 123, 158, 161, 162, 169, 202), and they're all an integral
part of the narrative and its ultimate point: communication is integral to
activism, therefore corrupt systems will implement distinct means of altering
or altogether destroying means of communication between activists.

491 Days: Prisoner Number 1323/69 is a pedagogical text: we, the
reader, are meant to learn from it. Its progressive intent is not incidental or a
post-construction implemented by the editors of the book, but is present in
the very content of Winnie Mandela's diaries and letters. Even under the most
profound duress, she understood that her position was not one that called
for lamentation or temporal isolation, but rather an awareness of herself
as part of a continuum of activism present within a continuum of systemic
oppression. After all, Mandela was not the first anti-apartheid activist to be
imprisoned and was not the last. In the same vein, apartheid was not the first
system of racial separation and oppression and, likely and unfortunately,
will not be the last. Therefore, what can be found in the book is not just the
importance of interpersonal and intercollective communication to activism,
but the importance of communication across time, as well. One must fight
colonial systems, those that would seize and pervert time and space from
the subjugated, through the recapturing and reconstruction of communion
across time and space and the intentional restoration of historical and spatial
context. In that, weaponized isolation and loneliness cannot prevail.

Bibliography

Madikizela-Mandela, Winnie. *491 Days: Prisoner Number 1323/69*. Ohio
University Press, 2014.

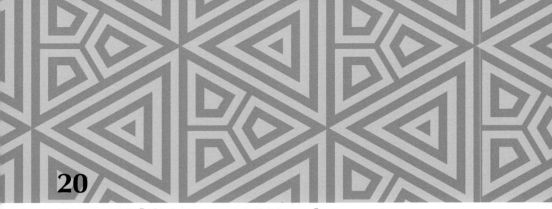

20

From Whimmen to Wombman to Woahmen

Maya Green

Winnie Madikizela-Mandela
You are a Mind Master, a Master of Minds
Keeping it together
When the world stands on your spine
You inspired
Teaching us how to battle
Even in the midst of struggle
You are a role model

You love for your people
The way you love for your life
You'll fight to the death
To bring better ways to thrive
We honor your Spirit
We honor your Heart
We honor your Valor
We thank you for proving apartheid is sour

Winnie Madikizela-Mandela
With an African Spirit
Strong as that of Colle Ardo[1]
You are recognized as a protector of generations
One who advocates for the love of all humans
For all people to be treated people

A woman in the herstory books
For being a hero to the oppressed
A philanthropist at heart
A soldier at best

You example the courage and strength
Of Wombman
In a time when they were thought to be
Whimman
By the oppressors

We are here to
Learn
Unpack
Value
Your lessons

We thank you for your battle
We laid you to rest
In nations' hearts
In generations' minds
You overcome time

We trailblaze on
To a future of Women
While you lay at peace in our souls,
Knowing you've passed the torch
To bright children

Endnote

1   Colle Ardo is Ousmane Sembène's courageous protagonist of the magisterial
     feminist film *Moolade* (2004).

21
Painting

Maya Green

22

Post-Script:
Movements After 1994 Respond to Exclusivity, Extravagance, and Hierarchy or Flesh of the City: From Section Ten Policies to Fees Must Fall

Tiffany Willoughby-Herard[1]

> Why Orji had been elected chief in the first place had been a puzzle to Ajuzia when he was much younger, but as he grew up and began to be better acquainted with the hypocrisy of the elders, who in spite of their long-winded orations about justice were prone to deviousness and chicanery, and who despite their frequent tributes to bravery in the past and present meekly submitted to cowardice under the scowl of the strong eye […] Orji had passed out bigger bribes than his opponents, and the village had voted overwhelmingly for him—in spite of the past, or perhaps because of it, since no one dared to take his money and not vote for him, even though the vote was by secret ballot.

> T. Obinkaram Echewa[2]

> We are more than champions, the people on our side, a people we are […] we celebrate this beautiful land drawn by its promise.

> Sibongile Khumalo[3]

This volume has created the opportunity to look back at the quotidian policies of social control and regulation that indicate how deeply embedded the cultures of state violence actually are. State violence is both the overt kind created by the military and police force, health system, educational institutions, etc. But state violence also represents the covert forms of interlocking and nested power that are normalized as the cost of bureaucracy, the cost of transition, the cost of bearing the dream of a free social democracy that is a moral beacon to the world. The context of normalized violence in the economic, financial, housing, welfare, health care, water and energy and infrastructure, regulation and insurance, and education sectors point to where the many fissures of rebellion are most likely to emerge.

One such rebellion occurred when Mary/Maria Rahube of Mabopane[4] went to court to sue for the right to purchase a home that she has lived in for four decades after her brother attempted to evict her. In a legal loophole taken advantage of by many during apartheid and since its demise, her brother became the legal owner of the home where she had raised her children and grandchildren. When South African courts had invalidated the discriminatory Section Ten Housing Laws of the apartheid era, her brother used the post-apartheid legal remedy that had been put in place to try to defraud her and her side of their family of their home. Prohibited under apartheid law (and criminalized for attempting to) as a black woman from owning land, she and other women could only own reside in urban housing if a male relative had a right to live there. Rahube was forced to take her case to court because the legal corrective, known as the Upgrading of Land Tenure Rights, converted rights of occupation to her brother, her adult male relative, ironically actually upholding the same land tenure system that obtained under apartheid. With his limited occupational right certificate secured under apartheid and a new body of housing law jurisprudence that sought to remedy the gendered racial wealth divide created by apartheid on his side, her brother began the process of eviction in 2009. After raising three generations in that home as the head of household, in 2017, finally the courts deliberated and parliament introduced legislation that would not automatically turn land occupied by women into commodity property for their male relatives.

Rahube's story illustrates for us how important a knowledge of the history of apartheid actually is for deciphering whether legal, cultural, and social remedies of the present actually do achieve the goals imagined by the people of South Africa or turn those goals on their heads. From housing displacement during the first era of mineral expansion to the 1913 Land Act, housing for black people has been largely a conscripted and gendered affair to make domestic, mining, industrial and sexual laborers easily available and easy to police.

Families like Mary/Maria Rahube's had experienced displacement several times over the course of the prior hundred years. They witnessed their land taken and their possessions destroyed after 1948 when her own family had been displaced from the Lady Selbourne area, a neighborhood established in 1905 by a Colored syndicate that by 1936 opened land ownership to black people. Hounded by laws and town council and national debates about "influx control," "slum clearance," and outbreaks of communicable diseases, the land set aside for Black residence inevitably became designated as places of social blight and economic stagnation

But so little of this history is accessible anymore. Instead the Rainbow Nation and World Cup Nation and the burgeoning Credit Card Nation are the social leitmotifs of the day as they create the terms for breezy social relations, easy affective responses, and interactions across persistent racialized, gendered, and spatialized class barriers. Schools, libraries, neighborhoods, universities, malls, and artistic societies are inclusive in name only—and only if Black people remain apologetic for their minoritized presence. Marikana and #RhodesMustFall/#FeesMustFall were not flashes in the pan, they were expressions of organized rebellion, despair, and demands for a political and economic order that has yet to materialize. In a way they were signals of a historical reckoning within black communities over the terms of national belonging and national meaning. Will the society continue to hold together in a context of airless and sterile consumer pursuits or will the art that is being made and the social challenges being leveled decisively puncture the ever more refined forms of exclusivity, extravagance, and hierarchy that signal the way black non-belonging is constructed in contemporary South Africa? What is the "Born-Free" Generation supposed to do with the knowledge that so much of what feels forced and strained is the result of concessions made, allegedly on their behalf?

Rhodes Must Fall/Fees Must Fall

In a country that is 80% Black, fewer than 25% of the premier University of Cape Town student body and fewer than 5% of the faculty is Black. How can that be? What sort of agreements made this possible? In a culture where white paternalism and promoting black mouthpieces who justify and benefit from the race, gender, and class divides that haunt post-apartheid, South Africa is facing a profound standoff with young people. Young people whose experiences, with the legacies of racism, expanding global apartheid, and deepening criminalization of and genocide against the poor, reveal that the promises of post-apartheid have not been kept—or even remembered. From throwing feces at the statue of Cecil Rhodes in September 2015 to Fees Must Fall in October of the same year, the national conversation about bringing the historically black technical schools and colleges under one administrative regime with the historically well funded and white universities was shifted forever. Young people had come to understand that the universities declared by Milner and Rhodes to have been built out of the flesh of their grandparents continued in that legacy undaunted. Susan Booysen's anthology, *Fees Must Fall: Student Revolt, Decolonisation, and Governance in South Africa* (Wits University Press 2018), is a key text for analysis.

Marikana Massacre

On the anniversary of the 1960 Sharpeville Massacre in mid August 2012, the owners of the Lonmin Platinum Mine (located about 100km away from Johannesburg) in the historic revolutionary area of Rustenberg responded to a wildcat strike among about 2,000 of their workers. The owners with the support of the National Union of Mineworkers called in South African Police and organized a day long stand off that resulted in the deaths of 44 people, 41 of whom were striking mineworkers killed by police. Also, during the same incident, at least 78 additional workers were injured. This launched a nation wide series of rolling strikes across the mining sector. One of the many important commentaries on Marikana is the Rehad Desai (2014) film, *Miners Shot Down*.

Landless Peoples Movement/ Shack Dweller's Movement

Marching under the banner "No Land, No House, No Vote" shackdwellers all over South Africa organized against electoral politics on election day in April 2004 sustaining arrests of 57 members who were tortured. Ongoing protests have faced police shooting rubber bullets, live ammunition, water cannons, arrest, arsons, and murder by the state and "middle class vigilantes." By 2008 various organizations including the Western Cape Anti-Eviction Campaign, the Abahalali baseMjondolo the Rural Network came together to found the Poor People's Alliance.

LGBTQIA Anti-Violence Activism

The names of activists like human rights and womens rights activist and filmmaker Bev Ditsie, photographer and visual artist Zanele Muholi and academics like Zethu Mathabeni have to be held up time and again for creating artistic and political spaces for responding to the violence of corrective rape and scapegoating Black LGBTQIA people. Ironically, they have been the most consistent in some ways about addressing black consciousness and the need to decolonize black heteropatriarchy and sex and gender normativity. Creating artistic spaces and community groups that represent and provide a black context for consciousness-raising about the toxic meanings and cultural logic of gender and gender based violence has been essential work.

Many of the spaces that they create work explicitly to name, condemn, and re-historicize the architecture of apartheid as a carceral state and society. Holding workshops and art exhibilitions at the Johannesburg Women's Prison about the lives of the women who were detained there and the policies that they had to live under are examples of the kinds of work that feminist and LGBTQIA activism continues to produce. Working explicitly in the spaces of state and interpersonal violence and criminalization was a choice and decision made by organizers to make sure that the history of black women's exclusion from public space (via immigration and employment and housing policies) and inclusion into public space (as representatives of the worst anti-black caricatures) is always being braided into the conversations about the possibilities of survival and self-knowing and the promises of rebellion.

Remembering the Past

In order to reclaim the institutions through which the social is organized, much more is required than hiring, access to credit for small businesses, access to high quality education, and more expansive pension plans. Indeed we learn from the miners and the students, contemporary activists that a fragile unjust peace continues. It is a threadbare seam that deserves to be explored in great detail. Sites of equal opportunity are producing ever more flagrant expressions of hierarchy and exclusivity and forms of entrenched and historical structural oppression operate with even fewer investments in remedies by the dominant electoral parties. Rape has not become an issue among social scientists and cultural critics for any prurient reasons or to get the attention of foreign donors, it is being raised because the context under which social reproduction is happening is shaped indelibly by the legacy of silence about sexualized torture and attacks on the body that are not a post-1994 phenomenon alone. For more scholarship on this topic see the following key texts: Pumla Gqola's *Rape: South African Nightmare* (Jacana Media 2016); Redi Thlabi's *Kwezi: The remarkable story of Fezekile Ntsukela Kuzwayo* (Jonathan Ball 2017);

Ronnie Kasrils' *A Simple Man: Kasrils and the Zuma Enigma* (Jacana Media 2018) and earlier works, especially Yvette Christianse's *Unconfessed* (2007) and *Deep HiStories: Gender and Colonialism in Southern Africa* (Brill Rodopi 2002) edited by Patricia Hayes, Wendy Woodward, and Gary Minkley, which describe and analyze these forms of gendering violence and sexualized subjection and the ways that rape has been established in the four centuries of making of modern South Africa.

How art is being made under such constraints, and the inability to guarantee that the future will be grand or safe or full of rainbow promises for everyone is a question that cannot be escaped. That black artists continue to make and sculpt the world according to their own imaginaries and in contradistinction to the world that is handed to them is both poignant and a testimony to not being wholly proscribed by being devalued, written off, and being reduced to living symbols of a country that so many people still wish to escape and to find an alternative to. While the rainbow imaginary is steadily fading, artists and critics and audiences who engage their work in the most robust ways possible stand still and look the history of apartheid and what it has made squarely in the face. So what might a return to the history remind us of? And how would certain aspects of this history especially using attention to the labors that are particular to nurturing, healing, and making the living sacred, help unpack the people who are on a move in South Africa today—organizing collectively to change the material conditions of desperation and institutionalized social disempowerment? Sasinda Futhi Siselapha is a project of witnessing where the transformation of conditions is actually happening.

In the history of urban housing laws we can access the historical antecedents of the forceable removals (from workplaces, housing, as well as from schools, libraries, and hospitals) and privatization of water and power (an other vital infrastructure) of today. In the practices of forceable removals and evacuation of the living and the dead—human and non-human we come to understand what compels feminist art making and practice because what is most often being removed and then denied again and again is life force, itself. These conditions though normalized today continue to be the central problems that animate the kind of artwork and cultural resistance that the authors herein explore.

In the words of Sibongile Khumalo, "This land, the whole land, it will be healed, it must be healed, it must be healed (*Breath of Life* 2016)."

Endnotes

1   The author wishes to express gratitude to Kia Lilly Caldwell and the 2016 African Diaspora Fellows Program Summer Institute at the University of North Carolina, Chapel Hill and Duke University. The program provides professional development to North Carolina teachers in African, African American, and African Diaspora Studies. Sixteen middle and high school teachers participated on July 12. This chapter was a presentation to these teachers and been incorporated into K-16 school curriculum standards in the state. It ends with organizing in 2017. Since that time a whole new set of organizing around Fees Must Fall has extended across the continent and transnationally, with expressions of its lessons all across Europe and North America. South African youth activists have been similarly influential across the globe on gender based violence. The August 2018 Total Shut Down March has been met with wide spread grassroots support and attention to levels of gender based violence and murder of womxn, children, and men across the globe.

South African artists and activists have been widely engaged in AfroFuturist convenings and the Black Lives Matter movement.

2   *The Crippled Dancer* (1986), p. 54.

3   "Warriors for Peace," Live Performance, Three Faces of Sibongile Khumalo, Market Theater, Johannesburg (Sept. 24, 2017), *Breath of Life* (2016).

4   Venter, Zelda. "Long arm of apartheid threatens woman's home." *Iol.com*, October 12, 2006, https://www.iol.co.za/news/south-africa/gauteng/long-arm-of-apartheid-threatens-womans-home-2079008. Accessed September 27, 2017; Venter, Zelda. "Gogo beats "racist, sexist land ownership laws." Iol.com, September 27, 2017. Accessed September 27, 2017; *Rahube v Rahube and Others (101250/2015) [2017] ZAGPPHC 651; 2018 (1) SA 638 (GP) (26 September 2017)*, South African Legal Information Institute http://www.saflii.org/za/cases/ZAGPPHC/2017/651.html. Accessed October 8, 2018.

Author Biographies

Ariana Bolton is an Afro-Latinx race and gender theorist alumna of the University of California, Irvine. Her primary research interests are introducing personal narrative to critical theory.

Zethu Cakata teaches Psychology at the University of South Africa. Nurturing young spirits in search of their true selves. On a personal journey of self-discovery and in demand of self-definition. Writes on the role of languages in the quest to reclaim African ways of knowing. Also writes stories and poems. Written poetry collection titled: *Twin Tongued: Azania Double Speak.*

R. M. Corbin is a fiction and essay writer from San Diego whose writing is concerned with isolation and loneliness with regard to literature and cultural production. His work has been published in the San Diego City Works Literary Journal and he was the recipient of the 2019 Howard Babb Memorial Essay Award. His current project, "In A World of One Colour": Conceptions of Loneliness in Post-WWII U.S. and Japan Literature explores literary conceptions of loneliness through the lenses of history and cultural production.

Kamerahn Francisco-Laititi is an alumnus of the University of California, Irvine who studied Criminology and African American Studies. Growing up in poverty in urban Los Angeles, CA, his capacity to question everyday life as a child influenced him to question why violence and inter-generational suffering exist so persistently in the world. While pursuing a post-grad degree in Sociology or Education, he plans to conceive a pedagogical scheme that makes radical, black scholarly work translatable and accessible for folks who lack the proper means to do so.

Callan Grace Garber is an undergraduate student in the School of Humanities at the University of California, Irvine. Her personal research focuses on Margaret Sanger and the "Birth Control Movement" in the United States, an analyzes the ways in which eugenics-centered narratives have been utilized to secure access to birth control for white women. She is an active participant in campus sustainability efforts, working alongside her colleagues to lower UCI's carbon footprint, as well as set a standard for other University of California campuses.

Maya Green is an undergraduate at the Cleveland Institute of Art. They studied drawing and painting at the Claire Trevor School of the Arts at the University of California, Irvine. Accepted to study medical illustration in fall 2020, their goal is to better represent African America and non-white skin tones in the medical field. Through exploring the artistic representations of people of color with varying medical conditions, they hope to bridge the gap between healthcare's knowledge and correct representation and identification of health concerns.

Our late colleague and friend, **Peter Hudson** (1950-2019), earned degrees from the University of Natal, Paris X (Nanterre), and Paris VIII (Vincennes). He taught in the Department of Political Studies at the University of the Witwatersrand from 1982 until his retirement in 2015. In 2002 he received the Vice Chancellor's Individual Teaching Award and in his last post was the honorary senior lecturer in the School of Social Sciences. Peter will be remembered as an inspired teacher and a dedicated craftsman of thought.

Ashraf Jamal is a Research Associate in the Visual Identities in Art and Design research Centre at the University of Johnnesburg, and teaches in the Media Studies Programme at the Cape Peninsula University of Technology. He is the co-author of *Art in South Africa: The Future Present*, co-editor of the *Indian Ocean Studies: Social, cultural and political perspectives* and the author of *Love Themes for The Wilderness* and *Predicaments* of *Culture in South Africa*. He has taught at the Universities of Cape Town, Stellenbosch, Natal, Rhodes, Malaya (Malaysia), and Eastern Mediterranean (N. Cyprus). In 2017 Skira published Jamal's edited volume on Robin Rhode and collected essays on Contemporary South African Art – *In the World*.

Sharlene Khan is a South African visual artist who works in multi-media installations and performances which focus on the socio-political realities of a post-apartheid society and the intersectionality of race-gender-class. She uses masquerading as a postcolonial strategy to interrogate her South African heritage, as well as the constructedness of identity via rote education, art discourses, historical narratives and popular culture. She holds a PhD (Arts) from Goldsmiths, University of London and is currently a Senior Lecturer in Art History and Visual Culture at Rhodes University. Professor Khan can be reached at s.khan@ru.ac.za and sharlenefkhan@yahoo.co.uk

Sydney Diane Lara is a graduate from the University of California, Irvine with a B.A. in Philosophy. During her studies she focused on ethics and made sure to not only study the authors in the standard Eurocentric philosophic canon but also to study Black Feminist Theory, Queer Theory, and Indigenous Theory. Angela Davis, bell hooks, C. Riley Snorton, Pumla Gqola, and Ariana Brown are among her top influences.

Alexa Dorsett-Levingston studied at the University of California, Irvine in the field of criminology law and society and African American studies. In her undergraduate years she focused on the systematic corruption of the criminal justice system and the intersections of race, gender, sexuality, and socioeconomic status. Her studies have inspired her passion in creative writing and social justice, where she can speak for the unspoken and shed light on the invisible.

Derilene (Dee) Marco lectures in Media Studies at the University of the Witwatersrand. Dee's research is in cinema studies and visual culture with specific focus on racial identities in post-apartheid South Africa as 'the Rainbow nation'. Her work also pivots around ideas of memory, narrative and the project of mothering and care. Dee also cohosts a podcast, Mamas with attitude and enjoys long walks, reading and yoga whenever her two small kids permit! In the words of black feminist bell hooks, Dee believes that people really do learn theory with greater ease through pop culture-something that is also a great source of joy and fun in her own life.

Aditi Mayer is a fine art and documentary photographer whose work explores themes of identity, displacement, and gender politics. She is a University of California, Irvine alum ('19) with degrees in Literary Journalism and International Studies.

Natalia Molebatsi is an acclaimed poet, writer, MC and recording artist/ producer. Her cds include *Natalia Molebatsi & the Soul Making* (2015) and *Come as you are: poems for four strings* (2013), both available on itunes. Her books are *We are: a poetry anthology,* as editor (Penguin books) *Sardo Dance* (Ge'ko) and *Elephant Woman Song* (Forum). Her academic writing is included in, among other journals, *Scrutiny2*, *Rhodes Journalism Review*, *Agenda* and *Muziki*. She has performed poetry and presented creative writing workshops in over 15 countries globally. www.nataliamolebatsi.com

Robert Muponde is Full Professor in the School of Literature, Language and Media Studies, University of the Witwatersrand, Johannesburg. His publications include: *Some Kinds of Childhood: Images of History and Resistance in Zimbabwean Literature* (Africa World Press, Trenton NJ: 2015); co-edited with Emma Laurence, *While the Harvest Rots: Possessing Worlds of Kudzanai Chiurai's Art* (The Goodman Gallery, Johannesburg/Cape Town, 2017); *Sign and Taboo: Perspectives on the Poetic Fiction of Yvonne Vera* (Weaver Press, Harare: James Currey, Oxford 2002), co-edited with Mandi Taruvinga; *Versions of Zimbabwe; New Approaches to Literature and Culture* (Weaver Press, Harare, 2005), co-edited with Ranka Primorac; and *Manning the Nation: Father Figures in Zimbabwean Literature and Society* (Weaver Press, Harare: Jacana, Johannesburg, 2007), co-edited with Kizito Muchemwa. He is currently working on a memoir/personal essay titled, *The Scandalous Times of a Book Louse*.

Lara Nguyen is a distinguished graduate from the University of California, Irvine with honors in International Studies and Public Health Policy. Born to Vietnamese refugees, Lara is innately drawn to understanding the discrepancies between binary contradictions that share space; the haves and have nots, the enabled and disabled, and the oppressors and oppressed. Beyond trailblazing a platform for silenced narratives and identities, Nguyen strives to continually unlearn her own institutionalized education and its built world in hopes of reimagining equitable justice. A 2018-19 Dalai Lama Scholar her previous work has taken her to explore conflict zones in the Middle East and grassroots development in Nepal.

Bhavisha Panchia is a curator and researcher of visual and audio culture, currently based in Johannesburg. Originally from Johannesburg, South Africa, her research interests are leveled at anti/decolonial practices, global South-North relations, production and circulation of (digital) media, including the politics of sound and music in relation to diasporic formations. Her works engages with artistic and cultural practices under shifting global conditions, focusing on anti-postcolonial discourses, imperial histories and networks of production and circulation of (digital) media. A significant part of her practice centres on auditory media's relationship to geopolitical paradigms, particularly with respect to the social and ideological signification of sound and music in contemporary culture. Of concern is the ways in which knowledge is given precedence, and systems which determine who is given the right to speak, and the right to be heard. Panchia holds a BA Fine Arts Degree and MA History of Art Degree from the University of Witwatersrand, including an MA in Curatorial Practice from the Center for Curatorial Studies at Bard College, New York.

Alyana Reid is a young filmmaker and graduate of the University of California, Irvine, originally from Berkeley, California.

Jeanne Scheper is an Associate Professor of Gender and Sexuality Studies at University of California, Irvine and author of *Moving Performances: Divas, Iconicity, and Remembering the Modern Stage* (Rutgers 2016). She has published articles on feminist visual culture and activism, student debt, and popular culture and is owrking on a book-length project on debates over the "don't ask don't tell policy," transgender military service and the role of popular culture.

Tiffany Willoughby-Herard is an Associate Professor of African American Studies (University of California, Irvine) and the Vice President of the National Conference of Black Political Scientists. Willoughby-Herard's research covers Black political thought and the material conditions of knowledge production, Black movements, and raced gendered consciousness and queer sexualities internationally. A widely published author and editor, Willoughby-Herard is also a poet, a reader, a mama, a member of the Christ our Redeemer, Irvine, African Methodist Episcopal Church Choir, a teacher, a friend, a research mentor, and a Black lesbian feminist internationalist who survived.

Abebe Zegeye, is a Senior Research Fellow at The Institute for the Study of Global Antisemitism and Policy. He has conducted and published extensive research on African and social identities. He has taught & worked in Africa, the Middle East, North America, Europe and Australia. Zegeye is the author of the highly acclaimed book, *The Impossible Return: Struggles of the Ethiopian Jews*, The Beta Israel (Red Sea Press, 2018). His forthcoming book is *Sites of Remembering* (Africa World Press, 2021).

Index

E

F

G

H

I

J

K

L

M